Life in the Slow Lane

Life in the Slow Lane

by Arthur E. Martin, NA

Peter E. Randall Publisher • Portsmouth 1990

© *1990 Arthur E. Martin, NA*
Printed in the United States of America

Design: Tom Allen

Peter E. Randall Publisher
Box 4726, Portsmouth, New Hampshire 03801

Available from the Publisher and
Martin Marine Company
Box 251
Kittery Point, ME 03905

Library of Congress Cataloging -in-Publication Data

Martin, Arthur E., 1917–
        Life in the slow lane / by Arthur E. Martin
                p.   cm.
        ISBN 0-914339-30-3 : $25.00
        1. Martin, Arthur E., 1917–   . Naval architects– –United
States– –Biography. 3. Yachts and yachting– –United States– –Design and
construction– –History– 20th Century. 4. Yacht building– –United
States– –History– –20th Century.   I. Title.
VM140.M26A3 1990
623.8' 1' 092– –dc20
[B]   90-39493
                                                                                  CIP

To Franklin Martin, my father, who introduced me to the Isles of Shoals, and to Marjorie, who encouraged me to return.

Acknowledgments

*f*rom the cradle to the grave lives are inevitably affected by numerous human cantacts along the way. This book chronicles many such contacts: people from whom the author learned about boats and the sea, and, more importantly, standards of honesty, integrity, and satisfying living. Many were family and friends no longer with us, while others are living proof that one can learn from the young as well as the old. My children and grandchildren inspire me and unobtrusively remind me of my lapses in the very standards of conduct which I have tried to pass on to them. To all who have contributed to making my life what it has been I am extremely grateful.

Many contributed to the actual mechanics of producing this book. First and foremost, my son Douglas patiently steered the manuscript through the treacherous reefs of a word processer, coming to the rescue each time I became frustrated to the point of looking for a sledge hammer to smash the arrogant machine.

Marjorie not only put up with endless hours as a computer widow, but played a very active role in collecting and arranging all of the photographs. Although photo credits are given elsewhere, special recognition is deserved by my father, Franklin Martin, whose trusty old Kodak recorded so faithfully the early years. Edwin Hills and Ann Grinnell contributed the highest professional standards to many of the pictures. Captain Richards Miller was instrumental in procuring the U.S. Navy photos, while Gregg Bemis loaned some valuable Cohasset pictures from his own collection.

Finally, Peter Randall's patience and expertese translated an imperfect computer disc into a presentable book, in record time.

Contents

Introduction

*t*he 20th century began at what was, by today's standards, a snail's pace. The automobile was known as a horseless carriage, fully appreciated only by those with the skill and patience to put up with endless flat tires, leaking radiators, and slow, unreliable engines. Worst of all were the roads, usually consisting of two parallel ruts in the mud, permitting passage of only one car at a time. It must have been quite a scene when my maternal grandfather, a volatile and emotional Irish doctor, who highly disapproved of my grown-up father courting his teen age daughter, found himself in his first automobile, following the ruts, face to face with my father, heading in the opposite direction in one of the vehicles that provided his hobby, profession, and livelihood.

Despite the ensuing altercation, things eventually worked out so that I was permitted to enter a relatively slow-moving world, two weeks behind schedule. With the passage of time, the world speeded up considerably, bringing ever faster cars, boats, and airplanes, and all kinds of instant communications. Partly by happenstance, and partly by choice, I seemed to fall behind the pace of progress. I did not get a driver's license until I was 20 and was able to drive an ancient Model A only on the rare occasions when my brother Franklin did not have our joint $75 purchase at Dartmouth. I had nothing but contempt for the new fangled outboard motors and used to delight in racing against them while rowing at full power in a Maine peapod. Although I actually owned one in later years, as auxiliary power for my little sloop, *Barnacle II,* I never came to think highly of outboard motors, particularly those monstrous ones with ever more power. I grant that there are many good uses for such readily portable power, but I do not consider such a use aimless speeding about, to the danger of swimmers, canoes, and small sailboats, by young children who would be better off

Early skinny-dipping at the Isles of Shoals. Franklin Martin, Jr., left, and Arthur E. Martin (AEM), right. Time did not diminish the pleasures of the sport. Photo: Franklin Martin.

doing something more mentally and physically challenging. One spoiled kid in an outboard can shatter the very tranquility of a quiet lake or creek that the adjacent homeowners have paid so dearly to enjoy. Perhaps I hate outboards because they remind me of mosquitoes. On the other hand, perhaps I hate mosquitoes because they remind me of outboards.

I have not been a complete stranger to skiing down a mountain at a speed beyond my ability to control, exceeding the speed limit in a car, casually hopping a jet, and indulging in the wonders of instant communication all over the globe. But in general I have always preferred an easier pace, allowing time to stop and smell the daisies, or, more correctly in my case, the salt air in fog, seaweed drying in the sun, pine or mahogany shavings. I have found time to meditate, and enjoy the company of my children and grandchildren, at the expense of a possibly more adventuresome and worldly successful life.

It might well be said that I have lived life in the slow lane, in contrast to the fast lane of highly organized pandemonium, rushing from one daring mental exploit to another, seeking interim entertainment vicariously in gunfights where six-chamber revolvers fire thirty or forty consecutive shots, and sex precedes introductions. If old-fashioned pace of living, values, and prejudices do not find favor, so be it. That is the way it was, and this is an attempt to tell it like it was.

AEM returns to the clear water in front of the family house on Appledore, in one of the now-familiar Alden Ocean Shells. Photo: Judy Kehl.

1 • *Return of the Native*

*f*or more than 270 degrees, there is an almost unbroken expanse of bright blue water. The curving line where sea and sky meet suggests unlimited horizons, stretching on forever, always in sight, but never in reach, unfettered by the petty machinations of man, always for me spelling freedom.

For the thousandth time I stick my head out of the starboard window for a closer look at the clear, deep water rushing by. The bow wave is a gentle partnership of boat and ocean, the former disturbing the latter as little as possible. There is no evidence of the usual power struggle as huge engines force an ungainly shape through the protesting water. The bow rises smoothly and gracefully as it meets the rounded swells that remain from now docile winds, multiplying the bow wave without the jarring motion of an automobile on a pockmarked road.

Off the port bow, Boon Island Lighthouse gradually takes shape, from a misty pencil to a towering granite structure. I sip a Heineken beer and munch a tasty sandwich which Marjorie has conjured up. We talk of many things, without raising our voices, for the little diesel is well insulated for sound. I glance at the compass from time to time, but the long, narrow double-ender has little tendency to veer from a straight course. My attention is more occupied in scouring the distant horizon for the first glimpse of the Isles of Shoals.

We are ending a glorious cruise "Down East." We could not count the beautiful islands, large and small, we have seen, many of which have provided anchorage for one or several nights, incredible rowing and sailing, delicious mussels and clams, invigorating swimming, and exploring on foot or bicycle. Christmas trees growing right down to granite shores or sloping beaches, most of the latter composed of mussel and clam shells, ground to tiny chips by the relentless waves and bleached by the sun to snowy white and subtle shades of

The Energy 48. The boat designed by AEM and used on all of the later cruises. Photo: Marjorie Martin.

blue. New friends and old, on other boats, from the familiar and beloved Concordias to our own Appledore 16s: neophytes trying out an Alden for the first time, satisfying our desire to introduce more people to the great sport of rowing: visitors to the Energy 48, for a drink or dinner, or just an inspection tour, some, old friends, and others friends we hadn't yet met, interested in the unusual boat but so far none ready, willing, and able to acquire a sister ship.

The cruise, as usual, has been a trip to paradise. The days, each so perfect, had rushed by with frightening speed. Now it was over, or almost over. One more delight awaited, just over the horizon. In more than 60 years of cruising, I liked to say, not without some poetic license and outright exaggeration, that my destination was always the Isles of Shoals. For me, life began when I first saw the magic isles, looming ever larger over the high bow of the old steam tug *Sightseer*. I was seven at the time but had been there previously as an unimpressionable infant. Dim memories of other events, almost all inland, during the early years, seem to be crowded out by my first impressions of the Isles of Shoals. There many of my ideas, hopes, and aspirations originated, and there I spent some of the happiest days of more than

65 years. Whenever I turn to ashes, I hope they will return to rest in those sparkling waters.

So I search the broad horizon with growing anticipation, and when I catch the first glimpse of the tower on Appledore, I feel the same inner excitement that had gripped me so many times before. Soon we would be secured at a friend's mooring, taking down the Aldens from their teak chocks on top of the deckhouse. It is Labor Day, and Gosport harbor is crowded with boats, power and sail, a few graceful and a joy to behold, most somehow out of place in those surroundings. But, one by one, they were returning to their marinas on the mainland, leaving us to enjoy a peaceful night and quiet morning.

I row over to the house we used to own on Appledore, looking better superficially than ever but lacking the presence of my mother on the front porch, my father out in his shop to the east, and the rest of the family all together, instead of scattered over the country. A few strokes take me on what used to be the long voyage to the Half Tide Ledges, where I had spent so much time in the miniature natural harbors among the seaweed-covered rocks. It is reassuring, as always, to find nothing changed. I try to tempt the bluefish off Cedar Ledge, but they ignore my Stan Gibbs plug, cast with difficulty in the big swells and chop bounced back by the unyielding granite of the island.

The next day Marjorie and I row around Star, Cedar, Smuttynose, and Appledore, as my father used to do so many years ago, stopping at the Shoals Marine Laboratory for a visit with dynamic J. B. Heiser, lunch, and a walk around the island, pausing at the little graveyard of the Laighton family and Celia Thaxter's garden, so beautifully restored by the Shoals Marine Laboratory.

Then down a newly cut path through the thick underbrush, the result of my daughter-in-law Faith Harrington's archeology expeditions, exposing foundations of centuries-old houses which used to shelter more than six hundred people before the country was founded. On to the back of our old house, where the now big chestnut tree contributes one of its shiny prizes.

A nostalgic visit and a fitting ending for a happy voyage. A little sad, for, despite my usually optimistic spirits, I cannot forget that my next destination will be Mass. General Hospital, to engage, once more, in the battle with the big C, mesothelioma in the left lung.

The family house on Appledore in 1924. The slip is on the right. Photo: Franklin Martin.

2 • *The Isles of Shoals*

*f*urthest to the east of the houses on the south side of Appledore Island stands one of local granite to the top of the first story. A simple, square design, consisting of cellar, three stories, and an attic, circumscribed by a porch with a roof. Perched on solid rock, far above high tide, it is not completely out of reach of the winter storms, as evidenced by the dry seaweed under the porch.

Just to the east of the house, two huge tree trunks slope down to the low tide mark, securely fastened to the rock with wrought iron rods leaded into laboriously pounded cavities. Ten by ten crossbeams, spaced roughly five feet apart, connect the two tree trunks, while two two-by-twelve planks, with cleats, serve as a walkway, bleached and dry at the top, offering secure footing, becoming more and more slippery with marine growth toward the bottom.

A big orange dory, with "U.S. Coast Guard"lettered on the bow, is hauled out on the cross-beams at the top of the slip. Further down is a small lap-strake skiff, with "Oceanic" branded on the stern seat and also the blades of the oars.Beyond the now-submerged end of the slip a gray dory rocks almost imperceptibly in the sparkling blue water, tied to an outhaul, that marine version of a clothesline loop so characteristic of the Maine coast. Further out, a 36-foot motor lifeboat, labelled "U.S.COAST GUARD Isles of Shoals,"rides behind the big white spar of a heavy mooring. A dark gray Coast Guard picket boat is moored to the east, while a mooring to the west secures a dark red double-ended power boat on a bridle leading to shore, with a dory tied directly to the spar. Inshore, another dory with a one-lunger engine rides at an outhaul.

A small boy runs down over the rocks to the slip (what small boy ever walks anywhere?). He sits down on the sloping walkway, knees drawn up to his chin, arms around his shins. He gazes out over the panorama of rocks, seaweed, clear blue water, boats, and the other islands beyond. He is dressed in khaki shorts and shirt, without hat or shoes, in blissful ignorance of the sun's threat to light skin, or the old wood's capacity for making splinters. He has no schedule of lessons in swimming, tennis, archery, or other activities. Neither does he have the inactive diversions of radio or television. He is totally dependent on his own thoughts and observations. Children naturally have great imaginations, and an infinite capacity for daydreaming. What impressions does this scene leave on the young mind? What thoughts and dreams does it inspire?

I should know, for I was that little boy. More than 60 years have dimmed many memories, and obliterated innumerable others, but that scene remains permanently etched on my mind.

I remember looking down through the crystal clear water, watching the seaweed gently swaying back and forth, like the grass skirt of a hula dancer in slow motion, in response to what we called the undertow. I was not smart enough to realize that "undertow" was really ocean waves, flattened to an almost imperceptible height by miles of travelling over windless sea. In later years I studied the trochoidal wave theory, observed countless natural wave formations, experimented with waves generated by all kinds of boats, from tiny models to full-size boats propelled by sail, oar, and power, only to realize that none of us will ever know all there is to know about waves.

Despite my youthful ignorance of boats and waves, I did have a powerful intuitive feeling that the scene before me was a preview of my life from then on. Those rocks and water and boats were destined never to leave that part of my mind reserved for the most vivid, pleasurable, and influential memories.

How sorry I am for all the children, born with enthusiasm, curiosity, wonder, imagination, and capability to reflect, similar to my own, who let these priceless gifts atrophy in response to the beguiling distractions of the modern world. Television at best reveals the secrets of nature with amazing clarity, dramatizes the best literature, captures live the world's best in sports, but leaves little to the imagination nor challenges young minds or bodies. As for the rest of TV, the less said, the better. Battery-powered toys perform entertaining feats for young owners, but soon become boring, or broken. Ever increasing organization allows little time for individual initiative or thought. Obviously, many thrive on these benefits of progress, but for myself, I am grateful that none of this was to be found at the Isles of Shoals when I was a child.

I could sit by the hour watching the tide come in. I still can. A periwinkle (penny wrinkle as we called them) sitting on a dry rock, several inches above the little ripples on the water below: one ripple wets a little of the dry area of the rock. Then another. And another. Then the lower part of the rock is permanently covered. The little snail occupies an ever diminishing dry area of the rock. Finally the first ripple splashes it. Not very exciting compared to watching television while someone fights a thousand-pound marlin from a half-million dollar sport fisherman. Who is to say which is better for a little boy?

I am grateful that I had the opportunity to use my imagination, to pretend, and to dream, and absorb and relish all the sights and sounds and smells of the edge of the sea and the various boats that were such a pleasure as well as a necessity.

My older brother, Franklin, and I each had colossal boats in which to play. His was a rock formation on the side of a hill, tapered toward the hill at one end, forming the crudest of half models. Mine was a cluster of old rotting timbers, overhanging the rocks at one end, making it possible to go down into the engine room. I learned to imitate the sounds of all the engines. The single cylinder, two-cycle, make-and-break engines used to propel dories and other small lobster boats, the easy-to-duplicate "put put", with the quieter "nin nin nin"of the diminishing speed after the spark had been cut off. An expert could connect the spark again at just the right moment and start it again without cranking, or reverse it by hitting the spark just as the flywheel bounced back after a final gasp. The bigger four-cycle engines had quite a variety of noises, and it was a challenge to imitate them all, particularly the whine of the gears in reverse and the periodic sound of water coming out of the exhaust pipe of the Coast Guard picket boat. The dark red double-ender went "che-chung che-chung", two beats close together, and then a space. I never could figure this out, but many years later Fred White, a member of the Sunday morning rowing club, solved the mystery by explaining that this was an old Sterling two-cylinder engine with an offset crankshaft to prevent stalling on

Hand-carved canoe paddles. AEM left, Franklin at right.
Photo: Franklin Martin.

dead center.Our boats naturally had tremendous engines, calling for considerable lung power.

We inevitably spent a lot of time in real boats, but never without an adult, usually my long-suffering uncle, Deane Freeman, who was very patient with crude models towed in the path of the oars, and sudden lurches to one side to look at the bottom. But we could not venture out by ourselves until we learned to swim. I remember my first trip out to our new summer home quite vividly. We arrived at Star Island on the steam tug *Sightseer* (engine sound: quiet, except for "fluff-flum fluff-flum"which represented the reciprocating main circulating pump pushing salt water through the condenser and out the side. How relaxing to hear nothing but the waves and the gentle murmur of a steam engine!). We were met at the float by our own 16-foot dory, propelled by a hired man named Walsh, who was very strong and very profane. It was blowing briskly from the northwest, and we faced quite a chop going across to Appledore. I sat in the bow seat, facing forward. As each wave advanced toward us, I felt sure it would engulf us. But each time, the bow would lift at the last split second, and we would be on top of the wave, instead of vice versa. The crash that followed as the flat bottom landed in the trough was equally unsettling. This was the first of countless experiences with dories. I gradually came to appreciate their remarkable seaworthiness, but the pounding never failed to disappoint me.

My father had an Old Town canoe, dark green canvas outside, and well varnished wood inside. Once or twice a summer, when the water was like a mirror, he would take it out for a paddle, and I can remember being a passenger on one of these trips. The canoe seemed so sleek, responsive, fast, and quiet compared to our dory that I could never forget the contrast. The Davis oarlocks were very convenient and quick to stow or use, but they were very noisy.

Needless to say, I could hardly wait to go out in boats by myself. The idea of putting a PFD (life jacket) on a non-swimmer and sending him out in a boat never would have occurred to any of us, and, besides, we did not have any life jackets except for the ungainly cork ones for adults found on ocean liners. So learning to swim had my highest priority. Every day we trudged through the bushes and poison ivy to the back of the island, where the Appledore Hotel, which had

Franklin and AEM off Star Island in a canoe paddled by their father. Photo: Margaret Martin.

burned to the ground in 1914, had included an enclosed little cove with a sandy beach, so that guests could swim in water warmed by the sun. The dam had long since deteriorated, completely obliterating the pond at low tide, and assuring refreshing cool water at high tide. Upon completing, unassisted, the required 25-yard swim across the pond, I dashed back across the island in the uniform of the occasion: long black woolen trunks, red and black striped woolen top, and high sneakers. The bathing suit itched and chafed when wet, and the

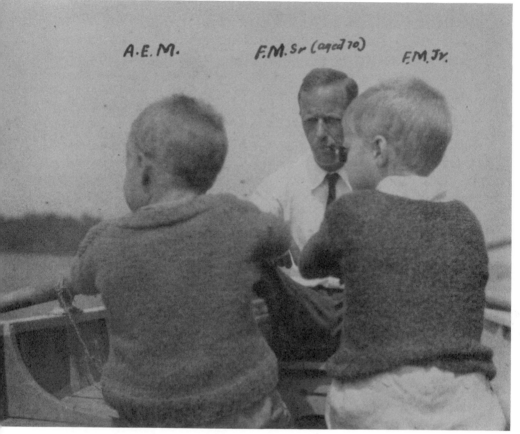

Rowing at Macmahan Island. Left to right, AEM, Franklin Martin, Senior, and Franklin. Photo: Margaret Martin.

sneakers sloshed and chafed as they filled with water dripping from the bathing suit. But all of that was forgotten in the heady knowledge that I could now go out in boats by myself, albeit only within strict limits, and always with my father's permission.

Franklin and I were soon allowed to row the dory over to the dock at Star, and bring back the crates of supplies that would be sent out periodically on the *Sightseer*. These rowing expeditions were really a necessity. My father had been rushed to the hospital for an emergency operation on a perforated ulcer. Although several years had passed, during which my grandfather, the esteemed Dr. Richard Freeman, tried repeatedly to explain that the scar had long since healed completely, my father was convinced that he would split open again "like a fish"if he were to lift anything weighing over 10 pounds. Hauling those crates up over the rocks was undoubtedly as good for our bodies and souls as rowing that heavy dory in tandem.

Franklin, being older, was always thinking of new things to do. One day, after a storm, he found a badly stove-up lobster trap, washed ashore. He brought it home, fixed it up, caught some cunners(perch to landsmen) for bait, and set it out by the moorings. The next morning we rowed out in the dory, and he slowly hauled it toward the surface, assisted no doubt by the excitement and suspense. While it was still far below the boat, we could see some dark green with orange trim. A real lobster! I am sure that the discovery of gold provides no greater thrill. We landed, pulled the dory out on the outhaul, and climbed triumphantly up the rocks toward the house, I leading the way, and he following,holding the lobster tightly by the back. I suppose to check the lobster for signs of life after this ordeal, he held it up to my back, and the captive obligingly took a bite of my shoulder with his sharp claw. Since the lobster was already destined for capital punishment, no further penalty could be imposed on him, but a punishment to fit the crime awaited my brother. I was awarded the lobster trap for two weeks. Thus began my very happy career in lobstering.

Our relationship with the Coast Guard was somewhat unusual by today's standards. They kept their dory and a dinghy at our slip without any bureaucratic or legal contract or financial agreement. In fact, as far as I know the subject was never mentioned. If they were going to the mainland to take a man on liberty, we, or any one else on the islands, could go with them. I roamed over all of their boats at will, crawling down into each watertight compartment of their self-righting, unsinkable 36-foot motor lifeboat known as *Old Sal*. We regarded them as our friends. The days when a foolish Congress would require them to fine anyone rowing out to a mooring without a PFD were far in the future, along with the stipulation that an underage and over priviledged child, driving a lethal high-powered outboard among swimmers, is not under the jurisdiction of the Coast Guard. Outboard

Uncle Deane Freeman departing from the slip with guests. AEM supervising. Photo: Franklin Martin.

motor manufacturers have plenty of money to contribute to congressional election campaigns.

Once I rescued a Coast Guard dinghy which had been inadequately secured. The score was evened later on. I was looking out of my bedroom window early one morning, watching the boats straining at their moorings in a rising northeast storm. Our peapod had an old, frayed painter. I had spoken to my father about this, knowing he had a whole coil of new three-quarter inch manila stored in the attic for a rainy day. The rainy day never came, and forty years later the manila was still waiting for its first job as an emergency fire escape. The old painter, however, figured it had done enough, and right in front of my eyes, it parted company with the mooring. I ran up to the Coast Guard Station and gasped out the details of the tragedy, and they very kindly lost no time in catching up with the rapidly departing boat before it could meet sudden death on the rocky shore of White Island.

One day two Coast Guardsmen set out from our slip in a skiff. An argument developed over who would row. Each allowed as how the other should row, a discussion hard for me to understand, as I always wanted to row, any kind of a boat, anywhere, under any conditions. The altercation became more and more vociferous, until finally one of them said, "Well, we'll float then." And float they did, until I got tired of watching. For all I know they are still floating.

Prohibition was in full force then, as we were sometimes reminded by the sound of powerful engines at night, and the stem of the *Ann* under our front porch. She had been run ashore at Broad Cove and burned. We never did see the rest of this famous rumrunner, but heard that her Liberty airplane engines, left over from World War I, could drive her at over 40 knots, giving her a comfortable advantage over 17-knot Coast Guard boats. History repeats.

While our friends in the Coast Guard were doing their best to enforce the Eighteenth Amendment, my father was doing his best to get around it. Starting with elderflower wine, and going on to various other wines, sherry, brandy, and rye whiskey, he did everything in a most scientific and at the same time devious manner. After using his still, he took it all apart, and hid the pieces in different parts of the house. He kept copious notes, recording dates, weights of ingredients, temperatures, and processes in great detail and accuracy. He was careful never to mention the word "still," however, for fear the law would find the notes and mete out some appropriate punishment. Instead, he would record "put through warm filter" followed by the time and the date. He had read that the best whiskey travelled in charred kegs in the holds of ships which went around the world. Not having any ships, he improvised. He mounted a charred keg of his best rye whiskey on a pivoting frame in the cellar of our house in New Jersey. To one end he attached a large spring. A long rope, tied to the other end, went through a series of pulleys up to the door of the front hall closet where we kept our skates, hockey sticks, tennis racquets, and miscellaneous clothes and sports equipment. Every time someone opened the door there would be a loud clanking down in the cellar, indicating that the whiskey was getting sloshed against the charcoal, removing the harsher ingredients. It must have worked, for it was the smoothest whiskey I have ever tasted. A keg of this most precious whiskey was left at the Shoals all winter. My father, ever the pessimist, feared that someone would break in, indulge in some whiskey, and top off the keg with water. Having read various pirate stories, some many times, he devised a scheme to detect, and possibly thwart, any such dastardly act. He put the keg on the floor in a corner of the cellar, its centerline lined up exactly on true north, using an old box compass. Then he carefully covered it with driftwood for the fireplace. Next June it was still pointing at true north, although the house had been broken into in other years.

My brief history, prior to that first summer at our house on Appledore, included a visit to the Thousand Islands, where I first traveled in a St. Lawrence Skiff, and a brief stay at the Oceanic Hotel on Star Island, neither of which I recall, being too young at the time.

I do remember spending a summer in a rented cottage at Macmahan Island, in the course of which my father paddled me across the Sheepscot River, and through Townsend Gut to Boothbay Harbor. My clearest recollection of the voyage is that my father, never one to squander money on unnecessary luxuries, bought me a stick of Black Jack gum, which I had never before had the privilege of sampling. For all of us, there is an age below which events remembered form no discernable pattern.

Looking back, I realize that life really began for me that summer of 1924 at the Isles of Shoals.

Mr. and Mrs. William A. Brewster in Portsmouth. Photo: Franklin Martin.

3 • Mr. Brewster

*h*is name would never appear in Who's Who, or the Forbes 400, or the Social Register. His social activities were almost non-existent, except as a member of the Shriners. But William Albert Brewster was one of the finest men I have ever known, as I am sure all of the few privileged to know him would agree.

His house and what he called his barn were just west of our house on Appledore, painted dark red. He and his wife, Annette, had lived there, year-round, for many years, and only recently had indulged in moving ashore to a modest house in Portsmouth for the worst of the winter months. He was not large of stature, but strong and sinewy. The lower part of his face was tan and gnarled, but his forehead was astonishingly white, for he always wore a cap or a panama hat.

He moved slowly and deliberately in a boat, every step well planned, and no wasted motion. It was always a pleasure to see him in a boat, for he seemed to be in perfect harmony with the motion of the boat and the water. People said he could land or embark from our slip in winter storms when no one else dared to leave the island. In a real storm, there is no lee at the Isles of Shoals. The giant waves, traveling at a speed equal to 1.34 times the square root of the distance from crest to crest, would move in the same direction as the wind, until one end would reach the shallowing water at the outer ledges. This would slow it down, while the other end continued at its natural speed, causing the wave to turn toward the island. Our slip, on the south side of the island, was thus subjected to almost as much wave action as the barren rocks to the northeast. A dory, attempting to land at our slip in such a storm, could be caught by a huge wave, lifting the stern so high that the bow caught under one of the crossbeams, pitchpoling the boat and throwing the occupant out onto the other beams, rocks, or churning water. I heard of this happening more than once, but not to Mr. Brewster.

He made his living catching lobsters. He usually rowed a dory standing up, facing forward, but for a longer distance he would occasionally row sitting down, with long, even strokes. For hauling lobster traps in the summer, he used the dory with the one cylinder two-cycle engine, which he called a Barker. In the winter he used his big boat, which was the dark red double-ender. In 1927 he replaced it with a torpedo-stern Jonesport, built by "Pappy" Frost. He was very proud of this boat, which would slide along very easily with a small engine called an Erd. I often pondered the question of why this boat could move through the water so easily, making scarcely any waves, while my father's Elco Cruisette, acquired the same year, seemed to drag the whole ocean up behind it. Almost without realizing it, I was getting interested in wave formations of contrasting boats. The Jonesport had a beautiful shear line, curving gracefully up to a high bow. Though somewhat wet, it never took green water over the bow, unlike our Elco.

Mr Brewster built me a little lobster trap, with only one head, light enough for me to lift over the gunwale of a dory. Being conservative (a leaning which time has not changed), I sold the lobsters I caught, sending them in to Portsmouth with Mr. Brewster and his weekly catch. He, in turn, brought me out the entire 37 cents a pound they were bringing at the time.

Lobsters, if their claws are not restrained, will injure each other or any one handling them carelessly, as I was only too well aware. These days, small elastic bands or plastic plugs are used for the purpose, but back then plugs were whittled out of white pine. Mr. Brewster was very adept at this task, and as I sat in his barn, enjoying the aroma of fresh pine shavings, I couldn't wait to try my hand at what seemed such a fascinating occupation. I soon acquired a jackknife, and a subsequent series of cut fingers, but I was hooked on whittling, and anxious to learn more about it.

One day Mr. Brewster put a big piece of pine in his vice and began to peel off great shavings with a drawknife. I watched intently as the wood gradually began to assume the shape of a boat. Further work with a jackknife, gouge, and sandpaper duplicated the distinctive shape of Mr. Brewster's Jonesport. He painted it with the same paint

Mr. Brewster and members of the Martin family in his Jonesport. Photo: Franklin Martin.

he used on its larger sister and handed it to me. Needless to say, it immediately became my prize possession, and traveled many miles on dry surfaces and in practically every salt water pond on Appledore, always accompanied by suitable engine noises. Thus inspired, I struggled with the task of whittling a shapely bow, at first always inadvertently slashing away the sharp, curving lines I had envisioned. But in the years that followed I learned to twist the knife with each stroke, preserving a sharp bow below the waterline. I made numerous models, always trying out new shapes. At that time catamarans were virtually unknown, despite Nat Herreshof's early experiments with the concept. I whittled one out of a single piece of pine, thus eliminating all the engineering involved in joining two hulls. It was only twelve inches long, but it beat a three-foot model of a Star Boat. Coming events cast their shadows before.

Mr. Brewster took each of us children, in turn, out lobstering. We would get up at five o'clock in the morning and run over to the Brewsters' house, where Mrs. Brewster always had fresh doughnuts and steamed bread. Then we would sit in the bow of the "Barker" dory and watch him haul as many as 90 traps (pots in Isles of Shoals jargon), all by hand. Hydraulic winches were yet to come. We also went "cunnering " with him sometimes in the afternoon. He had a big iron hoop, with a deep net attached to the circumference, forming a pocket at the bottom. Across the top was a line from which he suspended some of the crabs that frequent lobster traps, made more appetizing by smashing in their backs with a hammer. He would lower this to the bottom and look down through the clear water to see how many guests were arriving. When sufficient numbers appeared, he would pull up the net and dump the fluttering, splashing contents into the bottom of the dory. Meanwhile, we would jig for them with small mackerel jigs, and he would cut notches in the seat to record the length of the largest one we caught. Later he would tie half a dozen together, using a needle and string which went through the eyes, putting a string in each trap the next day.

Lobstering was a lot of hard work then, and it still is. There are bigger, faster boats, electronic aids to locate traps in fog, power winches, and purchased bait, but fewer lobsters. Starting with Mr. Brewster, I have always admired lobstermen. They have complete responsibility for everything they do. Unlike the bureaucrats who infest government, big business, and all too many other activities, they have no opportunities to pass the buck to others in a multi-layered organization. There is no one else. Mr. Brewster painted and repaired his boats and engines. If he neglected any one of the many potential trouble items, he, and he alone, would have to pay the price. When hauling a trap a few feet from giant waves breaking on a ledge, a faulty ignition, a dirty carburetor, or a stray line in the propeller can result in loss of everything, including life itself. There is no lengthy report, skillfully shifting the blame to someone else, nor are there a lot of foolish regulations drawn up by lawyers on shore. The lobsterman stands alone, independent, self-reliant, and completely responsible for his own life. He works hard and intelligently for every dollar he receives, and people pay for the fruits of his labor without any coercion. My admiration for Mr. Brewster has increased rather than diminished with the passage of time and the accumulation of experiences in school, college, big business, and finally our own small business, to say nothing of forced contact with numerous bureaucratic government agencies. He perhaps originally inspired my fierce independence (a little too fierce at times), contempt for political game-playing, and coercive and deceptive methods of accumulating money and power while contributing little or nothing of economic value in return.

Mr. Brewster was undoubtedly a strong influence in developing my lifelong love of boats and the sea, but he was even more influential in steering me away from the life of hypocrisy, dishonesty, and greed, which surround us.

My father acquired, in a junk yard in Portsmouth, an old forge, with a hand-cranked blower. With the help of various offspring, he hammered out numerous tools, including a curved knife which I used to hollow out models and make link chains out of a single piece of wood. The latter accomplishment was overshadowed years later when my son Douglas carved out a working pair of pliers from a single piece of pine.

Everyone at the Shoals used a spar buoy for a mooring. Holes drilled in the top and bottom of any old log could serve the purpose, but my father, ever the perfectionist, wanted something better. He bought a huge yard from an old square rigger, beautifully tapered from the large diameter in the middle to the finely rounded ends. He cut it exactly in half, and forged a U-shaped bale of wrought iron for the large end of each one. When the one in use became covered with blue mussels, despite the best copper paint available at the time, he simply replaced it with the other, using the mussels to make what he called mooring stew (no one ate mussels in those days; high prices for the same mussels are a comparatively recent development). Naturally, my father offered to make similar bales for his friend Mr. Brewster. The recipient was more than happy to join in the fun of fabrication. Over the sounds of the vigorously generated forced draft and the sledgehammer pounding the red hot metal, we recited lines from "Under The Spreading Chestnut Tree, The Village Smithy Stands." Often there was more truth than poetry in "Warned By The Smell Of Burning Flesh," but a quick dip in the cool salt water worked wonders. One year, after we had reluctantly returned to the mainland, Mr. Brewster located a tiny chestnut tree in Portsmouth, planted it in the sparse soil behind our house, and regularly spread old bait around the bottom. Over the years, the tree grew to magnificent proportions, and still flourishes today, one of the few if not the only real tree at the Isles of Shoals.

My father's success in alcohol production began with elderflower wine, there being an abundance of elderberry bushes right on our own property. On occasion, he would invite Mr. Brewster over to partake of a very small glass of this elixir. Invariably, after only a few sips, a high-pitched, rasping voice would shatter the tranquility of our living room, making its way across the small space between the two houses, and through the open window, repeating the one word "Albert" with ever increasing decibels. Poor Mr. Brewster, sometimes without even emptying his glass, would get up and quietly leave. He was without doubt one of the most henpecked husbands I ever knew. Along with everything else, he would have to listen, along with all of us, to unceasing descriptions of the desperate condition of his spouse's health, leading the unsuspecting to the conclusion that she would be unlikely to last the year out. Actually, nearly a century elapsed before she finally went to her reward, whatever that was. Despite her obvious faults, Mrs Brewster was quite a character in her own right. She used to sit by the hour on either of the port and starboard lantern boards which had been salvaged from the *Samuel Gaucher*, a coal-carrying schooner which had been wrecked on Duck Island years before. The red one was in front of the house, and the green one was in front of the "barn." No boat entering or leaving Gosport Harbor could escape her notice, for she had a big brass telescope retrieved from the same wreck. (The remains of the ill-fated ship were towed into Kittery Point, where part of the ancient skeleton resides today, rotting away between high and low tide, part of the scene as I row by almost every day.)

When my father was a young man, spending the summer at the

Appledore Hotel, it was the custom for the menfolk to walk to the back of the island to a miniature fiord in the jagged rock known as Siren's Grotto, where no female, by long tradition, would ever think of going. There they would strip and plunge into the icy water, unencumbered by the restrictive and uncomfortable bathing suits of the day. My father, cogitating over the irritating walks to the "pond," to say nothing of the return in wet bathing suit and soggy sneakers, decided that he and his three sons would revive the long-forgotten customs at Siren's Grotto. After a few such trips, however, he decided to find a suitable swimming area closer to home. Consequently, we found ourselves traveling a much shorter route to the western end of the island, ostensibly to look to see if the fog was coming in, even though it invariably came in from the east. No one questioned the deception, however, and the gently sloping rocks (due to the passage of the glacier from west to east, the west side of Appledore is relatively smooth and low, while the east side has steep cliffs facing the sea, challenging for young climbers), became known as Foggy Point. Further reflection convinced my father that we could improve nude swimming efficiency still further by simply diving in off our own slip.

Needless to say, it didn't take Mrs. Brewster long to become aware of this practice, and she complained with self-righteous ire to my father. He asked how she was able to distinguish various parts of the human anatomy from such a distance, and she proudly acknowledged that her old brass telescope was still in good working order, whereupon he suggested that if she did not like the view in that direction, she train her telescope elsewhere. Swimming continued, as before.

One year, the day before we were to arrive in our Elco 34 from New Jersey, Charles and Anne Lindbergh dropped anchor in their Elco 38, on their very secret honeymoon. Even they could not avoid Mrs. Brewster's telescope. She hated boats and never ventured off the island except to go to Portsmouth in the Jonesport if there was a "good chance across," and then if it breezed up on the return trip Albert got quite a scolding. But there are exceptions to every rule, and the chance to gawk at the famous flyer was too much to resist, and Mrs. Brewster set off in a dory to circle the honeymoon boat. When Mr. Lindbergh poked his head out to investigate the commotion, she said "Hi Lindy." It was probably the high spot of her life, but I doubt if it improved the honeymoon, and the Lindberghs soon left, while we were still several miles away, completing the trip from New Jersey in our own Elco, *Folly*.

For all her aches and pains, and sometimes abrasive ways, Mrs. Brewster was a good soul and generally quite companionable with all four of us children, particularly my sister, Mary. She would play double solitaire by the hour with any of us. She was very adept at picking blueberries, which were then plentiful on the island. She taught me a lesson in picking blueberries which I never forgot, because I think it applies to many other situations in life.

We would walk up through the poison ivy to where the blueberry bushes were, and she would settle down to pick, dropping the berries into a tin quart measure. I, on the other hand, was sure that there would be better picking a little farther on. I would rush ahead, stamping through the bushes right and left, stopping for a few minutes at a promising spot until the thought of possibly better picking somewhere else got the better of me, and I would move on once more. Meanwhile Mrs. Brewster would have filled her quart measure and we would start for home, I with little to show for my efforts, listening to her patiently explaining the error of my ways. Now I see others making the same mistakes I made, not with blueberries, but with life itself. I see people with large motorboats, drinking, watching TV, speeding heedless past all that life on the water has to offer, and counting the minutes to get back to the umbilical cord at the marina, all the while deluding themselves with the thought that a bigger boat next year will really make them happy.

So I like to think that Mrs. Brewster contributed something to my education, helping me to savor the simple pleasures of life by the edge of the sea, unbeguiled by the temptations of boundless riches and the material things they make available. Whenever I have thought of the grass being greener, I am reminded of the blueberries and am content to continue to get the most out of the blessings I now enjoy.

Mr. Brewster died of a stroke, out in his beloved Jonesport, off the Shoals. His life was complete, and he suffered none of the agonies of gradually failing life, dependent upon medication, artificial devices to delay rest for the body and soul, and the indignities of hospital life.

I was far away at the time, summer being over, and I attended no funeral nor ever saw his grave, but I still think of him fondly, and can never forget the many things he taught me. I can see him now, with his curved pipe with the silver initials "WAB" on the front, presented to him by my father so many years ago, giving me one of his rare but highly prized accolades, "You done good, boy."

Uncle Oscar at the helm of Twilight. Photo: Franklin Martin.

4 • *Uncle Oscar*

*h*e was not really my Uncle Oscar. He was everyone's Uncle Oscar. Although his several nephews and nieces were the only ones qualified to call him uncle, all of the thousands who met him immediately assumed the privilege.

He was the second of the three children of Thomas B. Laighton of Portsmouth, N.H. Mr. Laighton was active in local politics but was defeated, under questionable circumstances, in a race for selectman. Mr. Laighton left Portsmouth to become the lighthouse keeper at White Island, one of the islands at the Isles of Shoals. He took his young family with him and, although he later spent periods of activity in mainland politics, lived most of the rest of his life on the islands.

Out of concern for the education of his children, he invited a friend, business associate, and Harvard scholar by the name of Levi Thaxter to tutor them. They must have been awed by the intellectual accomplishments of their mentor, considered the foremost reader of Robert Browning in the country. Levi's grave is here in Kittery, under a tombstone inscribed with an epitaph written by Browning. Mr. Laighton's daughter, Celia, the oldest of the three, aspired to write poetry herself at an early age, adding to her natural attraction to the older man, the only eligible bachelor on the barren islands. The predictable result was that she was a bride at the age of 16, in a marriage which became most unsatisfactory and in later days would certainly have ended in divorce.

Mr. Laighton had acquired Smuttynose, one of the other islands, and Appledore, the largest. Toward the middle of the 19th century, he decided to build a summer hotel on Appledore. With transportation limited to horses, trains, and boats, a peaceful resort entirely surrounded by the protective moat of the Atlantic Ocean became quite an attraction. Furthermore, as Celia Thaxter blossomed into a talented poetess and cultural leader, she attracted some of the better known writers of the time, including Nathaniel Hawthorne, John Greenleaf Whittier, Henry David Thoreau, Ralph Waldo Emerson, Henry Wadsworth Longfellow, and Mark Twain, among others, artists such as Childe Hassam and Olaf Brauner, and famous musicians. Along with these talented guests, the island resort attracted many vacationers with no visible talent or claim to fame, including my great grandparents, grandparents, and my father, along with various other relatives including my Aunt Daisey, who died there. Counting my generation, my children, and my grandchildren, it adds up to six generations of my family at the Isles of Shoals, a record to challenge the Laightons, the fishermen, or any one else of whom I am aware. One of my grandsons, Caleb Martin, five days old, landed at Smuttynose from an Alden single, held, as one would expect, by his mother, and propelled by his proud grandfather.

As time went on, Oscar and his younger brother, Cedric, became more and more helpful in running the hotel, while Celia became more and more famous. This must have irritated Levi, who, for all his superior education, never created anything of note. Then one day Oscar and Levi were sailing out to the Shoals from Portsmouth when a vicious squall caught them, still far away from the security of the little islands. Oscar took it all in his stride, steering and bailing at the same time. Levi Thaxter, however, was petrified, and thenceforth sought any excuse to avoid the islands. Celia, on the other hand, spent as much time as possible at her beloved isles, cultivating her many friendships and her beautiful garden. She gave slips of her flowers to numerous friends, who planted them in their own gardens on the mainland. Years later John Kingsbury, founder of the Shoals Marine Laboratory, a joint venture of Cornell and U.N.H., had the great foresight to initiate a restoration of Celia's garden which was almost obliterated by years of neglect. He was able to obtain slips from the gardens ashore where Celia's original slips had flourished and bring them back to her garden on Appledore, now fully restored and lovingly tended.

As the late "Schnozzola" Durante used to say, "Every one wants to get into the act." A man named John R. Poor decided to cash in on the Laighton's idea and built a summer hotel named the Oceanic on Star Island. But he lacked the Laighton touch, and after a few years it failed, and the Laightons bought it. With the two hotels, their success was greater than ever.

My father was one of the leaders of a very active group of young people who returned to the Shoals year after year. He organized fierce naval battles in little rowboats in the bathing pond, and later led rowing trips around the islands. He would paddle his canoe around Appledore after a storm, to the consternation of the older people on shore who were watching the huge waves smashing into the rocks on the northeastern end of the island. Out in deep water where he was, the waves had flattened considerably for lack of wind, and they only built up menacingly in the shallow water near the rocks. However, if anything had happened to allow the the breakers to get a grip on the canoe, I would not be here to tell about it. To this day, I always like to have a friendly shore, permitting a safe landing, within easy reach.

Cedric Laighton had a daughter, Margaret, who, by all accounts, was a beautiful girl and very popular among the young men who frequented the Appledore Hotel. One of my father's cousins once took her rowing, that being one of the principal daytime activities at the islands. They went out to Anderson's Ledge, a small rock protruding from the relentless sea at low tide but entirely submerged at high tide, with nothing showing but the spindle which warned navigators of the hazard, a good distance southeast of Star Island. The tide being low, they landed on the ledge, and the young man decided it would be quite romantic to be stranded on a tiny island with a beautiful girl, and pushed the boat away. Margaret, however, being wise to the ways of the sea, and possibly also the ways of young men, put her foot on the painter, thus assuring transportation back to Appledore.

All who are so inclined may read of murders every day, and watch gruesome enactments on TV *ad nauseam.* But the murder at Smuttynose will be remembered forever because it was so out of character with the peaceful life of the Shoals and its unusual ramifications. Celia Thaxter wrote a gripping account of the circumstances in one of her books. I mention it briefly here because of its involvement with rowing.

Louis Wagner had worked spasmodically for some Norwegian fisherman who lived on Smuttynose. One day in March they came in to Portsmouth with a load of fish. Wagner happened by the dock, and during the course of conversation they said they would spend the night in Portsmouth, since it was already beginning to get dark. Later that night he rowed a dory out to the Shoals, landed at Smuttynose, and attacked the three women who remained on the island, using an axe. He murdered two of them, but the third escaped. He hunted in vain for her all over the island. As dawn approached, he gave up and returned to the bloody kitchen, where he made himself a substantial breakfast. He then rowed all the way back to the mainland, wearing the oak thole pins, which had been new, almost to the breaking point. He took a train to Boston, where he was apprehended and brought back to Maine, where he was tried and hung, the last to die at the end of a rope in the state.

Rowing to or from the Shoals was considered quite a feat in those days, and because of the murders, had connotations of evil. Nevertheless, my father rowed in to Portsmouth one day, played two sets of tennis with Margaret Laighton, and rowed back out to Appledore. Today, many people, young and old, men and women, from rank beginners to Olympic champions, participate in the annual Isles of Shoals race in Aldens, many rowing back as well as racing out. While no exact statistics are available, it is safe to say that neither Louis Wagner nor my father covered the distance as fast as the sliding seat oarsmen of today. It is gratifying to find many others rowing out to the Shoals in dories and peapods and other boats, including the famous Harvard rowing coach, Harry Parker, and Lloyd Dahman of the Union Boat Club, rowing out and back in real racing singles. To me, the most remarkable feat of all occurred in 1987, when Dwight Hamsley, a quadriplegic from Rye, New Hampshire, rowed out in an Alden single equipped with stabilizing pontoons. Details follow later.

Rowing played a big part in life at the Appledore Hotel and the newly acquired Oceanic Hotel on Star. Today it is hard to visualize a vacation without the distractions of automobiles, television, outboard motors, night clubs, and everlastingly organized activities. There was a certain grace at the Shoals, replaced today by frantic activity and boredom. An unhurried row refreshed the spirit and unburdened the mind, and the old families returned year after year to bask in the soothing atmosphere of the islands.

The internal combustion engine, particularly when combined with wheels, brought changes, for better or worse. Younger generations became too restless to settle for the lack of excitement at the Shoals. Guests at the Laighton hotels began to decrease in numbers. Death took its toll from the closely knit, loving Laighton family. Then in 1914, after the end of the summer season, the Appledore Hotel burned to the ground. The Oceanic continued, but the cliental gradually diminished.

Uncle Oscar had a most optimistic attitude towards life. He seemed to love everyone and appeared to be completely unaware that evil existed anywhere in the world. I have often wished in vain for some of his serenity. But, as he often admitted, he was not a businessman. Yet more and more of the responsibility of running the remaining hotel fell upon his shoulders.

Among the decreasing numbers of guests at the Oceanic were a group of Unitarians, who appreciated the peaceful atmosphere, the better to practice their religious activities. It was not long before they arranged to buy the hotel, and Uncle Oscar became a permanent guest each summer. He would sit in a rocking chair, his twinkling blue eyes showing under his black stovepipe hat, above his flowing white beard. He always wore a fresh blue flower in the buttonhole of his dark blue suit. In inclement weather he would sit just inside the lobby, but otherwise he would be out on the long porch.

When my father purchased the big house on the south side of Appledore in 1924, Uncle Oscar was one of the first to greet us, rowing over from Star Island to our slip in his heavy 18-foot dory. He showed my father how to make an outhaul, using a big iron casting (which looked just like Uncle Oscar's hat) for a mooring. In our house there were wooden bailers and birdhouses, crafted by Uncle Oscar himself, and oars, each branded with "O. Laighton." He had a strong affiliation for our house, having arranged for its construction. We had a certain empathy for the new owners of the Oceanic and always allowed their guests to land at our slip when they rowed over to explore Appledore. Sometimes problems arose, as when a rising tide caused the painter to submerge the bow, or a brisk southwester made it impossible for a landsman to row back to Star. We were always happy to help out in these frequent situations.

Uncle Oscar had an open motorboat, named *Twilight*, in which he took groups of hotel guests, mostly old ladies it seemed to me,

Uncle Oscar and guests, AEM checking the wake of Twilight. *Photo: Franklin Martin.*

around the islands, explaining various points of interest along the way. *Twilight* was a graceful, carvel-planked boat, except for the tombstone stern of a dory, which always seemed out of place to me. Power was supplied by a Lathrop engine, with little brass cups with petcocks on top of each cylinder. Uncle Oscar was no better at engines than he was at business, and my father, who ran the Marco Garage, was always happy to coax it back to life on the frequent occasions when it did not respond to Uncle Oscar's best efforts. The aging skipper always carried a scythe, suitably branded with his name, under the fore and aft

The Sightseer *arriving at The Isles of Shoals. Photo: Franklin Martin.*

seat on the starboard side of his boat. This was to free his propeller from lobster trap buoys which happened to be in his way. This was not appreciated by the local lobstermen, but somehow no one took Mr. Laighton to task for it.

One afternoon Uncle Oscar rowed over to our landing in his dory, accompanied by a man named Warren Shepard, a superb marine artist. They stayed for an enjoyable dinner, at the conclusion of which Mr. Shepard brought out a violin and proceeded to play in a way that would make Jack Benny sound like Oistrakh. Uncle Oscar leaned over toward my mother and said in a loud whisper "He don't play so good." This is all I remember of the occasion, except for the observation that Mr. Shepard had very dirty fingernails.

Long after Uncle Oscar celebrated his 90th birthday, he decided to write his book, *90 Years at The Isles Of Shoals*. He would row over from Star, tie up his dory at our slip, and climb up the rocks to our living room. There he would dictate his book to my father, who typed it out on his trusty Corona. My father persuaded him to cut down on the description of his trip to Europe, which so many have written about, and concentrate on the Shoals, which only he could relate. His great niece, Rosamond Thaxter (Celia's granddaughter), very kindly gave me the original typewritten pages.

At the end of the summer in 1938, we left the Shoals in the afternoon to spend the night at Uncle Oscar's house in Portsmouth. He was 99 at the time and as fit as ever, his jesting remark "I hope the good Lord hasn't forgotten me" apparently falling on deaf ears upstairs. I noticed an oil painting of the back of Appledore in the moonlight, with a wave breaking against the dark rocks. I stared at it spellbound for some time, awed by the beauty of the familiar scene, so faithfully reproduced. Uncle Oscar told me it had been painted by Warren Shepard, our violin-playing visitor at Appledore. He then asked me if I liked it. Although words failed me, he must have gotten the idea, for he said that he would leave it to me when he died. Coming from some one 99 years old, that was quite a promise. But when he passed away the following spring, there was nothing written about the painting. Rosamond Thaxter, however, who inherited all of his limited worldly goods, had heard about it, and sent it to me. It has occupied a place of honor on my living room wall ever since, save for a brief visit to an Isles of Shoals exhibit at the University of New Hampshire.

We left Uncle Oscar's house the next morning to drive to New Jersey in what turned out to be the great hurricane of 1938. The trip took more than 24 hours, and included all kinds of misadventures. After driving around numerous fallen trees and boats far from their usual element, we stopped before crossing a high bridge. My father and I walked ahead to check the structure and saw, to our horror, that the bridge ended in mid air, far above the receding salt water below.

In the summer of 1939 I was living alone in our house on Appledore. Rosamond Thaxter asked me to attend a belated funeral service for Uncle Oscar. He had been cremated when he died, and the ashes were to be buried in the little family graveyard near Celia's house, to join his mother and father and Celia and Cedric.

None of us can stop the clock, and the years which had finally caught up with Uncle Oscar brought changes to all of us. Young Margaret Laighton had grown up and married, not any of the eager young men at Appledore, but Edward Forbes of Naushon, in the Elizabeth Islands off Massachusetts. She had come to visit us for a weekend at Appledore, bringing her teenage daughter Anne. We were quite shocked to discover that the eternally young Margaret Laighton we had heard so much about was actually showing some signs of age, just like my father. The burial ceremony was to include Margaret and other descendants of the Laighton family.

I walked over to the little family graveyard on the appointed day, bringing a shovel to cover the remains of Uncle Oscar after the ceremony. It was a drizzly day and the bushes were wet. When I arrived at the grave, the others were already there: Rosamond Thaxter, Margaret Laighton Forbes and her four grown up children, her sister Barbara Durant, and the Rev. Lyman Rutledge, who owned the old Laighton cottage on Appledore. I cannot remember any one else being there. Considering all of Uncle Oscar's family and friends, there could have been enough store-bought floral arrangements to rival any gangster's funeral. Instead, there were only a few native wild flowers, picked on the way across the island. Mr. Rutledge spoke a few words and led a prayer, and then the four younger Forbes sang the Alleluia Chorus from Handel's *Messiah,* in perfect harmony, accompanied only by the wind in the bushes. It was as magnificent as any music I have ever heard, before or since. Elliot Forbes later became head of the music department at Harvard.

After the rest had left, I filled in the little grave and walked home with my shovel. On the way, the sun came out over the islands and the adjacent sea, and I burst out crying without restraint or shame. It was not that I was upset by the Lord finally remembering to take back Uncle Oscar; it was the simplicity, honesty, and shear beauty of the little ceremony I had just witnessed, so in keeping with the life that had finally ended.

Barnacle, *with AEM and Princess. Photo: Franklin Martin.*

5 • Barnacle

O ne Saturday, when Mr. Brewster was delivering his weekly catch of lobsters in Portsmouth, he stopped in at the emporium of one Sam Hooz. Situated in some ancient sheds, dilapidated by the elements and neglect, the business was about 10% antiques and 90% old junk. There Mr. Brewster spied an ancient butter churn. Most antique churns have internal paddles, but this one, probably being of an older design, was made to agitate cream by rocking the entire tub, like a rocking chair. It was rectangular in shape, 43 inches long, and 22 inches wide. The sides consisted of single pine boards, 14 inches wide, the ends rounded to become semi-circular. Grooves were cut along the inside edges to receive the ends of the 5/8-inch tongue-and-groove transverse planking. The small opening at the top was fitted with a removable cover, with a little round glass window to check progress of the butter making. Iron rods held the sides together, and iron trunnions were attached to the bottom to fit the rockers on which it swung. A pipe nipple at the bottom served as a drain for the buttermilk. It was painted with peeling yellow paint, and black letters proclaimed the name of the builder, M.M. Davis, I believe.

Mr. Brewster immediately thought it would make a great boat for children, but he considered the asking price of $5 excessive. When I heard of this great opportunity about to be lost, I couldn't wait to get to Portsmouth, fearing that each passing day invited some one else to walk off with the prize. The very next time my father's Elco Cruisette, *Folly*, went to Portsmouth, I was aboard, sitting on the vertically mounted steering wheel, rotating myself and the wheel with my feet, the better to see over the trunk cabin.

No sooner had we landed than I hotfooted it over to Sam Hooz's. I told him I wanted the butter tub, but not the rocker support, and held out two moist dollar bills, the total of my savings from my

AEM going to Portsmouth in Folly *to purchase* Barnacle. *Photo: Franklin Martin.*

lobster earnings. He thought for what seemed like an agonizingly long time, and finally consented to the deal.

When I arrived at Appledore with my new possession, I lost no time in taking it over to Mr. Brewster's barn, where he fitted a pine plug in the buttermilk drain, helped me enlarge the top opening and paint it battleship gray. He then painted the name I had selected, *Barnacle*, in black letters, 4 inches high, along each side.

I cut off the lower part of a broken oar, to provide some method of locomotion. Sinking the blade down perpendicular to the surface of the water, turning it 90 degrees, and prying it up against the round handle at the stern of the deck, I was able to force the ungainly little vessel ahead a few inches, where it seemed to stop until the next stroke. We called this method of propulsion "guinea boat," possibly because the Portuguese and Italian seiners used this method to move a seine boat sideways towards the mothership. It would not be easy to scull *Barnacle* because of the extremely short length. Besides, I was convinced that "guinea boat" was more efficient. How wrong I was! Years later my son demonstrated how much more efficient an oar blade is when it is getting lift like an airplane wing (as in sculling with a single blade moving back and forth at a proper angle of attack, or rowing with the new Douglas oars he designed) than just using resistance in a stalled condition (as in "guinea boat," or rowing with a sliding seat and an old-fashioned spoon oar).

I was only allowed to go out in *Barnacle* in the fresh water ice pond behind our house. Under this severe limitation I nevertheless learned to deal with the eccentricities of my new ship. Not only could it capsize very easily transversely like any narrow boat, but it could almost as readily capsize end for end. Nevertheless, in all the many miles I eventually travelled in *Barnacle*, I never capsized.

It was not long before some diplomatic persuasion, and a demonstration of capability, resulted in my father allowing *Barnacle* to venture out in the ocean...within limits. The limits were Mr. Brewster's outhaul to the west, the moorings to the south, and the Half Tide Ledges to the east. The latter, only a few hundred yards from our house, were for me a fascinating destination. They still are. At a normal high tide very little protrudes above the level of the sea, and breakers from the open ocean often make them untenable for boats

The fleet at sea. Left to right, dory, punt, Barnacle, Red Barn, *and* Seaweed.
Photo: Franklin Martin.

such as *Barnacle.* But as the tide recedes a whole new world opens up.
A little protected harbor emerges, and then, as the sea level drops farther, almost completely landlocked salt water ponds, accessible only to
very small boats. At each stage of the ever-changing tide it is always
possible to find a rock formation, reasonably flat on top, a few inches
above the water level, well padded with seaweed. A turn of the painter
around a suitable clump of the conveniently situated growth, with two
half hitches, serves to tie up a boat securely. I still inadvertently say to
visitors who want to join us in a row "tie up to that dock over there,"
forgetting that there is no dock within many miles. They look back in
bewilderment, but perhaps they learn a little bit about living in harmony with nature.

The water is always clear as crystal at the Shoals, and I never tired of looking down at the bottom at the Half Tide Ledges and in the deeper water outside. Red and blue mussels, sea anemone, crabs, flounders, and an occasional lobster venturing outside of the protective kelp. Life was never boring for me at the Shoals.

Before long I drilled a hole in the forward deck, and installed a little mast made out of a broomstick, and upper and lower yards. My mother made a square-rigged sail to fit, and *Barnacle* became a windjammer. She would sail directly before a brisk breeze at a remarkably slow pace, the turbulence behind her singularly inefficient stern emphasizing the importance of a well designed run on any boat. Having no centerboard or keel, in addition to her other limitations, the closest she could come to the wind would be about 175 degrees.

For all her faults, *Barnacle* served me well for several years, making many trips to far away places, such as Star Island, half a mile to the south. Perhaps her limitations encouraged me to try to design a faster, more seaworthy, and more stable boat some time in the distant future.

Some cruel person sent a black and white dog out to the Shoals to get rid of her. The Brewsters could not bear to see her die and adopted her, naming her Princess. She was one of the most intelligent and certainly the most obedient dogs I have ever known. The mildest scolding, almost never required, would give her pangs of shame and remorse, and the offense would never again be committed.

Princess loved to go out in boats, any time, in any kind of a boat, although most of her experience was with Mr. Brewster in a dory or bigger boat. One day she was at our house and heard me down at the slip. She came running down, head lowered to keep track of the cleats on the walkway. When she got to the water's edge, the only boat in sight was *Barnacle*, with me kneeling in my customary position in the cramped interior. She never hesitated, but jumped right into my lap, and seemed to sense immediately that the slightest motion on her part would result in a swim for both of us, and she hated to be in the water. From then on she was a constant companion in the little boat.

Years passed, and I grew a little bigger, but I was still able to squeeze into my little boat. Other boats claimed most of my attention, but *Barnacle* was never completely inactive in the summer, and always rested snugly in our cellar when we were not there. Then she was stolen, and my first boat seemed nothing but a memory.

AEM in Barnacle *half a century later. Photo: Marjorie Martin*

More than 30 years later I found her, much the worse for wear and abuse, the rigging gone, most of the tie-rods rusted away, and all the planking opened up. I must say that the spectacle brought a tear to my eye, but I carefully picked her up and brought her to Kittery Point. I painted her again, battleship gray, and my wife, Marjorie, painted the name on the sides, in big black letters, just as Mr. Brewster had done so many years before. I made new spars and sails, not, I fear, quite as good as the original.

One of the first activities of the restored little ship was to form one end of the starting line for the first Isles of Shoals Race, her tiny pennant fluttering from the masthead. The Barnacle Cup, a perpetual trophy engraved with the names of the winners of this annual Alden race, was named in her honor.

It would be almost impossible to make *Barnacle* watertight again, but I wanted my grandchildren to have a chance to try her out. So I covered the entire outside temporarily with clear plastic and launched her once more. Today she occupies a place of honor in my boathouse, with a photograph on the wall, showing the gallant little ship in all her glory, off our house on Appledore, with Star Island in the background. Princess and the young captain are aboard, and all is well.

6 • *The Punt*

*t*he Coast Guard station on Appledore was run by Captain Sprague. He was undoubtedly a C.P.O. or Warrant Officer, but we were generous with titles at the Shoals. In his spare time, which was plentiful, he liked to fish and catch lobsters.

One day he was fishing in a dory for cod and haddock with a local fisherman, anchored about a mile or so to the west of Appledore. It was a good, warm day, with a gentle breeze from the south, but a line of hard thunderheads began to appear over the mainland. Then it turned very black, so that all of the boats at their moorings and the nervous seagulls, appeared very white, as though freshly painted. My father went out to *Folly* and prepared to start the engine, fearful that the front would bring high winds to threaten the mooring. The big, black, clipper–bow schooner *Constellation*, anchored in Gosport Harbor with the Sears family aboard, put out a second anchor. A wall of spray appeared far to the west, and in almost no time we were hit with a mighty blast of wind, turning the placid sea to a white froth, followed by menacing breaking waves. To our horror, we saw *Constellation* starting to move rapidly backwards, despite the two anchors, and she would have been wrecked on the breakwater had they not started the engine.

Captain Sprague and his partner crouched in the bottom of their dory to keep it from capsizing, one bailing and the other steering for Appledore with a single oar. They were lucky to be on the windward (windud) side of the island, for they never could have rowed against such winds.

Having survived the ordeal, the stalwart captain resumed his lobster fishing. He had obtained, from sources unknown, an old Maine peapod, which he seemed to use mostly for transporting lobster bait, in the form of bluebacks, of the herring family, which he acquired

The punt with our Irish setter Fleur and AEM. Dory and Smuttynose Island in background. Photo: Franklin Martin.

from the guinea boats. I was quite taken with the idea of a rowboat with a bow at each end, little realizing what a part this very boat was to play in my life.

In due course, Captain Sprague was transferred, and Mr. Brewster bought the peapod. He called it the punt, which it certainly wasn't, but the name stuck, and it was never referred to by any other name from then on. He cleaned it up, repaired it, and painted it, white topsides, green bottom, white inside above the seats, and dark green below. Needless to say, I was dying to try it out, and Mr Brewster was only to glad to oblige. I suppose a 16–year old youth, having achieved the privilege of driving the old family station wagon, must get quite a thrill from getting behind the wheel of a real sports car, but it could not compare to the ecstasy I experienced the first time I rowed the punt.

It was 13 feet four inches long, and four feet wide. The midship section consisted of pretty rounded bilges and some deadrise. The garboard strakes went from nearly horizontal in the middle to nearly vertical at the ends. It is not easy to twist a plank this way, but it makes all the difference in performance. The adjacent planks are similarly twisted, but less and less towards the shear strake. This makes the hollow curves which distinguish a good boat from a mediocre or poor one. In whittling a model, the knife must be adroitly twisted with each shaving toward the bow to avoid a spoon–shaped bow with a rocker bottom, which is not the same at all.

I was astonished at the difference between our dory and the punt. For all its good qualities, a dory does not go through the water very gracefully. The bow does not have the subtle, sharp shape, with a hollow waterline, to cut through the water easily. The tombstone stern comes to a point only at the bottom, and thus presents a wider and wider transom the further it is immersed, creating turbulence and therefore drag like a small transom. In waves the dory's graceful shear, flaring sides, and high freeboard combine to lift it up rather than letting it become inundated. But when it lands in the trough, it is with a bone–jarring pounding motion, which seems anything but pleasant to me. Furthermore, it tends to stop all forward motion, so that the glide is not all that much more than that of *Barnacle.*

The punt, on the other hand, would lift itself over waves equally well, but it would land with a satisfying "swoosh," throwing the water out several feet to either side. It was like riding over a bump on a soft cushion rather than a stiff board. Furthermore, it would not lose headway as much. It seemed that I would never get enough chances to row the punt, in glassy calm water, where it seemed to glide silently forever, in average waves from wind or boats, where its motion was so graceful, and in really rough water where its seaworthiness was so reassuring.

To my great delight, Mr. Brewster sold the punt to my mother for

$10. I became the punt boatman, to add to my other title of head of The Department of Dumping and Burning, my own glorified title for garbageman. I bailed it out after each rainstorm, and many times besides, for it always "sweated a little," a euphemism for leaking considerably. I painted it each year and did my best to keep caulking in its ample seams, which no amount of swelling could close completely. I replaced the rotting wood that held the oarlock sockets and shaped a block with my jackknife to hold together a split plank at the stern.

Folly was secured to a cable, called a bridle, running from the spar buoy at the mooring to a ringbolt on shore. I tied the punt directly to the spar, using *Barnacle* as a tender to get back and forth from shore. One day, immediately after a heavy rain, I went out in *Barnacle* to bail out the punt. As usual, I couldn't resist going for a row, heedless of the old warning "wind before rain, go out again; rain before wind !!!__***!!." Just as I got back to the mooring, untied *Barnacle*, and was about to tie up the punt, a fierce wind came up from the southwest, although there was not a cloud in the sky. A big chop came up in no time at all, and "Folly" really strained at the mooring, pulling the big spar right out of my hands and under water. I was left with nothing to hold on to, and nothing to leeward (louard) but Spain. I quickly secured *Barnacle*'s lobster pot warp (wop) painter to the inwale at the stern, and rowed as hard as I could to windward (windud). It was quickly apparent that I was making progress in the wrong direction. It is doubtful whether I could have prevailed against that wind in the punt alone, but with the waves crashing against the bluff bow of *Barnacle* and beginning to come over the top to swamp her, there was no way I could win. I turned broadside and headed towards the nearest rocks, letting the wind carry us sideways as fast as it would, hoping that I would not be carried beyond the east end of Appledore before I reached terra firma. This was a lesson I never forgot, and I have had harrowing revues in the years that followed. In a self–propelled boat there is no substitute for the power to get to windward in the emergency circumstances that may come as a surprise at any time. Many well meaning but ill-advised people equate stability to seaworthiness and think that a wide, blunt skiff, with toothpick oars, assures safety.

As time went on, we depended less on Mr. Brewster for fishing opportunities and created our own. We acquired several lobster traps and caught our own cunners for bait. When a "guinea boat" would set its purse seine around a school of mackerel, I would often row out in the punt to observe the proceedings. As they circled the fish in the mothership, towing the seine boat, a beautiful double–ender about 28 feet long, men in the latter would pay out the net, with corks along the upper edge to keep it afloat and lead weights along the bottom to keep it hanging straight down. There were also big steel rings along the bottom edge through which a rope, called the purse line, led. After they had gone a full circle, and the ends of the seine were together, a gasoline-powered winch in the seine boat was used to haul in the purse line, thus closing the bottom of the net and allowing the hapless fish no escape. Then all but one or two of the crew would get in the seine boat and start the laborious task of hauling the seine back, confining the fish to a smaller and smaller area of ocean. When the mackerel were sufficiently concentrated, they would be scooped up with a big dipnet, raised by a line running over a sheave on the boom and down to a power winch on the mothership. During this operation, the corks would be inclined to bunch together, and I was only too happy to volunteer to tow them out with the punt. The fishermen were invariably very friendly and would often offer a few mackerel. If the catch included bluebacks, which they could not sell economically, they would give me all of them. I would row up to the side of the mothership, following instructions which were sometimes difficult to understand, due to the language barrier. Then they would open a scupper port and the fish would come cascading down until I thought the poor punt would surely sink. After thanking them profusely, I would row back in triumph, mixed with apprehension, for the dried out seams of the upper topsides, now mostly submerged, were admitting the ocean at a prodigious rate. I would salt down in buckets enough for our use and give the rest to Mr. Brewster, who would do the same but in wood barrels. The mixture of oily bluebacks and salt, after a few weeks, produced an aroma that not every one would appreciate. The liquid which gradually surrounded the bodies of the departed we called Brewster's Snow Puff. It was said to be good for the skin, but this was of little concern to me. All I know is that after immersing our hands in it we were not very popular at the dinner table.

AEM and Franklin rowing dory. Photo: Franklin Martin.

For what we called deep-sea fishing, we would use the dory, first procuring some of the big red mussels known as "mussel a bush" at the Half Tide Ledges at low tide. Then we would row out to the south of the spar buoy that used to mark Halfway Rocks. Rowing a heavy dory, with several people in it, is not my idea of fun, but our dory was a very necessary part of life. We would anchor, shuck mussels, bait hooks, and lower our heavy cod lines to the vicinity of the bottom. Cod and haddock were plentiful, and it did not take them long to discover the mussels. My brother Franklin and I followed the Isles of Shoals method of landing a fish, which consisted of hauling the line in as hard and fast as possible over the gunwale of the boat. All of the dories at the islands had grooves in the gunwales (gunnels) from this practice. It worked well for cunners, which had very tough mouths, but we lost many a good many cod and haddock because of this practice. As the fish would make a desperate attempt to escape, the line would be snubbed so much by the gunwale that it would hardly give an inch, and since something had to give, the hook would come out of the delicate mouth. A rod and reel, such as I use today in the Alden, were strictly for landlubbers. My sister Mary, holding the line over the side, where her little arms would give at every tug of the hook, was quite successful.

Fortunately for me, my older brother, Franklin, did not seem to appreciate the fine points of the peapod design and was quite content to take the dory when we took the two boats mackerel fishing. We would troll lead jigs, shined up with a jackknife, through a school, rowing as hard as possible to make the jigs challenging. These days, I have to remember to slow down to troll at the same speed. I rigged a little bell in the punt to warn of a strike, but it proved more effective to just tie the line around my bare ankle.

One day we were both trolling for mackerel off Star Island in my brother's canoe, which was called the *Black Junk.* The second word in the name derived from the fact that the old canoe had suffered too many years of wear and abuse and was indeed a candidate for the junk heap. The first alluded to the fact that it had been painted several times with a mixture of tar and turpentine. This treatment was the equivalent today of fiberglass over an old wood hull beyond repair. The tar precluded the future use of paint or anything else, as it is not friendly to other materials. It is nothing if not durable, as evidenced in the black splotches on the bleached rocks, quite visible today, where lobstermen soaked the heads (hand-knitted nets at the entrances) of their lobster traps. Durable though the tar solution was, it was incapable of stopping leaks or preventing wracking of the hull in waves. Nevertheless, with two young paddlers the *Black Junk* was fast enough, and, warned by the ankle, we each pulled in several good mackerel.Then, just as Franklin started to pull in another, a huge shark broke the surface, swallowed the mackerel, and headed for the depths. It pulled the line from my brother's hands but not his ankle. The stern made a sudden downward lurch, and swamping seemed inevitable, but fortunately the line parted just then, and the stern bounced back up. With my heart racing, seemingly in my mouth, I gingerly pulled in my jig, praying that the mackerel would leave it alone for once.

Franklin acquired a 1000–hook trawl, which we used to set from the dory. This gave us a first-hand idea of what dory fishing on the Grand Banks must have been like. Not an easy life, and we only had to row back to a comfortable and stable house on Appledore instead of a bobbing schooner far off in the fog or other hostile weather.

Although many of our activities took place in the dory, or other boats, the queen of them all remained the peapod (punt). The shear joy of rowing that boat was always the frosting on the cake for me. When we did not have the crates of food that required the dory, I would row over to Star in the punt to meet the noon boat, gawk at the city folk getting off the *Sightseer*, talk to Uncle Oscar until the mail was sorted, and row back with our mail. I usually planned it so that I could catch the waves from the *Sightseer* before she slowed down to make a landing. I would row just as hard as I could, directly into the waves, never tiring of the smooth, cushioned motion of the boat which had evolved from the experience of many a smart lobsterman and boat builder. The former were able to row out in the worst weather Maine winters could produce. No wonder the *Sightseer*'s waves were so easily and pleasantly traversed. Not infrequently, the *Sightseer*'s ancient scotch boiler would blow a tube, and another steam tug, the *Mitchell Davis*, would be pressed into service for the day. The waves from the *Mitchell Davis* were steeper, and therefore something of a refreshing novelty to ride. To this day I do not understand this phenomenon, although I have certainly devoted more than a little time in an effort to reduce wavemaking in boats large and small.

One day I was rowing out between Star and White Island in quite a brisk southerly. I was having a great time in the white-capped waves, high enough to block my view, except when riding crests. All of a sudden two of our Coast Guard appeared from out of nowhere in a powered lifeboat. They asked if I needed any assistance, and, when

The family crew in dory. Photographer unknown.

assured that I did not, went surfing back to Appledore. The Coast Guard were our friends; not our adversaries.

One morning while I was rowing outside of Smuttynose Island, I came upon a school of tunafish. I quickly rowed back and borrowed a harpoon, complete with "lilly iron," spliced to many fathoms of line which was tied to a keg, very kindly loaned by one of the Coast Guard. I rowed back out until I was right over the fish, shipped the oars, and scrambled to the bow. I picked up the harpoon, and aimed it at one of the fish below. I hesitated in letting it fly, first checking to make absolutely sure the line and keg could make a hasty departure from their cramped location without entangling my legs. By this time, the fish had moved, and I had to go back to the oars. This was repeated several times, but, for lack of courage or skill, I never connected. Thus ended the first of my two unsuccessful encounters with tunafish.

When Franklin and I were away at summer school, my father decided to surprise us by rigging the punt for sailing. He had the best of intentions, but he was no naval architect, and he was overly cautious about how much sail his young sons should expose to the unpredictable winds. The result was a short, heavy mast, with a miniature loose–footed sail made out of some old canvas that must have come from a square-rigger. Furthermore, there was no keel or centerboard. After a few experiments, I removed the entire business, as tactfully as possible, and the peapod (punt) went back to being the finest rowing boat at the Shoals, or the whole world, as far as I was concerned.

Not that I didn't try many other rowing boats. I never hesitated to test any rowing boat I could get my hands on, with or without permission. The lap–strake skiffs at the Oceanic Hotel were always available while the guests were at lunch. They were nice and light, but their transom sterns and typical unshaped bows kept them out of the class of the punt. I persuaded visiting yacht owners to let me try their dinghies, which they were only too happy to show off. There were skiffs, and Whitehalls with beautiful wineglass sterns, and even peapods, all well painted or varnished. But a few strokes on the oars quickly revealed that the shabby old punt was still the fairest of them all for performance. The wineglass stern is a great advantage, for it can travel light without any transom in the water, and yet there is a great addition in capacity and stability as weight is added. This is just what the Whitehall watermen wanted. They could race the competition out to a newly anchored square-rigger, pick up a fare before someone else, and row them back at a comfortable speed. The lines of the stern, however, must slope up to the transom, causing turbulence at slower speed than do the straighter buttocks of a properly designed double–ender. To put it another way, the wineglass stern results in a shorter effective waterline length than has a double–ender of the same length. Not just waterline length, but effective waterline length is all important in the ease and speed of rowing. The peapods I rowed were either wider overall or had harder bilges (resulting in more stability but greater waterline beam). It was never a disappointment to get back into the punt after one of these many trials.

For many years I wanted desperately to own the cherished peapod. I asked for it as a combined Christmas and birthday present, all to no avail. It was eventually given to my younger brother, Bill, who named it *Ole Possum*. He was generous in letting me use it most of the time, although he complained that it made the sides go in and out when I rowed hard. Perhaps there was a message in the fact that I never could own the boat I loved so much: if I wanted such a boat, I would have to design it myself.

Rebuilt Forge

The forge, making the shepherd's crook for the outhaul. Left to right, Henry Freeman at bellows, AEM, Franklin Martin, Sr., and Franklin. Photo: Martin.

7 • Kent School

*L*eaving the Shoals at the end of the summer was always a sad experience for me. As August waned, a sense of gloom began to pervade the atmosphere. All too soon, the boats, one by one, would have to be hauled up for their winter hibernation, either at Star Island or in our cellar. The cistern would have to be drained and cleaned, all the pipes blown out by lung power, and storm windows put up. Then we would row over to the dock at Star for the last time, and board the *Sightseer*. As the beautiful islands gradually faded away in her wake, I usually cried, for I was all too well aware that it would be many months before we returned.

The year 1931 was different. Schools postponed opening for two weeks due to a polio epidemic, a blessed reprieve. By then the *Sightseer* had stopped running, and we were planning to depart in Mr. Brewster's Jonesport. Dawn broke on the scheduled day to the accompaniment of a screaming wind from the northeast (no-theest; landsmen said nor'east and sou'east, just as everyone said nor'west and sou'west, but at the Shoals no one would have thought of saying anything but no-theest and sou-theest). It would have been pretty wet in the open Jonesport, even with the canvas spray hood up, considering the overload of people, dogs, and gear.

We rowed over in Mr Brewster's dory to Star, where a former Isles of Shoals Coast Guard member named Calder was anchored in his new command, a 75-foot patrol boat. These boats had more dignity than any I knew of, with their flaring bows, high bulwarks, and forward wheelhouse, followed by a long trunk cabin containing two huge Sterling engines. At full throttle, they could achieve a speed of 17 knots. Since their duty was to chase rumrunners, most of which could go more than 40 knots with their surplus World War 1 Liberty aircraft engines, they were not particularly effective. With their round bottoms, they rolled

55

alarmingly, and even when the small waves of a passing vessel had long since passed by, they seemed to continue rolling indefinitely. Nevertheless, I had watched them with fascination for years, and now thrilled at the possibility of riding in a real storm in one.

Calder was a good friend of my father, and readily agreed to take us to Portsmouth. As we got out from the lee of Appledore, the full force of the storm became apparent. I stood in the wheelhouse, holding on tightly against the awesome rolling, in seventh heaven. Great sheets of spray would be thrown out against the wind by the flair of the starboard bow, to be blown back in a beautiful curve, and smash against the vertical windows.

I was enjoying myself immensely, but I had some mixed emotions, not without some apprehension. We were leaving the Shoals for the winter. I was about to start life at Kent School. I looked forward with happy anticipation to rowing with a sliding seat, a device unheard of at the Isles of Shoals. How much difference would the added power of my legs make? How fast could an eight-oar shell go? As fast or faster than Mr. Brewster's one-lunger dory? As fast as the Elco, or the *Sightseer*? What would it be like rowing with a single 12-foot sweep? My father had organized a crew for the dory on several occasions. My mother and brother Franklin sat side by side on the after seat, each with a trusty ash oar. My brother Bill and I sat on the middle seat, likewise each manning an oar. My father rowed with two oars in the bow, while Mary, the youngest, sat in the stern and steered. I thought it was quite good fun, but the younger members of the crew soon tired of the sport. The dory made magnificent waves, just like a motorboat, but it didn't actually go very fast. I figured that a 62-foot shell would go somewhat faster.

I also looked forward to playing hockey, which was by far my favorite game, possibly because it was played on my favorite element, in one of its two other forms. At Carteret Academy, a day school in New Jersey, I had been coached by a remarkable, wiry, little man named Mr. Boyson, who was always referred to as Baukey. He was tough, and he had quite a temper, as evidenced by a story of one of his golfing experiences. He was taking an inordinate number of practice swings before driving, and an impatient member of a following foursome knocked his ball off the tee. Baukey calmly replaced the

Kent School. Photo: Kent School.

ball, and said to the agitator, "Go ahead, knock it off again, I haven't had a fight in two weeks," and continued his practice. For all his belligerence, Baukey was a great hockey coach. He rightly figured that skating is the key element in hockey, and he really knew how to teach what he called "skating from the hip." Although there were not enough boys in the senior class to make up a team, Carteret regularly beat much larger schools, including Kent. His boys knew how to skate better.

Academic work was not my favorite school activity, but circumstances put me on the honor roll at Carteret. The circumstances were that the administration found it a little difficult to attract enough paying students to meet expenses. One useful device to alleviate the situation was to make sure that junior made the honor roll, regardless of effort or ability. My experience in French, taught by a Mr. Laity, was a good example. He showed little interest in the subject or the progress of his charges, being instead more concerned with the virtues of his powerful Chrysler and the remarkable flying speed of 800 miles per hour, which, he claimed with a straight face, was achieved by the deer fly. Nevertheless, my report card indicated a proficiency in French which made my parents proud, up to a point.

The scholastic standards at Kent were considerably higher, as became evident when I received a mark of 6 on the entrance exam in French. No, gentle reader, that is not a misprint for 60, it is 6 (six). The threat of harder academic work didn't bother me, but some other doubts remained.

Kent School was Episcopal, High Episcopal, founded and run by Father Frederick H. Sill, O.H.C. (Order Of The Holy Cross).My religious experience up until then had consisted of walking to the Church Of The Holy Communion in South Orange, with my family, including my grandmother and my Uncle Jack.

After walking about a mile to the place of worship we always sat in the front pew on the right side of the aisle. I often wondered what would have happened had any one else ever attempted to sit in that pew. As it turned out, no one ever dared. On the wall in front of the pew was a large bronze tablet, given by my grandmother. The title of it was "The Great War 1914-1918." The text was as follows: "All honor and grateful tribute to God for those who, daring to die, survive." This seemed like a generous way to give thanks that Uncle Jack was still among us, but it didn't do much for those who did not come back. Uncle Jack lived with my grandmother in a house she built just behind ours, which my father called "Peepover," a sarcastic reference to the fact that she watched every move we made, and the Shoals was our only escape from her constant supervision. When she was well over 90 she gave the house to Uncle Jack, in a devious effort to outsmart the I.R.S. Unfortunately, he dropped dead on the golf course shortly thereafter, and she was forced to pay inheritance taxes on her own house.

My father always sat next to me in church, and when the sermon was about to begin he would pull out a large stop watch, hold it up ceremoniously, and as the minister uttered the first word, turn it on with a loud click. At the conclusion, there would be another loud click, and my father would announce, in a whisper that could be heard at least five pews away, "31 minutes, 23 seconds", or some such figure, displaying obvious pleasure if it happened to be shorter than usual.

This background hardly prepared me for the very serious religious activity at Kent School, but I had decided to make the best of it.

What really concerned me was the fact that I was inclined to be quite independent, and I cherished freedom more than anything in the world. I was accustomed to making my own decisions, for there were no organized activities at the Shoals. I never wasted time sitting around waiting for something to happen, as so many young people do today. I could always think of plenty of things to do, if Franklin had not already thought of them, and they were usually good fun, good exercise, or somewhat creative. I had already developed an aversion to what I called "Rule by the dumb," even though so far I had managed to escape it.

These characteristics, which I am sure many would consider personality defects, were hardly destined to mesh harmoniously with the structured life of Kent School. Thus, while the big Coast Guard boat plunged toward the safe haven of Portsmouth, it was taking me on a journey with an uncertain destination.

Father Sill was a man of great strength of character, with innovative and sound ideas about education, indomitable courage in adversity, and the magnetic personality to persuade others to help him reach his goals. In reading about the early days of the school, one wonders how he was able to build such a great school with absolutely no financial resources, facing continuously the brutal fact that there was not enough money to feed the boys and provide enough heat, let alone paying the long-suffering masters. But Father Sill persevered and never gave up or let up until he accomplished what he wanted to do.

Whether out of necessity or philosophy, he required every boy to participate in taking care of the school, cleaning the halls, washrooms, and schoolrooms, waiting on the tables, washing the dishes, and keeping the furnaces going. This was just the medicine for lazy sons of rich parents who were used to being waited on hand and foot.

He found good masters, many of them great, willing to accept the challenge and stick with the faltering little school until it became a strong institution and a real force in education.

Last but not least, Father Sill, having coxed the varsity eight at Columbia, had his heart set on making rowing a significant part of Kent. From the most humble beginnings, Kent grew to be a major fac-

Father Sill and athletic coaches. Back: D. Tirrell, C. Bragdon, W. Worthington, K. Moore, G. Hall. Front: B. Titus, M.D. Nadal. Father Sill, J. Humphreys, T. Evans. Photo: Kent School.

tor in scholastic rowing. Even much later, when I was there, there was so little competition among schools that Kent was forced to race against college freshmen a good part of the time. Kent Crews traveled to England to win the Princess Elizabeth Cup at Henley more than once.

Kent was a great opportunity for me, which I did not fully appreciate nor take full advantage of. Although I did put considerable effort into many phases of the school life, I gradually found myself in disagreement with some of the policies. I had an unfortunate tendency to accent the negatives rather than the positives, a fault which is difficult to overcome. Sad to say, there are no institutions or individuals completely devoid of negative qualities, if one chooses to seek them out.

My father, whatever his failings, was honest and fair to a fault. At Christmas, in addition to all the presents, one or more of us would receive a check for an odd sum, such as $2.37. This represented the balance to make the dollar value of presents equal among the four children. Years later, if he had to borrow a stamp for a letter after the post office was closed, he would insist on repaying the three cents, even if it required writing a check.

Hypocrisy was a word unknown to me, because my father was always straightforward, even if it meant being brutally frank. In his automobile business, he periodically reviewed in his mind the performance of each of his employees. He asked himself in each case what he would do if faced with the decision to give a raise or lose the employee. If he decided on the former, he would immediately give the man a raise. If any one asked for a raise, it was always refused, for the decision had already been made, strictly on the basis of merit. The men were happy to remain, year after year.

I suppose that my father's example had a profound effect on me. Although I, like almost everyone else, cannot claim to be 100 percent honest, I still have very strong aspirations in that direction. While I try to respect the biblical injunction to "judge not, that ye be not judged." I cannot condone the blatant dishonesty which is all around us. Advertising, particularly on television, is often designed to give a false impression, and sometimes gives product information which contains outright lies. Major media news is deliberately slanted to favor the causes the perpetrators believe in, and more and more often contains inaccuracies. Politicians, particularly members of Congress, indulge in any number of dishonest words and actions, some of which are illegal, but they figure, correctly, that if they bring enough benefits to special interests, they will always be reelected. In big business, government at all levels, and some professions, such as teaching, advancement depends less and less on merit, and more and more on fawning loyalty to superiors,and groups such as unions, right or wrong, to say nothing of race, creed, or color. All of these concepts were, and still are, contrary to what I had come to believe in. I was more comfortable with the simple laws of nature, as experienced at the Isles of Shoals, where the unforgiving sea cannot be fooled, and lack of effort or ability can be punished swiftly and relentlessly.

Academically, the very capable masters were of great benefit to me, and I took full advantage of the opportunity, with one exception:

French. Despite years of French governesses, Mr. Laity, and summer school, French was still my downfall. My brain, such as it is, seems to be lopsided in the direction of analyzing and figuring, leaving little space for memorizing foreign languages. My French master, a most precise and meticulous man who appeared to weigh close to 300 pounds, was known as Tiny Baker. He could scarcely conceal his contempt for such a poor student as myself and informed me that I "would never pass the baaahds (College Board Examinations) in June. One day, as he was writing the next assignment of idioms on the blackboard for us to copy in our notebooks, he started talking about the best student he had ever had. It seemed that this gifted youth would just copy the idioms on the top of his desk, in chalk, and have them all memorized before the class was over. The next time he turned around, he discovered that I was writing down the idioms in chalk on my desk. I don't know to this day why he did not suffer a stroke or a heart attack, but the incident did facilitate my transfer to the class of Cap Harrington, who was much more tolerant of what he called the dummies, and he succeeded in steering me through the final reefs for the absolute minimum passing mark. For mathematics and physics it was another story. I was so confident in algebra that I bet someone that I would get 100 in the College Boards. I had to pay up, however, as I only got 99.

Hockey was somewhat disappointing. My first experience involved a four-mile walk to a lake which had frozen before the school rinks. When my class got there, we played keep-away for a while, and then Cyrus Vance and another of the top players of the year before (the second form; I had entered in the third form) chose up teams in the usual way. I was one of the first to be chosen. Just as we were about to start a game, our coach, a very "intellectual" English teacher named John Park, arrived on the scene. He announced that he would pick out teams, although they told him they had already done so. As a result, I found myself standing around in the cold after the long uphill walk, watching twelve boys, some of whom could hardly skate at all, play all afternoon. Being somewhat vindictive, I took advantage of an opportunity for revenge later on. He came in to English class one morning bringing some newspaper clippings. He said that we should be informed about current events, and right then the schooner *Bluenose* was racing the *Gertrude L. Thebaud*, which he pronounced

"Thee-bud." It's"Tay-bow," I immediately announced in a loud voice. He countered in a stern voice "it's Thee-bud." I stood my ground and repeated, a little louder, "it's Tay-bow." It went back and forth several times, until he finally said, "Martin, if you're trying to get my goat, you're certainly succeeding." Thus the battle ended, and everyone learned the correct pronunciation. I had not been entirely unprepared for this encounter. The Thebaud family were friends of my family, and we had, in fact, inherited from them the big Packard we used to go from South Orange to Portsmouth after the 1929 stock market crash ended the career of *Folly* in the family.

The coach of the varsity hockey team was assistant headmaster Bill Nadel. He was a very pleasant man and completely loyal to Father Sill. In my opinion, however, he was not first in line when they were passing out brains. In fact, I had nothing but contempt for his methods of coaching hockey. I was appalled by what seemed to be team selection without regard for merit. I longed for the days of Baukey, where you knew what you had to do to get on a team. Needless to say, I never made the varsity, due, no doubt, in part to my ornery nature.

At first I went at the heavy religion hammer and tongs. I took confirmation classes from Father Sill, was confirmed by the bishop, learned to serve at the altar, and joined the group practicing ringing the big bells in the chapel. I even went to confession, a practice unheard of in our version of the same Episcopal religion in South Orange. I seemed to detect a lack of interest on the part of Father Sill when I confessed to having "smutty thoughts," inspired, no doubt, by the only females one saw for months at a time, the wives of masters who sometimes ate in the dining hall. It appeared that he was more interested in infractions of the school rules, by others as well as the confessor. This brought up the subject of the selection of prefects, those chosen to take care of discipline. As I saw this system in action, I was happy to have no part in it.

One incident I will never forget involved one of my classmates, Morris Littell. He had a sensational mind, being able to read an entire page at a glance, and he could remember long passages of prose or poetry, seemingly without effort. He was also far ahead of his time in being able to kick a football very far with his bare foot. But he had some kind of a mental block which I think any one interested in education could readily detect. Even I, with none of the knowledge of the human mind which I later tried to acquire, could see that he was not responding to the school discipline and needed some more understanding attention. Nevertheless, at the daily job assemblies, where the prefects read off reports of jobs improperly performed, the name of Morris Littell would come up with dismal frequency, and he would be given another hour of detention, to perform extra work. Finally one Thursday night, when the prefects and council members met in Father Sill's study for a kind of kangaroo court of discipline, one of the prefects came down to the study hall to select a culprit. You could hear a pin drop as he picked out poor Morris Littell. He was led up to Father Sill's study, where he was soundly beaten with a wooden paddle.

The next morning, when attendance was taken at breakfast, Morris Littell was missing, and he was not in his room or anywhere else. This was something of an emergency, for if he had strayed into the rattlesnake country in the woods, anything could happen. For some reason the school doctor took charge and immediately organized a search by groups of older boys. Fortunately, Morris was unharmed, but he never returned to Kent School.

Father Sill selected the prefects very carefully. They were invariably good athletes, liked and respected by their classmates. But did they also require a certain loyalty to Father Sill rather than their classmates? Was attendance at confession a requisite? Was there true separation of church and state? Whatever the answers, it seemed to me that prefects faced an inner conflict. On the one hand, they were typical mischievous schoolboys, anxious to be accepted by their peers as equals in the usual discussions, pranks, and roughhousing that are a part of life in a boys' boarding school. On the other hand, they were Father Sill's lieutenants, a kind of Gestapo, or K.G.B. One always kept an eye out for the approach of a prefect and quickly altered activity and conversation to what was expected. One prefect forgot himself and joined happily in a big roughhouse scuffle on the porch of one of the dorms. All of a sudden he remembered his position of authority, and announced "You all get an hour of detention, including me."

Only in the classroom were the masters in charge of discipline. Cyrus Vance, the senior prefect in my class, took advantage of this situation to resolve the dilemma of trying to be two different people at once. Outside of class, he was the stern disciplinarian feared by all wrongdoers, particularly lower classmen. In class, however, he could be one of the boys. I remember a Latin class which was held in a room adjacent to the porch in front of the old main building. It had windows facing the porch, only three feet above it. There would be a bell five minutes before each class, and then a final bell which was the signal for all students to be sitting at their desks or be recorded as late by the master, resulting in an hour of detention (work). The game was to see how close one could get to the final bell before coming to class. Coming through the window provided a shortcut, with a saving of several precious seconds. As a latecomer breathlessly approached the open window, several of the earlier arrivals would rush to the window, close it, and attempt to hold it down until the final bell. We were all happy to have Cy Vance participate in this game, and I am sure it provided a welcome outlet for him.

The majority of boys were either not aware of any faults of the system, or they attached less importance to them than I. I sometimes wish that I had had a more easygoing, optimistic attitude about it, but none of us can rewrite history, though many try. Whatever the problems of church and state at Kent, they pale by comparison with the bigotry, suffering, and wars related to religion over the centuries. It seems deplorable that man's highest aspirations toward knowledge of the Supreme Being who loves us all should so often degenerate into bitter quarrels over specifics.

While I had become disillusioned by what I perceived as hypocrisy in religion at Kent, I never lost faith. I could never believe that any one specific religious doctrine could constitute the one and only path, rendering all other religions evil. Many years after my school days, my son Carl led me to a simple little building in Cohasset called the Vedenta Center. Inside each of the ten plain glass windows hangs a small round stained glass medallion, depicting one of the world's ten major religions. Guyatri Devi, an extraordinary woman from India, conducts very direct and simple services there, without a trace of pomp and circumstance. She says "Truth is one; men call it by different names." This expresses my feelings better than anything I have heard or read, and I could never bring myself to support any religion which condemned all other religions.

For the most part, the place where I worship is the great outdoors. I often think of God when I am rowing, always with gratitude for the privilege of enjoying the magnificence of the edge of the sea. Often I row by the old Congregational Church in Kittery Point, where George Washington once worshipped. In the late afternoon I hear the bells playing a familiar hymn, just like it was at the Kent chapel so many years ago. This always gives me a feeling of peace and tranquility and a sense of continuity in life. The best of everything in life lives on.

There is a little old stone church near the highest point of Star Island, looking out over the other islands and the surrounding sea. There is a foot-pumped organ, for there is no electricity for music or lights. At night the good Unitarians pick up lighted candles on the porch of the hotel and climb up a winding path to the dark church. One by one they hang their candles on sconces, until the building is fully lighted. This is a moving little service, whether as seen from our house on Appledore or as a participant. It is the simplicity and continuity that appeal to me, and I hope they continue to have it forever, just as I first saw it more than 60 years ago. I sense the same continuity as I sit in the old Congregational Church in Kittery Point, listening to Christmas carols sung by the local choir in perfect harmony, remembering that George Washington sat in that very spot. Tyrants have tried to crush various religions, from within as well as from without, for all of recorded history. They have never succeeded. They never will.

Early in my career at Kent, I decided to become a naval architect. Typically, I thought I had accumulated enough practical experience without any formal training. Fortunately, I was persuaded otherwise. There were only three colleges having undergraduate naval architecture courses in the country, M.I.T, University of Michigan, and Webb Institute of Naval Architecture. The latter was founded by William H. Webb, a very successful 19th-century shipbuilder. He left enough money so that the income alone could pay the entire cost of running it. This immediately appealed to my father,who informed me in no uncertain terms that no funds would be forthcoming to finance four years at either of the other two institutions. I soon found out that getting in would not be easy. The first step was to have high marks in all of the mathematical subjects, along with physics, English, and chemistry. This I considered quite within reach, providing I was willing to work hard during the remaining years at school. But these qualifications would only allow me to take the competitive examinations on which admission was based. It was quite clear that with a completely free college education at stake, there would be many capable contenders for the 15 openings in the freshmen class.

Thus my last months at Kent became quite serious. I was determined to get in regardless of the odds, which seemed to get worse as time went on. In due course, Webb sent copies of previous entrance exams, so that I would have a preview of what I would be up against. It was quite a shock. The mathematics seemed far beyond what I had found so easy. I turned to the venerable Deac Anders, head of the mathematics department at Kent, for help. He had an intimidating voice and a dark, severe look. He had little patience with wayward boys and an obvious contempt for the ones who would not, or could not, cope with mathematics. He and I, however, got along famously. I would go down to his room after supper. He would smoke one cigarette after another, until I could hardly see across the room. He got out a slide rule, which was a complete mystery to me at the time, and attack the problems, one by one. He would complain about the utter impossibility of solving any of them, using language that I'm sure would have shocked Father Sill. I saw my chances of getting into Webb diminishing with each session, but I kept at it, more determined than ever. I wanted to concentrate on the upcoming Webb exams, but my father insisted that I also take the College Boards, just in case. With the school finals, this made three sets of exams in a row. I was losing weight, ultimately down 30 pounds.

At this juncture, there occurred an event which seemed to summarize my life at Kent and my reactions to it. It was a week in June known as "cram week." The regular school year was over. Classes and athletics had ended, school exams were over, graduation and prize day had come and gone, and the remaining boys were cramming for the College Boards. One morning Father Sill informed the manager that he wanted the varsity crew to row that afternoon. This rather unusual request was complied with and eight of the nine members of the crew agreed to give up studying and go out on the river. One, however, refused. He was Frederick "Chuck" Blair, president of the class below me, a great athlete, a good student, extremely popular, but not a prefect (by his own choice, it was said). As we assembled in the dining hall for lunch, Father Sill rang the bell at the head table and said with considerable emotion that he wanted Chuck Blair to meet him out in the Hall. Blair walked out with his usual smile, while the whole dining hall buzzed with conversation. It would have been impossible for any one to be unaware of what was going on. After a few minutes, Father Sill returned, livid with rage, while Blair, unchanged, returned to his seat. Father Sill rang the bell again, a little harder, and when all was quiet, announced that the entire school would have to go out that afternoon and either participate in some sport or just walk around for at least an hour. There was a second buzz of conversation, involving the entire student body and faculty members who were there. The subject was obviously the unprecedented command and the disagreement which was the cause.

That evening, Father Sill convened all the students in the assembly hall and asked that any one who had said his outdoor exercise command was motivated by the Blair incident stand up. Two people out of the entire school complied. One was Smith IV (boys having the same last name had numbers rather than first names), a little second former whose parents hadn't yet come to get him. I was the other. Father Sill looked over his glasses at the two who were standing and promptly told Smith IV to sit down. He then proceeded to deliver a tirade against me, pointing out all of my faults and character defects, and, worst of all, complete lack of school spirit.

I often look back on the events of that day, and ponder the question of whether I was the one bad apple in the barrel, defying our spiritual and temporal leader, and challenging a system of governance generally accepted as being beneficial to growing boys. Or was I the only one in the student body with sufficient residual integrity to stand up for the truth, regardless of the verbal lashing sure to result? In any case, I never regretted my small part in the drama of the eight that did not row.

A few days later I was spending as much as six hours each on the toughest exams I had ever faced but already gaining back weight.

8 • *The Housatonic*

*W*ith Father Sill's great interest in rowing, he could not have selected a better site for his new school than the west bank of the Housatonic. This gently flowing stream wound its way through the valley, becoming almost straight a little downstream from the school, providing either the Henley distance or 2000 meters for races in eight-oared shells. When I was at Kent, the boathouse was located a little below the campus. It was filled with gleaming eights, all neatly stored upside down on racks. The managers took good care of them, wiping off the remains of the muddy river water after each use.

It was a great thrill for me to step into the boathouse for the first time, which, needless to say, I did at the earliest opportunity. None of the many dories, skiffs, Whitehalls, and peapods I had rowed so much, and with so much pleasure, could even be mentioned in the same breath as these shiny, varnished racehorses of the water, each more than 60 feet long. I looked forward with eager anticipation to my first chance to step on board one of them, and pull one of the beautifully hand-carved 12-foot sweeps.

My feelings were not without some ambivalence, however. I missed the Shoals and the clear salt water of the ocean. A quiet river is a suitable substitute, in the minds of many, and preferred by some. But for me, nothing could ever take the place of unlimited, unrestricted, blue water. The feeling of the gentle and graceful rising and falling of a good boat as it first meets the ocean swells can never be duplicated, for me, by any muddy river, however choppy.

Previous to my years at Kent, I had always spent the winters far from the Shoals and the sea. Despite the tears as the islands faded into the distance astern, I never felt that I was inexorably confined inland. There was always the possibility of talking my parents into taking me down to the New Jersey shore to watch the waves breaking on the deserted beach and to swim briefly in the invigorating salt water, even when it meant running through the snow to get there.

At Kent, I couldn't help feeling oppressed by the finality of restraint as each term began. These days a prisoner may read, watch TV, or exercise, just as he might do outside the walls. But he is always conscious of the walls, and the locks, and the activities which are not possible within. I am sure that I should not have felt this way about Kent, and I should have forgotten, controlled, or hidden my extreme aversion to what I called "rule by the dumb." But that is not the way it was.

I often looked out at the peaceful Housatonic, flowing gently away from Kent, toward its ultimate destination. I was reminded of my favorite poem, "Land-locked" by Celia Thaxter. I repeat it here, with permission, from the book, *Sandpiper- The Life & Letters of Celia Thaxter* by Rosamond Thaxter, published by Peter E. Randall Publisher, Portsmouth, N.H.:

> *Black lie the hills; swiftly doth daylight flee;*
> *And, catching gleams of sunset's dying smile,*
> *Through the dusk land for many a changing mile*
> *The river runneth softly to the sea.*
>
> *O happy river, could I follow thee!*
> *O yearning heart, that never can be still!*
> *O wistful eyes, that watch the steadfast hill,*
> *Longing for level line of solemn sea!*
>
> *Have patience; here are flowers and songs of birds,*
> *Beauty and fragrance, wealth of sound and sight,*
> *All summer's glory thine from morn till night,*
> *And life too full of joy for uttered words.*
>
> *Neither am I ungrateful; but I dream*
> *Deliciously how twilight falls to-night*
> *Over the glimmering water, how the light*
> *Dies blissfully away, until I seem*
>
> *To feel the wind, sea-scented, on my cheek,*
> *To catch the sound of dusky flapping sail*
> *And dip of oars, and voices on the gale*
> *Afar off, calling low,- my name they speak!*

O Earth! thy summer song of joy may soar
Ringing to heaven in triumph. I but crave
The sad, caressing murmur of the wave
That breaks in tender music on the shore.

There was a room in the old main building which smelled always like a locker room but far more concentrated. There were two rows of rowing machines. Each had a small, form-fitting wood seat, running with rollers on tracks, and still called, paradoxically, a sliding seat. Within reach was a single, heavy, wood facsimile of the inner end of a rowing sweep, connected to a hydraulic resistance mechanism that could be adjusted for tension. Wood clogs, with leather open-ended shoe uppers, called stretchers, completed the device. Some were rigged for starboard, and others for port. Before setting forth on the Housatonic, one had to work on these machines, which was a good idea. They were also used for practice in inclement weather.

Rowing with a sliding seat is an entirely different motion from that used with a fixed seat, such as found in all of the boats I had rowed heretofore. With the latter, one leans back, and pulls oneself up to a vertical position, and some forward lean, using the arms for power and the oar handles to pull against. The oar blade is forced back, resisted by the water(the blade is more effective as it moves down and up vertically, creating lift like an airplane wing instead of just a turbulent resistance). The rather brisk motion of the arms thus accelerates the boat from its minimum speed at the end of the recovery phase of the rowing cycle to its maximum speed just after the oars come out of the water.

With a sliding seat, on the other hand, the powerful leg muscles are supposed to do the accelerating, with the back leaning forward in a comfortable arc, and the arms straight and relaxed. Following the leg drive, the back and arms provide a smooth finish of the stroke, maintaining the speed caused by the legs, but not attempting to increase it, and particularly not pulling up on the oars with a jerky motion, causing some further acceleration but at the expense of a disastrous checking or decelerating of the boat at the finish, and usually causing washing out, which is throwing a small amount of water violently back as the oar is lifted out of the water.

Kent 3rd Form 2nd Crew (AEM #2) April 29, 1932

Kent third form crew. AEM #2. Photo: Franklin Martin.

As I took my first strokes in an eight, I was thrilled by the tremendous speed it made, despite the numerous errors and deficiencies of the novice crew. I was also impressed by the satisfying run, or glide, it had after the oars were out of the water. The contrast with *Barnacle*, which seemed to come to a complete stop at the end of each stroke, and even with the peapod, which had always seemed to maintain its speed so well between strokes, was truly astonishing to me.

Coxswain and coach shouted repeatedly that I was "washing out." Unfortunately, I had a firmly fixated notion that nobody but nobody could or should have the temerity to tell someone from the Isles of Shoals how to row. Some forty years later I took one of the first Alden Ocean Shells up to the Union Boat Club on the Charles River in Boston, so that Lloyd Dahmen, who was then in charge of equipment for Union, and Harry Parker, the great Harvard and national coach, who was coaching at Union that summer, could try out the unusual new boat.

It was rigged with a very low seat for added stability, and seven and one-half foot oars which did not overlap, to make it easier for the average non-rower to learn to use a sliding seat. It was not a matter of ignorance of the way sculling boats were rigged, for by that time we had been using a racing single for several years. I just thought that the short oars and low seat were more suitable for this boat. Harry Parker and Lloyd Dahmen both tried it. Harry said the boat was fine and had a good run for such a short boat, but he said it really should have a high seat and full size (9 foot-9 inch) racing sculls.

Characteristically, I didn't agree with him, but said I would come back another day with a Rube Goldberg arrangement to simulate the rigging of a racing shell. At that time our riggers were made of a fiberglass and foam sandwich, attached to the fiberglass deck, but portable. I cut them in half and added a wood spacer to each, wrapping the area with fiberglass tape. I added several layers of foam rubber to the low seat, and brought the boat back to the Charles River, hoping to convince Harry Parker that he was wrong.

Lloyd Dahmen and Harry Parker both tried it out with various pairs of sculls, while I rowed around in a broad comp (a near racing shell used for training would-be scullers), made by my friend Francis Hagerty. At the conclusion of the tests, Lloyd turned to me and said, "You know something, Arthur——," and paused. I thought to myself, he's going to say something nice about our Alden. Instead, he added, "You don't row very well." He recently maintained that he never said any such thing, and I am sure that he never intended to hurt my feelings. In any case, the happy result was that I finally set out to learn what I should have learned forty years sooner at Kent. Today, when I am teaching rowing to so many people, I find that those who have had a lot of experience in fixed seat boats have a tendency to pull themselves up with the oars, making a hard and jerky finish, usually resulting in washing out, just as I had done for so long.

At Kent I was very small for my age, but I fancied myself a muscular Tarzan and had no interest in becoming a coxswain, which my physical dimensions suggested. On the other hand, my tendency to be insubordinate, added to my limited physical dimensions, precluded my ever sitting in the varsity eight that went to Henley. Many years later, however, I did row the Henley course: in an Alden. It was January, and there were only cows along the banks to deride or applaud the performance or observe what may have been the slowest time ever for that legendary course.

I did row and race in the second crew of the third form. I remember one race against a similar crew in the class above mine. My brother Franklin was stroking it, while I was in one of my two usual positions: bow or number 2. Whether from sibling competition or not, Franklin kept up an unusually high stroke the entire race, winning by a small margin. Immediately after crossing the finish line he collapsed over his oar, and he, among others, thought he was dead. But he quickly recovered and paddled victoriously back to the boathouse.

My father, having rowed enthusiastically all his life in fixed-seat boats of all kinds, was naturally as fascinated as I by the shells at Kent. They had a Fathers Day weekend every year, and, by way of entertainment for students and parents alike, they managed to get the old fossils out in an eight (needless to say, one of the oldest ones). My father was always first in line for this event and took a keen interest in the sport. Although he was indifferent to many activities, such as the opera, which he referred to as the "uproar," and invariably fell asleep during the performance, if he became interested in anything, he "put some study onto it" and became very much involved. Rowing was such a subject.

He took some photographs of the varsity crew, which we still have. They showed a layback so exaggerated that it appeared that the oarsmen were about to take a nap. This was pretty much the style of the times, but no two coaches ever agreed on exactly how much layback was optimum. Although today all agree that excessive layback is counterproductive, in those days the subject had not been given too much thought. My father was far ahead of his time in figuring out that the tremendous layback of Kent crews was wasting a lot of energy. He explained his ideas to Father Sill, whom he admired tremendously, and Father Sill apparently agreed with him, for he began insisting on less layback, and even went so far as to hit oarsmen with a strap if he thought they were going back too far.

In those days, only a few of the Ivy League schools had rowing in eights, and it is doubtful if many of them took the sport as seriously as

Kent varsity crew. Note extreme layback which my father later corrected. Photo: Franklin Martin.

Father Sill. Consequently, many of the races were against college fresh-men. When we came out with the Alden Ocean Shell, I enjoyed many contacts in the other world of rowing and went to the annual meet-ings of the National Association of Amateur Oarsmen (now the United States Rowing Association). Before one of the banquets, I was talking to a man named Rutherford, a Princeton oarsman who later became a famous sculler. The subject of schools came up, and when I told him the name of my alma mater, he laughed and asked if I knew about the famous Kent School start. When I pleaded ignorance, he explained that when he was on the Princeton freshman crew, they raced Kent in a race on the Housatonic, conducted entirely by Father Sill in the flowing white robes of the Order of the Holy Cross. When the two shells were lined up for the start, Father Sill gave the command "Forward all. Ready all. Back water a little Princeton. Row." This gave Kent a much needed lead of about half a length at the start. Since that time, I have heard similar stories from others, so I guess there must be some element of truth in it.

It wasn't long before I found out that among all the eights in the boathouse, there was a Pocock single wherry. This venerable craft was a completely open lap-strake wooden double-ender, designed to be the first step for a beginning sculler. It was shorter, wider, and much heavier than a racing shell. The idea in those days was that anyone aspiring to scull in a racing boat would start in a wherry. After getting over that first hurdle, one advanced to a broad comp, a lighter, narrower, and longer boat, with the same fabric deck and smooth hull construction as a racing scull. Then on to the narrow comp, and finally the true racing scull. Following the example of the Europeans, the Americans gradually realized that all these steps were not really necessary, and all the intermediate boats began to disappear as they got older and were not replaced. A sculling school such as Craftsbury in Vermont, or Florida Rowing Center, can teach a novice to row a racing shell in a week. An individual need not purchase and sell a series of boats before buying a racing boat. Nevertheless, I was very grateful that Kent had the old wherry, and I couldn't wait to try it out.

It employed almost the same body motions as the eight, but it had the great advantage, for me at least, of complete freedom. Freedom to come and go as I chose, at whatever speed I chose, and without anyone barking orders at me. Without being disloyal to the peapod (punt) at the Shoals, I developed quite a fondness for the wherry and went out in it at every opportunity. Father Sill at one point gave orders that I was not to go out in the wherry. If this was an attempt to develop in me a better school spirit, it was not altogether successful. Recently I was reminded of a compensating kindness of the good headmaster. We were required to wear caps in the winter, a different color for each class. Somehow I lost mine, and Father Sill loaned me his, which I think came from his crew days at Columbia.

I have always had a phobia about wasting time. According to my criteria, if I am neither enjoying myself nor accomplishing something useful, I feel that I am wastefully squandering the unknown number of minutes allotted to me on this planet. By these standards, sitting on a rock watching the tide come in is not a waste of time; filling out a ridiculous form devised by a government or other bureaucrat is. This basic philosophy did not mesh well with the structured life at Kent. Meals, jobs, job assemblies where the prefects announced all imperfections and meted out suitable punishments, classes, organized sports, more jobs and assemblies, chapel, study hall, and mandatory lights out left little time for anything else. Nevertheless, I tried constantly to find time for more interesting or productive activities.

Cliff Loomis, an excellent English master, assured me that I would not pass the upcoming College Boards in that subject. Faced with indisputable evidence, I could but agree with him. Having avoided almost all but compulsory reading, I had little interest in words and found Shakespeare and other classics rough going. I felt challenged to prove the good Mr. Loomis wrong and devised a program which I could superimpose on the already full schedule of school activities.

I began to read extra books at every opportunity—some thirty-five in one winter. Whenever I found a word which I didn't understand, I jotted it down. Later I looked it up in the dictionary and typed it and the various meanings on small cards, using the little portable Corona my father had given me. I carried the cards around with me all day and surreptitiously studied them during job assembly, chapel, and any odd moments of waiting for the next compulsory activity. This resulted in a 90 in the English College Boards, which consisted entirely of essay questions, and I heartily recommend the procedure to anyone interested in improving communicative skills. Today's multiple-choice questions make life easier for lazy teachers who have tenure or influence with the union, but they do little for useful education.

My first crude attempts at whittling boat models out of pine at the Shoals continued over the years, with gradually improving skill. One early effort was an attempt to make a speed boat with a V-bottom, like *Miss Wentworth*, which occasionally took wealthy guests of the Wentworth Hotel in New Castle out to the Shoals. Since I had little opportunity to see this craft, except at a distance, I did not understand how the V-bottom ended up at the bow. Consequently, in my ignorance, I brought the chines right up to the deck at the stem.

Long after I learned that the chines of V-bottom boats of that era came up only a few inches above the waterline, I still contemplated my mistaken model of *Miss Wentworth*, and thought, why not? I figured that if I made the deck much wider at the bow, there would be a tremendous flair, which would lift the bow over almost any normal waves. Furthermore, the sharp bottom of the bow would knife through waves without the pounding of the conventional boats, and the flaring concave curve of the bow sections would split the waves and throw the water out to either side in a most satisfactory manner. I made a series of models at the Shoals and tested them by pulling them with string attached to a long stick. Each model was designed to be an improvement on the previous one. Towing them in salt water ponds and the ocean revealed weaknesses to be corrected in the next model. At this time, Norman Bel Geddes figured prominently in designing not only stage sets, but also numerous industrial products. He was very keen on streamlining cars and trains, and even designed a streamlined ocean liner (which was never built). I went for the streamlining, hook, line, and sinker. Having an aversion to transom sterns, almost all of my models came to a point at the stern. With the shear well rounded, and a forward deckhouse in the shape of half a teardrop, wind resistance was greatly reduced at the expense of very limited usable space. Such practical considerations held very little interest for me. In the course of these experiments, I found out for myself that the slightest upward curve of the buttock lines at the stern would cause the stern to squat, prohibiting satisfactory operation at high speeds, and causing pounding because the bow would be elevated so much that the model would be riding on the flatter sections aft. Even with the flat buttocks of later models, pounding persisted if the waves were big enough. Little did I then suspect that this problem would be solved by Ray Hunt's deep-V.

It was far from easy to continue this work in the structured atmosphere of Kent. But there was, after all, water in the Housatonic, I had my special knife that my father had made on the forge at Appledore, along with a jackknife and gouge, and good white pine, all carefully hidden and shavings swept up when not in use. Even so, some bureaucratic young inspector would report any deviation such as my typewriter, pictures, or models which broke the dreary monotony of the typical dormitory rooms.

Thus I continued my development of what I called the Tripoliss bow (triple "S," for speed, sex, and seaworthiness). I towed my latest models in the shadow of Mount Algo and completed the final model in my room at Kent. I also sent and received endless correspondence, pecking out letters on the little typewriter. I engaged a patent attorney with my rapidly depleting funds and received a patent on my design. I wrote to Doris Duke and Betty Carstairs (famous speedboat racer, and friend of Greta Garbo, as I found out later) among others, suggesting that they build a boat to this radical new design. Needless to say, no replies were forthcoming. A man named J.O. Chesley, of the Aluminum Company of America, very kindly answered all of my letters and sent me considerable technical data on aluminum for boats, along with samples of various alloys which I tested for corrosion resistance, between high and low water at the Shoals.

As my days at Kent were drawing to a close, my thoughts and efforts became more and more concentrated on getting into Webb. I had few illusions about besting in the competitive exams all but 14 of the other applicants, and I began to think of other ways to help the cause. I wrote to W. Selkirk Owen, Professor of Naval Architecture, assuring him of my extreme interest in his subject. He wrote back a very nice letter but assured me that everything depended on the exams.

Included in the application requirements were letters of recommendation. I figured that a letter from a prominent graduate would carry more weight than one from the family lawyer or minister. Mr. Alfred E. Luders seemed to be a likely target. After graduating from Webb he had acquired and run the very successful Luders Marine Construction Company in Stamford, Connecticut. We had stopped there on several occasions in the Elco, on our way to or from the Shoals. My father was quite friendly with Mr. Luders, who very kindly let me climb all over all the boats in the yard, as I always attempted to do wherever we were. One time we tied up to the Luders dock at high tide without much slack in the docking lines. In the middle of the night, awakened by ominous creaking on deck, we discovered that the Elco was hanging by the docking lines.

Considering this sufficient introduction to Mr. Luders, I journeyed to Stamford during a vacation, carrying my latest model of the

A model of the Tripoliss design in a pool on Appledore. A patent resulted in controversy and an article in Yachting. *Photo: Henry Freeman.*

Tripoliss with me. Mr. Luders was cordial and looked over the model very carefully. He said it was a very good model, but the design was not practical. He then gave me a good letter of recommendation to send to Webb, which, after all, was my chief objective.

I was astonished to find at the next New York Boat Show a little yacht tender with the Tripoliss bow, displayed by the Luders Marine Construction Company. Later, there was an article in the design section of Yachting showing the plans of a launch for Imperial Airways. In those days overseas flights were in flying boats, and passengers were taken out in high-speed boats. The launch design showed the familiar Tripoliss bow, and it was to be built by Luders.

I sent Imperial Airways a bill for the design, and they wrote back after quite some time that the project had been cancelled. I also wrote a letter to Herbert Stone, the great editor and publisher of Yachting. Unlike some conglomerate publishers of today, who wouldn't think of becoming involved in a controversy between a large advertiser and a student, Mr. Stone wrote back that if I would write an article about my development of the Tripoliss bow he would publish it and pay me for it. The article appeared in the issue of September, 1938. Mr. Stone was a great editor, as was his successor, Bob Bavier, who wrote a very good editorial about his Alden and his other small boats, years later.

Life on the shores of the Housatonic was somewhat monotonous and confining for me, but I became used to it, and did not expect much else until each term finally ended. The announcement that there would be a talk and slides one Saturday night did not result in any exciting anticipation on my part, expecting, as I did, an account of missionary work in Africa or other such entertainment.

It was quite an overwhelming shock to see none other than Roderick Stephens standing on the platform, with his eyes half shut, describing in a low monotone the European trip of *Stormy Weather*. I had read with avid interest all about the phenomenal success of the firm of Sparkman and Stephens, led by the brilliant designs of Rod's older, but still very young, brother, Olin. *Stormy Weather* was one of the earliest of the great Sparkman and Stephens ocean racers. As Rod talked, he showed slides of the beautiful yacht crossing the ocean to England, winning the Fastnet race, and sailing through the canals of Holland without any motor at all, slowing down for bridges by easing into the mud. I sat on the edge of my seat, hanging on to every word, relishing every minute of this vicarious trip so far removed from the placid Housatonic. Rod Stephens had been the skipper for the trip, as the owner, Phillip Le Boutillier, was not on board. His son, Phil Le Boutillier, Jr., about my own age, was one of the crew. As inept as I was at remembering anything French, I had no trouble remembering this French name, although I never suspected that I would ever have any further association with its owner.

Several years later, when I was working at the Bethlehem Shipbuilding yard in Quincy, Massachusetts, I learned that a group of young bachelors working in the area had rented a house, employed a man and wife as cook and butler, and were living in luxury for twenty dollars per week in nearby Hingham. As one would get married, or otherwise move away, a new recruit would be selected, after careful screening, to take his place. Thus I became a resident of "Deadwood," as the house was called by its mostly nautical inhabitants. While there I heard numerous tales of previous occupants, none of whom I had met. One of these was Phillip Le Boutillier, Jr.

Many years later I was rowing an Alden around the harbor in Kittery Point, admiring a large double-ended power boat named *Dragoon*, which was just leaving. Suddenly it stopped, and a voice called down: "Are you Arthur Martin?" When I admitted that I was, the owner of the voice, and the boat, disclosed the fact that he was none other than Phil Le Boutillier, Jr. He said he wanted to get a wood Appledore 16, which he subsequently ordered and picked up at Kittery Point. Since then he bought one of almost all of our other models and was largely responsible for starting the Toledo Rowing Club and the Toledo Rowing Foundation. These organizations made it possible for all Toledo people, eventually including the severely handicapped, to row for a modest fee. They also provide fours and eights for the University of Toledo Crew, among others, run a yearly regatta for all rowing shells, from eights to Aldens, and ran the first Alden National Championships. Phil is a great competitor, having been captain of the Princeton crew, and he has done well in numerous Alden and Martin races, from the Charles River to Mackinac Island to the Isles of Shoals. Phil's son, George, is now a very successful Alden dealer, and his grandson has driven east to pick up boats. Thus, it could be said that a very pleasant association began, in a roundabout way, at Kent School on the shore of the placid and muddy Housatonic.

9 • *Nelda*

i have always had an insatiable appetite for investigating boats of all sizes and shapes, from kayaks and prams to battleships and ocean liners. To me, they are all related, though they may often be very distant cousins. They all must obey the Archimedes principle and other laws of nature. The unforgiving sea usually catches up with those that don't. The endless fascination is in discovering how some of the best brains of the past and present have attempted to meet the varying requirements of war, commerce, transportation, fishing, and recreation on the waters of the world.

At the Isles of Shoals, I never hesitated to row up alongside a visiting yacht or fishing boat, and ask if I could come aboard or row a beautiful Lawley yacht tender, in later years prefacing the request with the explanation that I hoped to become a naval architect. Usually the owners would be glad to grant my request, allowing me to inspect such gems as a William H. Hand motorsailor from bow to stern, and from bilge to masthead. Any boats that I rowed were immediately compared to our peapod, and I always looked for natural waves or the wake from a passing vessel to make a thorough test. Although almost all the yacht tenders, with their brightly shining varnish, and graceful wineglass sterns, put our shabby old peapod to shame, not one of them could equal it in performance.

In South Orange during the winter, such opportunities were difficult to arrange. At Kent School they were out of the question. Nevertheless, I tried ceaselessly to find out more about anything that floated. I struggled with endless red tape to get permission to visit the Brooklyn Navy Yard. On the appointed day, I walked across the Brooklyn Bridge (to save money) and checked in at the main gate, full of anticipation at the thought of finally getting to see how a battleship operated. I was assigned an armed escort, who led me down to the dock where the *Wyoming* was tied up. There we stopped, and it soon became apparent that no dangerous character such as myself would ever be allowed to set foot on so vital and secret an element of our first line of defense. The Japanese were more successful a few years later.

Following this disappointment, I arranged through family connections to actually go aboard the *West Virginia*, when she was anchored in the Hudson River. This was a great thrill, but once again I was disappointed, for visitors were only allowed on the main deck. It would be many more years before I could see, at first hand, just what made a battleship move through the water.

To get from South Orange to New York one took the steam train to Hoboken. There were two ways to complete the journey to Manhattan. One was the tube under the Hudson River, which offered a most unpleasant, dusty, dirty, noisy, bumpy, and evil-smelling ride, but it delivered the rider to mid-town with great speed. The other was to take the ferry, a true double-ender which never had to turn around. The crankshaft of its huge steam engine was connected to a propeller shaft at each end. I used to sneak down into the engine room until discovered and chased out. I feel sorry for the growing numbers of people who will never experience the joy of watching the great piston rods, connecting rods, valve rods, and crankshaft performing their slow ballet, to the accompaniment of the subdued and relaxing sounds of hissing steam and well lubricated metal sliding on metal, with the smells of oil and steam mixed. What a contrast to the high-pitched, staccato whine of an outboard motor, and the dreadful smell of the synthetic oil with which it pollutes the air and the water!

Standing on the bow of the ferryboat, one could smell the salt air from the sea beyond and watch and listen as the steel bow crunched into floating ice. And there were always tugs and barges and giant ocean liners to see. Needless to say, I never went in the tube, unless forced to by my mother. My father felt as I did and always went on the ferry.

Adjacent to the ferry docks in Hoboken was a dock where the Lackawanna Railroad tied up their tugs when not in use. These were mostly typical harbor tugs, with high wheelhouses and funnels (smokestacks). But one, named the *Bronx*, stood out from all the rest. She had a beautiful shear curve with a high bow, but her superstruc-

The Bronx, *in which AEM spent the day transferring barges and waving to* Nelda. *Photo: Franklin Martin.*

ture was nice and low, and the funnel was no higher than the pilot house. She was low so that she could get under the numerous bridges on the Harlem River. The low funnel required a forced draft for her big Scotch boiler, provided by a jet of steam. She was said to be the most powerful tug in New York Harbor, and to my eyes she was certainly the best looking. I never failed to walk over and admire her graceful lines whenever I went to the city, and my father very kindly took a picture of her, which he had enlarged and framed.

I was most anxious to go out on this special tug, so the Lackawanna Railroad was added to the receiving list of letters from the little Corona. To my surprise and delight, they answered, and, after my parents signed a release, arrangements for me to spend a day on my favorite tug were completed. I took an early train to Hoboken on the appointed day, brimming over with excitement and anticipation.

Nelda Audibert came from Paris, and she was a good friend of my cousin, Nat White. She had natural blonde hair, a very pretty face, a figure to rival Marilyn Monroe, a charming French accent, and an irresistible vivaciousness. At a dance, she would always be surrounded by boys jockeying for a chance to cut in. I had told her about my upcoming trip on the *Bronx,* and as we steamed by her family's suite at 10 Gracie Square, I blew the whistle three times. As we proceeded down the East River, she appeared at the end of one of the streets in a taxi. She waved and shouted frantically, getting back into the taxi after we had passed, only to reappear a few blocks further downtown. This performance was repeated all the way to the Battery, much to the amusement of the crew of the *Bronx.*

Shortly after this, my father purchased, second hand, for $100, an Amesbury knockabout. This was a 16-foot lap-strake skiff, decked over at the bow, with a typical Marconi mainsail, and club-footed jib. It was the first real sailboat for us. Being at that time the only sailboat at the Shoals, it was also the fastest, and, carrying our provincialism to extremes, the fastest of its type in the world. In any case, it opened up a whole new world of boating activity, although for me, no day would ever be complete without some rowing in the "punt," regardless of how much sailing it also included. By unanimous consent of the new owners, the sailboat was named *Nelda.*

Whales often frequent the waters around the Shoals, and today whale watching excursions are quite popular. I know of nothing more graceful than the slow, smooth motion of a whale breaking the surface to breathe and returning to the depths without any of the jerky motions associated with automobiles or bouncy outboards. Also, recent studies have revealed not only extraordinary communications skills but feelings and souls to rival the best of humans.

I had been given a copy of Clifford W. Ashley's book, *The Yankee Whaler,* when I was quite young. From my first perusal of the pictures to repeated reading of the text and studying the lines and plans of whaleboats and whale ships, I was fascinated by the whole industry in the days of wooden ships and iron men. It was my pleasure to climb all over the whaler *Charles W. Morgan* when she was owned by the late

Franklin shooting at whale from bow of Nelda. *AEM at tiller. Photo: Franklin Martin.*

Colonel Greene, with many encores at Mystic Seaport, including a chance to pull one of the massive oars of one of her whaleboats. Often when I have had occasion to visit Marion, Massachusetts, for an Alden race, I have stopped at Burr Brothers Boatyard, to gaze in awe and admiration at one of the whaleboats made by the Beetle company. Subtle differences in the underwater lines make this boat far superior to the other surviving whaleboats, in my opinion. I tried to imagine what it would be like to be in that fragile boat, towed at high speed by a harpooned whale, through rough seas. As form follows function, due to brilliant design based on endless experience and trial and error, this boat seemed to be the ultimate in perfection, a well proportioned double-ender ideally suited to its challenging task. A thing of beauty is a joy forever.

The slaughter of whales today, using powerful ships, sophisticated sonar gear, and brutal explosives disgusts me. But no matter how enlightened one may become, he cannot alter the events of the past. To my shame and regret, my brother Franklin and I did one summer attempt to harm these beautiful, peaceful mammals. We would sail out to the east of Appledore in *Nelda* in response to the old cry of "Thar she blows." When we reached the scene of activity, we would remove the jib completely, and Franklin would stand on the bow deck, leaning against the mast, holding his 30-caliber Lee-Enfield rifle, while I handled the tiller and the main sheet. When a giant whale would break through the surface close aboard, my heart would come up in my mouth, pounding like a triphammer, especially when the huge flukes would come right out of the water, and we would get a dose of spray or a whiff of the malodorous vapor which accompanied the exhaled air. My brother would try to get off a shot before the whale sounded. I hope and pray that if any of these shots hit, they did no harm. A craving for excitement is part of youth, along with streaks of cruelty. Hopefully, most of us overcome the latter.

One method of fishing which brought the most delicious food to the table was flounder spearing. We forged a multi-prong spearhead from a Ford engine valve, heat-treated and sharpened to perfection. On the end of a long pole, this could reach a flounder resting on the bottom in pretty deep water, but only on a windless day with no ripples to interfere with visibility. There was no waste, for, after the removal of the fillets, the remains were used for lobster bait.

Although fishing remained a great pleasure, as well as a virtual necessity, the passing years brought other interests: girls. *Nelda* proved to be quite effective in the pursuit of the new quarry. The Oceanic Hotel employed a number of waitresses, mostly college girls, who were, in the earlier years, older than ourselves. But, having as bait the only sailboat at the islands, the situation was not altogether impossible. It took a lot of courage for a young boy to go up to the hotel, find a likely prospect, and talk her into going sailing. I seemed to be chosen as a volunteer for this job, while my brother remained at the tiller of *Nelda*, tied to the float. When I arrived with a fair maiden in tow, we would get aboard and cast off. Almost immediately, Franklin would offer to teach the girl to sail, which necessitated her sitting in the stern with him. He would guide her hand on the tiller, which seemed to require his arm to be around her shoulder. Meanwhile, all by myself in the bow....

I finally corrected the situation by inviting two girls. This worked out very well, although it was not conducive to the best of seamanship. Four of us were sailing in a good sou'wester on a moonlit night. We were on a long run toward Smuttynose Island, and I, in the bow, pulled up the centerboard to increase the speed. As we neared the island, Franklin put the tiller hard over to come up on the wind, forgetting that we had neglected to lower the centerboard. The boat went sideways at a lively pace, right for the rocks, now only a few feet away. I hastily, too hastily, pulled an oar out from under the bow deck. Unfortunately, the butt of the oar hit Franklin square in the jaw with considerable force, knocking him out cold, draped over the tiller. I don't remember exactly how we recovered from this situation, but we all, including *Nelda*, survived.

With increasing age, our pursuit of the fair sex became more successful, but one day our position was challenged, if not shattered, by the arrival on the *Sightseer*, of a great young brain surgeon. From then on, all we heard from our feminine friends were tales of the exploits of the great doctor, who numbered sailing among his many accomplishments.

Out of desperation, we invited him to go sailing, knowing that with him aboard, the boat would be more appealing than the shore to the young ladies. Soon after we left the dock, it appeared to me that his experience in small boats was somewhat limited, to say the least. Franklin, studying to become a doctor, began to question openly the great surgeon's medical knowledge. These observations were treated as sour grapes by our feminine companions, and we appeared to be defeated.

The next morning, however, a high-speed boat arrived from Portsmouth, bearing an armed sheriff, and the great brain surgeon was escorted back to the mainland in handcuffs. He was wanted in several states for various crimes, including passing numerous bad checks. *Nelda* and her crew returned to the good graces of the young ladies of Star Island.

Arriving at Webb, September 1935. Photo: Franklin Martin.

10 • *Webb*

*W*hen I arrived at Webb to take the competitive exams, I was somewhat intimidated by all the bright-looking applicants, some brandishing slide rules, those prehistoric predecessors of the computer, whose functions I had yet to master. Some of the exams lasted six hours, with a lunch break interspersed. It was assumed that the aspiring students would pick up on the Webb honor system and not assist each other during lunch. They did discuss the problems in a general way, and I was aghast to find that several had encountered far less difficulty than I. After the three days of exams were over I left for the Shoals to recover physically from what had been a very tense and exhausting spring. I was not feeling very optimistic about getting into Webb, but I was confident that I had done my best.

I awaited the results impatiently, and rowed over to Star in the peapod every day to attack the mail ferociously, looking in vain for a letter from Webb. I had almost given up, deciding that they would not bother to notify the many unsuccessful applicants, when the fateful letter arrived. I tore it open with trembling fingers and couldn't restrain a gleeful shout when I read the good news. I would have a chance to become a naval architect!

When our class drifted in to the old original Webb building, overlooking New York City from Fordham Heights, at various hours of the morning, we learned our first lesson. The Institute was administered by Admiral Rock, and he left little room for doubt about who was in charge. He informed us that in the Navy, orders to report on a certain day meant 0800 and not a second later. Further proof of the admiral's pompous style was furnished by little signs on all the urinals. In a neat typewritten command, each one advised the user not to dispose of cigarettes or other foreign matter in that particular receptacle. Below was his imposing signature, followed by

Old Webb building in the Bronx. Photo: Webb Institute of Naval Architecture.

the following translation: "George H.Rock, Rear Admiral (CC) U.S.N., Retired."

I soon found that the work load was absolutely staggering. We were taking as many as 16 courses at once. After an early supper, we had to work until utter exhaustion set in, trying to complete the various assignments. Benjamin Keeler, the head of the mathematics department, was, without doubt, the greatest teacher I ever encountered. He employed his spare time in a never-ending quest for problems which seemed to defy all attempts at a solution. His exams were such that 90s and 100s were far out of reach of even the best of students, and, while he never gave out marks, I suspect that on some exams no one could have earned more than a 50. His idea was to find out how each student would go about trying to solve an apparently impossible problem. The most logical approaches, and creative efforts to find solutions, earned those students the privilege of remaining on campus until the next exams. I shudder to think of facing some of those problems today. But I did learn one thing that I will never forget: there is no such thing as a problem which has no solution. This applies not only to problems in designing boats but also to all of life's problems, whether personal, family, political, or global. This conviction results in a positive, constructive approach to whatever fate has in store. Not easy to practice, but worth trying.

Professor Keeler believed in approaching the unknown by applying the fundamental principals that apply to any situation. Most engineering schools teach students how to apply formulas to solve problems. At Webb we had to derive the formulas from fundamental principles. For instance, we actually had a course in celestial mechanics, in which we had to derive equations of motion for a satellite or planet. With this background I read with scorn about the Union of Concerned Scientists, consisting largely of biologists, psychologists, etc., pontificating about how impossible it is to design a defense against Soviet or other missiles. Nonsense.

Despite the grueling academic work, I took to the life at Webb like a duck to water. I was elected president of my class, a position I held all four years. As freshmen, we were subjected to hazing which was carried much too far. As sophomores, we refused to participate in the barbaric practice, and the junior class attempted to take our place. We interfered with their efforts to a considerable extent, and the old tradition never fully recovered.

The Consolidated Boatbuilding Company was within walking distance of the campus, and I spent quite a lot of my spare time there. Anthony Fokker, the famous German airplane builder, was having them build his dreamboat, which was named *Q.E.D.* It was a beautiful big yacht, with many innovations based on the owner's vast engineering experience. It particularly appealed to me because it was a double-ender, having a stern somewhat like the rounded reverse rake Jonesport stern, but it came to a point. It had one Wright Typhoon and two Curtiss airplane engines, with Vimalert marine conversions and reverse-reduction gears. It was extremely well insulated, as Mr. Fokker wanted it as quiet as possible in the luxurious living area. I naturally climbed all over the boat many times, and among many other things, I noticed that there were foam rubber pads on the hull above each propeller.

Later on, Webb students were allowed to attend the annual meeting of the Society of Naval Architects and Marine Engineers, where

The Class of 1939 arrives as freshmen. Top row, l..to r. Dick Anderson, Harold Bretz, (flunked out), AEM, Walter Michel, Mario Iaccabucci (Andrea). Second Row: Lewis Cooper, Dick Stearn (deceased), Cedric Nevitt (deceased), Bill Donovan, Ralph Bradway. Bottom Row: Walter Ramshaw (deceased), George Dixon (transferred to West Point), Harley Ferguson (deceased), John Ennis, Les Durant. Photo: Webb Institute of Naval Architecture.

they were supposed to be seen and not heard. Several technical papers were presented by eminent Naval Architects. At the conclusion of each presentation, comments from the floor were invited. One of the papers concerned ship vibration caused by the propeller, the water spinning off the tip of each blade hitting the ship in a regular sequence, which at certain speeds would be in harmony with the natural frequency of the hull area. This had been quite a problem on the French liner *Normandie,* solved by going to five-bladed propellers. At the conclusion of this interesting paper, I brazenly stood up and described the rubber pads on *Q.E.D.* This was duly printed in the annual Transactions book.

There was an upperclassman named Al Mason, who was a real

The Class of 1939, fifty years later. Standing, left to right, Walter and Ann Michel, Bill Donovan and Ellie Chester, Dick Anderson, June and Ralph Bradway, and Margaret and Lew Cooper. Sitting: Elma and Mario Andrea, Joan and Les Durant, and Marjorie and Arthur Martin. Photo: Webb Institute of Naval Architecture.

boat and yacht enthusiast. He had already designed successful boats before he came to Webb. He was later to become chief draftsman at Sparkman and Stephens and still later to design some beautiful and very successful auxiliary sailing yachts under his own name. I admired him then as I do today, and whenever I read about Mason boats in ads or editorials, I think of the designer and how lucky the owners are to have such sound and seakindly boats. Al had a way of printing an "A" with the first diagonal curved instead of straight. I started copying this distinctive touch at Webb, and used it for years.

Al had a nice little Scandinavian-type double-ender which he stored at City Island. He offered a deal to other students whereby he would pay for their carfare and lunch in return for work: sanding and painting his boat. Naturally, I jumped at this opportunity on many occasions. After completing the day's work on Al's boat, there was always time left over to wander around the island, examining all the boats under construction and in storage at the various yards. I spent a lot of time at the yard of Henry Nevins. This was certainly one of the finest , if not the finest, yacht-building concern in the country. At the time, they were building the New York 32s, the famous racing-cruising boats designed by Sparkman and Stephens, and one of which, *Mustang*, did so well under skipper Rod Stephens.

At Nevins I met not only the owner, but, more importantly, the great naval architect, George F. Crouch, who had his office there. George was considered the dean of American motorboat designers. He had designed numerous successful racing boats, including several winners of the historic Gold Cup. The most famous was *Baby Bootlegger*, which was extensively written up in all of the yachting magazines I perused so avidly. It was a unique design in that the shear was rounded between the deck and the topsides, achieving adequate strength with minimum weight, and reducing air resistance, which I had done with the *Tripoliss*. Also, to make it even better in my eyes, it was a double-ender. Mr. Crouch gave me a paper written by a Mr. Sotorff, documenting tests of pointed steps on hydroplanes conducted at the towing tank in Hamburg, Germany. This confirmed my belief that even on planing boats, double-enders were faster, if properly designed for the circumstances.

George Crouch had been dean at Webb, but left when he felt that there was too much Navy influence. He gave me copies of his propeller and speed formulas, which are still widely used today and are included in Skene's Elements of Yacht Design. He challenged me to derive the speed formula in typical Webb fashion. I am ashamed to say that I was never able to accomplish this task, although I was to use the formula extensively for many years.

All students were required to go to sea for at least eight weeks during the summer following the freshman year. I was fortunate enough to secure a job as cadet officer on the ocean liner *Washington* of the United States Lines. Over 700 feet long, she carried more than 1000 passengers, in addition to cargo in six holds, one of which was refrigerated. She had a cruising speed of 24 knots and went back and

AEM on the bow of the Washington. *Photo: Franklin Martin.*

forth between New York and Ireland, England, France, and Germany, alternating with her sister ship, *Manhattan.*

On the day of departure, I left South Orange early, nervous and very excited. As I purchased the necessary uniforms , consisting of dungarees, dress whites, dress blues, and white sailor hat, just as worn by gobs in the Navy, I looked at my watch a dozen times, fearful of being late, though the Army-Navy store was only a stone's throw from the pier. As I walked up the gangplank I was struck by the immensity of the ship, which seemed as immovable as a building attached to the pier. As they were still loading cargo through the open hatches, the decks were as dirty as the city streets below. It was hot and dusty, resulting in the uncomfortable sweat which I associate with life in the city during the summer.

Finally the hatches were closed, the cargo booms secured, and the last passenger ascended the gangplank just before its removal. There was a long blast on the whistle, and the great ship began to move, stern first. It gained speed very rapidly, and there was a loud report, like a gun shot, as one of the docking lines, which had not been released quickly enough, parted. It was an awesome sight to see

The Washington, *United States Lines. Cadet AEM took three voyages to Ire-land, England, France, and Germany in 1936. Photo: Franklin Martin.*

such a massive ship moving so fast in the narrow space between the piers. But with no tugs, there can be no hesitation once the stern gets into the current of the Hudson.

I was put to work stowing the heavy docking lines. The exercise was most welcome, and soon the tension and nervousness disappeared. As we passed the Narrows, the great ship came to life, and the bow began to lift slightly, in a most satisfying way, as it met the first of the ocean swells. As the city faded away in the wake, I relished the clearer and clearer salt air. The water gradually changed also, from the dirty brown of the river to the clear blue of the ocean. It was quite an experience for me, and one I would always recall with pleasure.

I was a deck cadet, one of three, while the other three, provided on ships carrying the mail, were on the bridge. My duties at night consisted of holystoning the teak decks, using a heavy stone with a handle, which was pushed back and forth in a liquid which was very irritating to bare feet. During the day, I worked in the bos'n's gang of seamen, chipping rust and painting. They would swing a lifeboat (all double-enders, I noted) down and out over the water, and we would get in with our buckets of paint and go to work. One old sailor was known as "seagoin'," because that was every other word he used. The other word he used was f—g. He was constantly discussing f—g Hoover and the seagoin' farmers. He spilled a whole bucket of paint in a lifeboat, and neither reported it nor cleaned it up. This general lack of responsibility was quite a shock to me.

In port, my job was to check cargo being loaded and unloaded. In Le Havre my French was no more effective than it had been at Kent, and I could not prevent the stevedores from smoking or eating the kippered herring that we always seemed to carry in barrels, just like our lobster bait at the Shoals. Whenever we carried Scotch whisky, there was always a most pleasant aroma in the hold, and the stevedores were always in good spirits. In sharp contrast, we always seemed to be carrying untreated cow hides in both directions. If the shippers and receivers on both sides of the ocean had been able to get together, they could have saved a lot of money, and the aroma of the ship would have been much improved. On the voyage before I came aboard, bars of gold had been carried. In addition to the cadet, there were representatives of the banks and governments, all checking each valuable billet as it was stowed or taken out. Nevertheless, at the start of my voyage a stray bar of gold was discovered. Not by me, however, so I had to make do with my $35 per month.

On subsequent voyages, I was on the bridge, which was much more fun. I learned to navigate by shooting the sun. My father, when I told him about it, became most interested in the subject and purchased a quadrant (generally still miscalled a sextant), along with the latest books to supersede Bowditch. He made little concrete number markers at Appledore, between high and low tide, so that he could always judge the height of eye, standing on our porch. It is amazing how that island moved around at first, but it gradually settled down.

Steering was the job of the quartermasters, two hours out of the four of each watch. On calm, clear days, they were allowed to turn the job over to the "iron mike," the Sperry automatic steering device, but at night, and in fog or stormy weather, they had to steer manually, which they elected to do with a tiny wheel connected to the Sperry electric system, requiring very little physical effort. Naturally, I was most anxious to have a chance to steer a great ship, and the quartermasters were only too glad to be relieved of the chore. Consequently, I steered most of the time, first shifting to the big wheel which ran the hydraulic telemotor. The wheel was hard to turn, and was self-centering, so it afforded good exercise as well as fun. It was exciting in a storm, controlling all that power, to contend with waves such as I had never before faced.. The bow would shudder when crashing down from the crest of a giant wave, even though they had reduced speed.

I was quartered far up in the bow, near the waterline. I could put my head out of a porthole and watch the bow knifing through the water, and the wave curving back along the hollow bow, to break just below me in a cascade of tons of water, the pure white of the foam blending into shades of aqua and green, in contrast to the dark blue of the undisturbed water beyond. A light mist would rise to sting my face, and add to the delicious smell of salt.

In a gathering storm, this off-watch diversion became far more exciting. As the bow cut into a wave the water would rise along the bow. I would quickly remove my head and shut the port, trying to get it dogged down before it was engulfed by the sea. This game would end when a man with the unlikely title of carpenter's mate would come around and dog down the solid steel deadlights with a wrench. All that would remain was the sound of the angry sea outside and the pitching of the ship, which allowed me to make sensationally high jumps if I planned the takeoffs at the right moments.

The captain of the *Washington* was Giles Steadman, who was married to an heiress to the Schick Razor fortune. He was quite fond of the ample social life aboard. He would appear on the bridge just before dinner in an elegant outfit which was a cross between a tuxedo and an admiral's uniform. He would issue instructions not to disturb him under any circumstances until late in the morning, and head for the first-class dining room, where the action began. Where it ended I never knew, but I heard that it apparently led to some marital difficulties. Back on the bridge, we would enter in the log a heavy fog as a light mist, as the captain was supposed to be on the bridge in the conditions that actually prevailed.

One morning we were knifing along at our usual speed through a heavy fog in the North Sea. I was out on a wing of the bridge, peering through the gloom, looking in vain for other vessels, as were other lookouts on the bow, up in the crow's nest, and on the bridge. As anyone who has ever done this can testify, after an hour or so the fog begins to play tricks on you. You either imagine you see something when nothing is there, or you become mesmerized and are no longer alert.

All of a sudden I spotted a boat, rapidly taking shape directly ahead of us. I shouted to the mate, who quickly verified it and called for full right rudder. The quartermaster began to turn the wheel in a manner which seemed a little slow and deliberate. "Hard over, you stupid son of a bitch," the mate bellowed. The wheel went over smartly, the ship lurched to starboard while taking quite a list to port, and a little trawler passed very close aboard on the port side. This experience left me shaking like a leaf, and from then on I kept creating shapes of ships from the drifting clouds of fog. My father's cousin, Sabina Barbey, had been on deck early one foggy morning on the *Manhattan*. She suddenly saw the *Isle de France* heading in the opposite direction at full speed, only a few feet away. The captain, whom she knew, denied it out-of-hand.

I never had time to go ashore, except in Hamburg. A German seaman offered to show me the city. First we stopped to visit a rather pretty lady friend of his, who ran a wine shop. After a couple of drinks of excellent wine, we headed for Two Mark Alley, which he was anxious for me to see. This is the well known street which is closed to vehicles at both ends and is lined exclusively with government supervised houses of ill repute. Having walked the entire length of the street without being seduced by any of the professional beauties, he led me to a bus which would get me back to the ship, giving the driver instructions in German to signal when I should get off.

Shortly a young German sat down beside me, and said, in perfect English, that he would be glad to help me. He went on to say that he was an officer in the German Navy and had been treated most hospitably when he was in San Diego. He invited me to come with him and meet his cousins. Consequently, I found myself having dinner with the officer, two girls, and their mother. We visited at least two night clubs after dinner, had more than enough Rhine wine, and danced until the wee hours. After that I was invited to spend the night at the family's house. In the morning, when we were having breakfast, the father appeared, wearing the typical brown shirt and arm-band swastika that had come to symbolize terror for so many people. I

The new Webb Campus in Glen Cove, Long Island. Photo: Webb Institute of Naval Architecture.

returned by way of a small ferryboat, which carried me close by a shipyard, where a new airplane carrier was about to be launched. Hitler was there, giving one of his tirades which passed for a speech, and I could hear it clearly, although I couldn't understand a word.

The entire experience in Germany left me quite depressed. Despite all the drinking and dancing and laughing, it seemed to me that the air was heavy with gloom and foreboding, and efforts to appear carefree with all those uniforms around seemed hollow and fruitless. When next I saw the Statue of Liberty as we approached New York, my eyes filled with tears of joy, as I am sure so many other eyes have done, before and since. Freedom is a priceless gift, which all too many fail to appreciate until it is gone. History repeats.

Captain Steadman always liked to be photographed on the bridge with celebrities, whom he always invited up. One exception was Edsel Ford and his family. Henry Ford met his first wife on the *Washington* while I was a cadet. But none of the Fords ever appeared on the bridge, perhaps because of the lingering fear of kidnappers. The American ladies tennis team was another matter. They came up to the bridge in force, and the captain naturally called for the ship's photographer. He wanted the Wightman Cup, which they had just won, to be in the picture, so he sent me down to Alice Marble's stateroom to get it. She, unfortunately, was already on the bridge

This was my second experience among the tennis greats. The first was at the Orange Lawn Tennis Club in South Orange, the former home of my great grandparents. John Doeg, the American amateur champion, was playing a decisive match on one of the grass courts. Paying spectators lined the stands on one side. Outside the fence at one end there was a grass-covered bank. This, with the green canvas at the top of the fence, gave a perfect background. It was here that I chose to sit and watch my tennis idol play. Doeg walked over toward me, and said in a soft voice, "Hey, kid, get out of there."

With this impressive background in tennis, plus the fact that I was one of the few students with a tennis racquet, I became captain of the Webb tennis team. Although there were no other athletic facilities on the small campus, there were two good tennis courts. The admiral liked to play tennis, although his form left something to be desired, and his age had curtailed his running ability considerably. It was his custom to call on the captain of the tennis team to organize two others for doubles.

The admiral summoned me to his spacious office at 0800 one day to make such a request, or, in the translation, issue such an order. The appointed day was extremely hot, with the high humidity which I find so unpleasant. I was playing against the admiral and his partner, carefully returning the ball right to him, as was the unwritten law. After we each won a set, I looked forward to the end of the deciding third set, and a cool shower. However, when the set finally ended, the admiral made an announcement which utterly shattered my hopes, along with my charitable consideration for my aging opponent. "At the Academy, we always used to play three out of five," he said as he was catching his breath from the latest exertion. At this point, I threw discretion to the winds and began to place the ball out of his reach. It was one of several occasions when I feared he might expire from a stroke or a heart attack. He never asked me to play tennis again.

11 • *Cynthia*

i was very happy at Webb. Many of my questions about calculating displacement, stability, speed, etc., were being answered. Also I was gaining confidence that any problem could be solved by analytical means. The professors were, for the most part, tops in their fields. I surmised that the Webb education would serve me well, whatever I chose to do after graduation.

New York City offered unlimited cultural opportunities, even on my stupendous allowance of eight dollars per month. The subway would take you anywhere in the city for a nickel. I skated outdoors in Rockefeller center and at various rinks indoors. I went to the theater and the opera. The old Metropolitan Opera had rows of balconies above the main floor and the boxes, topped by the Family Circle, which was as close to the roof as you could get, and admission was only seventy-five cents. Needless to say, my meager funds dictated attendance in this area. There I would be surrounded by real music lovers, many with foreign accents, and some with no command of the English language at all. Some would have scores, which they followed intently. At the end of each act they would stand and clap strenuously, shouting "bravo" and other epithets which I did not understand, sometimes with tears in their eyes. Up there, so close to heaven, among all those good people, I felt myself a part of the performance.

Sometimes, the very next day, I would attend the same opera under somewhat different circumstances. Thanks to my uncle being a senior partner of J.P.Morgan and a director of the ill-fated Johns-Manville Company, we would be invited to occupy either the Morgan box or the Manville box. The latter proved to be somewhat ironic, as I was to acquire lung cancer from exposure to Johns Manville asbestos, many years later. When we all walked into one of these boxes, lorgnettes would immediately be raised and trained on us, like the guns from a battleship zeroing in on a target. You could read their minds and guess that they were asking each other, "What are those hicks doing in that box?" I never forgot the contrast, and to this day question how much the ostentatious display of wealth adds to the enjoyment of the arts and nature, specifically the sea.

Being listed in the Social Register, which was owned by family members, I received invitations to various coming-out parties in New York and New Jersey, even though I sometimes did not even know the object of the elaborate celebration. Boys were inclined to line up at the bar and discuss football, so the pages of the Social Register were scoured for additional young men to ensure that the dance floor would not remain vacant. At one dance in New Jersey the young swains were double-crossed. At the bar there was only milk and Coke, which was greeted with howls of disappointment. Much to my delight, the money thus saved was used to employ Chick Webb and his orchestra, and Ella Fitzgerald. With a lifelong love of almost all kinds of music except rotten roll, I was in seventh heaven, and today I regularly play a C.D. of the immortal Ella singing with Count Basie, his superb rhythm section, and the rest of his band, sometimes accompanying them on the bass, which they seem to tolerate good-naturedly.

On another such occasion in New York, each girl was required to have three escorts. There being a scarcity of girls to talk to, I found myself having a long conversation with one of the other two escorts, David Rockefeller. He told me that he was planning to get a fleet of Elco 38s, and run a glorified taxi service from the city to the 1939 World's Fair.

I never saw him again, but many years later his son and daughter bought two Aldens and a bright wood Appledore 16 from me.

Despite all these diversions, and the ever present necessity of trying to keep up with the grinding academic schedule, something was missing. Although there was daily exposure to ships and boats, and I had the freedom which I so missed at Kent, I longed for the ultimate freedom: to be out on the water in my own boat.

An upperclassman named Pearson had built a kayak from a kit made by Mead Glider Company. It was between 16 and 18 feet long. It had aluminum transverse frames inside wood longitudinals, covered with canvas. It had a plywood sole in the large open cockpit area. Pearson was about to graduate, and offered to sell me his boat for ten dollars. I thought it over for about 30 seconds and took the plunge, callously ignoring the dent it would inflict on my finances.

I painted it dark green, with a white deck. I named it *Cynthia*, after a charming English girl in South Orange, and painted the name in the form of half a circle, on the stern deck, with N.Y. at the center.

At first I launched it in the Harlem River, which was almost as disgustingly dirty then as it is today. This was a terrible letdown after my years on the clear waters at the Shoals, but it was my first chance to experience the unique joys of kayaking, and I gladly put up with it. Whenever I went out, I always headed out through Spuytan Dyval, at the northern extremity of Manhattan Island, into the Hudson River. The water was much clearer by comparison, and there were always waves to test the seagoing capabilities of *Cynthia*.. I soon found a canoe club near Dykeman Street, and, for a modest fee, joined. *Cynthia* seldom entered the Harlem River after that.

I was often joined on the river by one of my classmates, particularly my roommate, Lew Cooper, who went into aeronautical engineering upon graduating, and the late Dick Stearn, who designed the Marine Travelifts and became the owner of an Alden. With two paddling, we made pretty good speed, and I thoroughly enjoyed the new experience of kayaking. Unlike rowing, you could see where you were going, instead of where you had been. Being long, light, and double-ended, my new boat went through the water easily, but the construction dictated that the lines lacked the subtlety which would have made the motion in waves much more satisfactory. While not wishing to be critical of my little yacht, I was always comparing her to the peapod, and other boats, and thinking of ways to improve her performance.

There was a paddle wheel ferryboat which ran between Englewood, New Jersey, and Dykeman Street. She was said to travel at 17 knots, and I had no reason to doubt it. The paddle wheels, in their inefficient effort to propel the ferry, piled up very steep and high following waves. At the canoe club there were some beautiful little boats called cedar canoes. They had considerable shear, in a fair curve unlike the traditional canoes, and their lapstrake cedar planks were varnished for the bright finish so cherished by yachtsmen. They were not long enough for more than one person and were decked over.

One of these boats would paddle up just as the Dykeman Street ferry was leaving the slip, and get immediately behind one of the paddle wheels before the ferry had gathered speed. It would then surf down the first wave, all the way across the river to Englewood. Needless to say, we tried to do this in *Cynthia*, always to no avail. She was too long for her other dimensions and shape, and lacked reserve buoyancy at the bow. Lesson number 537, never to be forgotten.

A tugboat towing one or more barges was another matter. It was easy to paddle up to the turbulent water behind the square stern of the last barge. With the water being dragged along at the speed of the tow, we could have a complete rest, while moving along at a good clip. Between vigorous paddling and such hitchhiking, we could cover long distances. We went all the way down town to where the real action was. With tugboats and ferryboats coming from all directions it was sometimes quite exciting. Once we crossed in front of a ferry slip, just as it was leaving. They blew the whistle and went into full reverse, missing us by inches. I am sure the captain must have used some salty language, but it could not be heard above the sound of the churning water and the rumbling machinery.

We checked out the ocean liners which were in port. I remember holding on to the bow of the *Queen Mary*, and looking up toward the sky along that towering stem, wondering how even the spray from a wave could reach the deck. But during World War II, when she was carrying troops to England, a rogue wave actually pushed in that very deck. We can pollute the sea, but we can never really conquer it. Size of a vessel can seem to be the answer when you look up from a bouncing rowboat to the motionless mass of big yacht in the chop of a protected harbor. But there are conditions where a well designed little boat is safer than a poorly designed one many times her size. He who underestimates the power of the sea is likely to suffer from his arrogance.

Although I never circumnavigated the island of Manhattan, *Cynthia* did, paddled by Dick Stearn and Lew Cooper when I was away. Quite a trip for a kayak, but recently people have swum it. I paddled in the Hudson River quite often in the early evening. New York is at its best when seen in the distance from a boat. I was accompanied by various girls, including my sister, Mary, on these occasions. Since the time on the water included the dinner hour, it was only fitting that the yacht provide a suitable repast. This invariably consisted of a loaf of white bread and American cheese, washed down by a little beer.

Cynthia was a great addition to my college life, and when I graduated, I sold her, reluctantly, to a freshman for ten dollars, thus retrieving my heavy investment. She was my first kayak but by no means the last.

The modern towing tank at the new Webb campus. Photo: Webb Institute of Naval Architecture.

12 • *Towing Tanks*

*a*ll children like to play with toy boats in the bathtub or anywhere else where there is sufficient water to float them. I was no different from anyone else, but in this respect, as in many others, I fear, I never grew up. As I pushed or towed various models, most of which I whittled out of pine in later years, numerous questions arose: Why did a good sailboat tow so poorly at high speed? Why did green water come over the bow of one boat and not another? What made any boat assume an angle with the bow in the air, and the stern below its normal waterline? Lifting of the bow? Or dragging down of the stern? Or both? If a double-ender was so good, why should both ends be the same? Is not the function of entering water, rough or smooth, quite different from the function of leaving it? Despite all of my experiments with the Tripoliss bow, I had no idea of the power it was consuming, for I had what amounted to infinite power at the end of a stick, and I had no way of measuring how much was required to make the little model skim across the water in a most satisfactory manner.

With all these unanswered questions, I was particularly fascinated when the curriculum at Webb turned to the study of resistance. The first part of resistance is frictional, and it is easy to understand and analyze. Water seems very slippery, even when it is not in the form of ice. Actually it tends to cling to anything in its clutches, like molasses or honey, but the effect is so much less that it is hardly noticeable to the uninitiated. Any floating object presents part of its surface area to the clinging property of the water. The total holding back effect depends on the amount of area, the coefficient of friction of water having been determined years ago by precise experiments. Considering this phenomenon alone, the way to design a faster ship or boat is to reduce the area exposed to the water. Thus the optimum shape would be a hemisphere: a ball immersed exactly half way, no more, no less. This would obviously not be a very satisfactory shape for a boat, so the next best thing is to stretch out the hemisphere to a suitable length. White water kayaks and racing shells are good examples.

When I was at Webb, the Meyerform hull had incorporated this apparently logical thinking to cargo ships, and when I was on the *Washington* I observed several of them in Germany. Norman Bel Geddes, whom I admired tremendously for his revolutionary streamlined designs, incorporated the Meyerform hull on his proposed streamlined ocean liner. Unfortunately, the designers had not known about, or ignored, other phenomena. At infinitesimal speeds, frictional resistance is indeed the only force holding back any floating object. As speed, in relation to length, increases, the vessel begins to make waves. The energy imparted to these waves is known as residual resistance. As the speed-length ratio (V, for velocity in knots, divided by the square route of the waterline length) increases, the residual resistance becomes a more important part of the total resistance. Planing boats, which are designed to rise above the water as much as possible, contend with different problems. This discussion applies only to displacement boats, which, as the name implies, must displace, or move out of the way, water equal in weight to their own, at any speed.

A cargo ship, hundreds of feet long, and traveling at a comparatively low speed, nevertheless has a significant speed-length ratio. The rounded rocker bottom of the Meyerform hull, so helpful in reducing wetted area, proved to be a real liability as far as causing unnecessary residual resistance. Furthermore, it tended to make steering very difficult. The concept disappeared entirely from ship design, the sole province of trained naval architects, years ago. The amateurs who design many of the smaller boats do not seem to understand the phenomena involved, to this day.

A racing single shell, twenty six and one-half feet long, with only eleven inches in beam, just gets under the wire as far as residual resistance goes. Some superman could apply enough power to increase the residual resistance to an intolerable degree, and a different design would be called for. But for ordinary mortals, the present design, with the minor subtle modifications that builders always seek, appears to be the optimum. A fin, or skeg, is required to keep it going in a straight line, because of the rocker bottom. A shorter and wider version of the same thing runs into a serious residual resistance problem and can often be beaten by an even shorter boat, properly designed for the circumstances.

A white water kayak, being shorter and wider, will always turn one hundred and eighty degrees, even in perfectly flat water, if not held to the course by the paddle. Because of the rocker bottom, the stern drags down at an unnecessarily low speed, demonstrating the importance of residual resistance. But for the criteria it is designed to meet, i.e. quick turns in white water, it is a great design.

I learned to calculate residual resistance for a ship using Taylor's Standard Series. Admiral David W. Taylor was far ahead of his time, and the Navy's excellent model basin is named for him, a fitting tribute to a real pioneer. He towed a series of models of ships of normal design, carefully and accurately recording the resistance at various speeds. Separating out the easily calculated frictional resistance, he had left the all-important residual resistance, which he published in tables.

No education would be complete without actually performing model tests, and we were fortunate in being able to have some of our classes on resistance at the towing tank at Stephens Institute. Ken Davidson, for whom the tank was eventually named, was one of the most brilliant men I have had the pleasure of meeting, and he ran the show. Tank testing sailboat hulls used to consist of towing the hull through flat water, straight ahead, on an even keel. This could give an accurate forecast of speed on a spinnaker run on sheltered water, but little else. Dan Strohmeir, who was later to be my distant superior at Bethlehem Steel company's shipbuilding division, while studying at M.I.T., contrived a method of measuring resistance under conditions of yaw and heel. Ken Davidson developed and perfected this technique, and was a great help to Olin Stephens as he was establishing his reputation as one of the greatest of naval architects. Ken Davidson could answer any of my many questions quickly and succinctly. I did not follow all of his advice, however, when he, perhaps facetiously, suggested that I push one of our professors into the tank. But for my restraint, I might now be a lawyer or member of Congress (perish the thought) instead of a naval architect.

It was a great satisfaction to be learning, finally, how naval architecture was practiced in the real world, with time-consuming and accurate calculations. The late Harley Ferguson, nephew of Homer Ferguson, the Chairman of Newport News Shipbuilding and Drydock Company, was a classmate and good friend, and one weekend he visited us in South Orange. With my father he turned on the southern charm and listened patiently to a long discourse on repairing clocks. This was an all-consuming hobby of my father's for many years. I was aghast one day to find him, in his late sixties, high up in the tower of the old Unitarian Church in Cohasset, fixing the ancient clock, with wood mechanism, which hadn't run in years. My two children, Douglas and Lorna, aged 5 and 4, were up there with him. I never found out how they climbed up so high, but they were good climbers and my father was a good clock fixer. The children survived and the clock runs to this day.

After Harley had listened for an hour or so about the care and feeding of clocks, my father decided to reciprocate and give him a chance to tell about what he was doing at Webb. Later my father remarked about what a smart young man my classmate was. "Do you know," he said, "he can tell them where to paint the waterline on a ship before it goes in the water, and when it is launched, that is where it floats?" Returning some of his sarcasm, I couldn't resist asking him what he thought I had been doing during the years at Webb. Actually, he loved all his children, despite his usually humorous, but sarcastic, ways of expressing it, and years after his passing, I still miss him, and wish I could take him out in some of the boats I have designed. I am sure he would delight in rowing an Alden.

As interesting as the work at Webb was, life there was not quite all work and no play. There were dances on the campus every month or so, and I became chairman of one of these. My interest in music dated back to childhood, when we used to go from New York to Boston on the Eastern Steamship Lines ships, named, appropriately, the *Boston* and the *New York*. On board, I divided my time between watching the wake, wondering what it would be like to row through it, and watching the drummer in the orchestra. Later I was to play the drums in what was called the Webb Saloon Orchestra, and later still, to play either the drums or the acoustic base in various jazz groups, sometimes for money when real musicians were scarce, such as New Year's Eve. Now I play along with various great bands on tapes or C.D.'s, whenever I feel like it. With this interest in music, it is not surprising that I went out of my way to find some better music than that performed by the so-so groups that were usually hired for these dances.

I went downtown to audition a group that sounded promising. Being convinced that they would more than fill the bill, I hired them on the spot. They were black. Word quickly spread around the campus, and I was ordered to appear in the admiral's office at 0800. Admiral Rock appeared quite upset, and his face was redder than usual, contrasting vividly with his snow white hair. He cleared his throat a number of times and then explained that he had learned that I was considering having a Negro band for the forthcoming dance. He cleared his throat several more times, and then explained that at the Naval Academy they were not (hrumph hrumph) prejudiced, but Negroes were (hrumph hrumph) different. Webb had certain standards to maintain. Negroes were apt to be noisy. So, (hrumph hrumph hrumph) it would be better if I would arrange for a white orchestra. "Well," I said, "I have hired these good people, and I am not going back on my word." His face changed color further, but, for once, I had the last word.

At these dances it was the custom to select one of the faculty, with spouse, to chaperone. On this occasion, the admiral ordered out the entire faculty to help quell the riots that were sure to ensue. I happened to know, but had not disclosed, that this group had no trumpet or trombone, but instead had a very smooth rhythm section, including a bass and an acoustical guitar (the electric guitar, which can make that magnificent instrument sound like a chicken squawk, had yet to be invented). The dance was a great success, in a quiet way, and I was glad to note that the same group appeared at almost every dance thereafter. Prejudices are hard to overcome, but it has been my observation that unpublicized little heartfelt actions do more to open doors than do the dramatic speeches and affirmative actions that do little other than, so far, garner votes.

One of the requirements for graduation was a senior thesis. A satisfactory one required months of work and original thought, supposedly contributing something to the general knowledge of naval architecture or marine engineering. With my great interest in model testing, it was natural that I turned to that phase of the science for a thesis subject. I had made models of motorboats with several different types of sterns. These were only about 12 inches long, whittled out entirely by eye, and in no way suitable for obtaining accurate quanti-

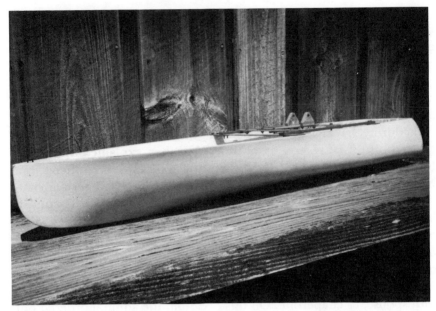

Model of George Crouch design on which spray strips were tested. Photo: Marjorie Martin.

tive resistance data. My thought was to develop accurate lines to a larger scale and make corresponding models to test in a towing tank.

One day I packed up my models and took them down to the offices of Sparkman and Stephens. Olin Stephens very kindly listened to my plans and wisely advised me that such a project was far too ambitious for a senior thesis. Making and testing so many models, and trying to factor out the many other variables outside of the stern shape, would be a gargantuan task. I was somewhat discouraged, but had to agree.

Next, I went to City Island, to consult with George Crouch in his office in the Nevins Company. He told me that a few years previously he had designed a twenty-five-foot motorboat to run in a displacement or semi-planing mode. The owner, like so many motorboat owners today, wanted more speed. Mr. Crouch thought of an idea which, as far as I know, was revolutionary at the time, and as original as anything ever is in the boat business. He reasoned that strips added along the bilge area would reduce the wetted surface and give some dynamic lift to the whole boat. He had a model built and tested at the Taylor model basin. This confirmed his theories, and subsequently similar spray strips, as they came to be called, were installed on the full-size boat, with great success. He said that he often wondered if he had picked the optimum location for the strips and also the optimum width. Tests with variations of both width and location would shed some light on the subject, in his opinion.

Seeing the interesting possibilities of such a project, I immediately accepted his offer of the lines and offsets, together with the dimensions and location of the spray strips. At this point my roommate, Lew Cooper, became a partner in the thesis effort. We made waterline lifts of pine boards, and glued them together, and made templates for each station. Then while I faired up the hull, he fabricated the metal parts for attaching it to the towing and resistance measuring apparatus. Since we were dealing with the high speeds of planing, the Stephens tank was not adequate, and we used the tank at N.Y.U., which was used primarily for testing floats for airplanes.

The testing procedure was that after we had set up the model and the instruments, one would run the drive controls, while the other rode on the carriage to check things out and take pictures. In addition to the manual stop and start buttons, there was a limit switch near the end of the run, to stop the heavy carriage automatically. One day Lew was at the controls, and I was riding on the carriage, watching the model plane down the tank at a breathtaking speed. As we neared the end of the tank, Lew pressed the stop button several times, but nothing happened and the carriage sped on. The automatic limit switch also failed to perform its duty. There was a mighty crash, and I found myself lying down among a pile of shattered cast iron gears and other pieces of the metal structure. At first I thought I was surely dead, but on closer inspection I was astonished to find not a single scratch. The towing tank, however, was out of service for several weeks, and we were hard pressed to finish the project before the deadline. But, as the finished treatise proudly announced, we did accomplish what we set out to do. Subsequently, a slight altercation ensued between myself and Admiral Rock as to who should retain possession of the model I had so painstakingly faired and smoothed. I still have it.

One of the early Higgins boats. AEM drew the plans after the Navy had tested the first boat out in the Pacific. Photo: U.S.Navy.

13 • Summer Jobs

*O*ne of the advantages of Kent was the long summer vacation, spent at the Isles of Shoals. At Webb, at least eight weeks of off-campus work each summer were required for graduation. The first summer, as soon as the *Washington* landed in New York after my second voyage, I called my family in South Orange. My plan was to go immediately to the Shoals, for the two voyages had taken exactly the required eight weeks. I could not understand why the family was not already there, and I began to suspect that further inertia might leave our house on Appledore vacant for the rest of the summer. I felt called upon to deliver an ultimatum then and there: If we were not going to go to the Shoals immediately, I would sign on for another voyage. It would be more fun on the ship than in hot, dull South Orange, and besides, I would accumulate more money. There being no opportunity to make purchases at sea, I could save the entire month's pay: thirty-five dollars.

My cavalier threat broke the log jam, and we went to the Shoals as usual. This did not please the admiral, who worshipped the work ethic. He seemed so upset that I signed on for another voyage just before classes began in the fall, in the hope that it would pacify him. It didn't.

After my sophomore year I worked at Federal Shipyard in Kearney, New Jersey, a subsidiary of U.S.steel. The pay was somewhat better, but the work was something else. At the time they were building two of the few destroyers commissioned between the wars. They were very fast, but limited beam curtailed their effectiveness. I was very interested in having a part in their construction, but my first assignment had nothing to do with ships at all.

The Lincoln Tunnel was being constructed, and the big tube was gradually pushing its way through the silt and mud at the bottom of the Hudson River, like a giant earthworm. There was not enough substance to support the tremendous weight, so steel towers, or caissons, as they were called, were required to support the tunnel above the solid bottom below. My job, with a partner, was to regulate plates and shapes that had been bolted loosely in place by the riggers. One of us would pound in a drift pin, a tapered steel pin like a marlin spike, through the rivet holes in the two members, thus lining them up accurately. Then we would put a bolt through an adjacent set of rivet holes, and tighten up a nut on the other side, using large open-end wrenches. Then others would ream out all the other rivet holes, and finally the riveters would apply red hot rivets with air hammers. It was hot, dirty, and unbelievably noisy, so that communication was almost impossible. There is nothing to compare to a busy shipyard with hundreds of chippers, riveters, and caulkers, all using pneumatic tools at once.

One afternoon, the whole yard suddenly became quiet, save for some spasmodic hammering on distant ships. The C.I.O. was organizing, and this was one of the first sit-down strikes. I was somewhat terrified, but at the same time fascinated, by the spectacle that unfolded. The leaders cursed at the sound of the few still working, and set off in their direction. I followed out of curiosity. I heard the leader threaten to kill several of the men who were not participating in the strike. Before long, all work had ceased.

Later the same leader tried to persuade some other college students and myself to join the union. We tactfully declined, on the grounds that we would have to return to college shortly. A few days later, I was sitting on a narrow beam at the very top of the caisson, trying to follow what my partner was doing without the aid of words, which could never penetrate the general din. For some reason, I happened to look behind me, and there, coming straight for me, was a load of steel beams, swinging from the hook of a crane. I dropped down quickly, holding on by my fingers, while the load passed just above my head. The crane operator was not visible, but he was being directed by none other than the union organizer. By such tactics the union won out, and Federal, along with many another good American shipyard, are no longer with us. Collective bargaining, which was so necessary to correct corporate evils, such as the goon squads of Ford's Harry Bennet, had introduced its own problems. Whatever sympathy I may have had for the C.I.O. did not last long.

Later in the summer I was promoted to shipfitter's helper on one of the tankers, on the night shift. At first I was apprehensive about working so far above the ground, but you get used to anything when you are young, and I soon began to take a sandwich and a bottle of beer up the mast for a cool supper. But the dreadful inefficiency and endless waste of time filled me with disgust. No one could do anything outside of his classification. Thus a welder had to wait for an electrician to plug in a welding machine, a shipfitter could not touch a burning torch, and so on. One night one of our group let all the oxygen out of a burner's tank, just to get an hour of rest, while the burner went through the long process of getting a fresh tank. If our boats were built according to the procedures I have observed in both public and private shipyards, only millionaires could afford them. When the required eight weeks were over, I was more than happy to walk out the gate for the last time, and head for the Shoals.

At the end of my junior year, I drove to New Orleans with my classmate Harley Ferguson in a model A Ford with a rumble seat. I had applied for a job there in one of my original, and possibly eccentric, letters to Higgins Industries. Andrea Higgins, the older daughter of Andrew Jackson Higgins, was a secretary at her father's boatbuilding company. She had been intrigued by my letter and claimed responsibility for my being hired.

I was one of three in the drafting room and already more knowledgeable about speed and propeller calculations than the other two, although I would be the first to admit that I was slow and inefficient in the day-to-day detail drafting work, which I was never to enjoy. Mr. Higgins was quite pompous and overbearing and had a large bay window to front for him. He had a loud voice, a contagious laugh, and the natural charisma which attracts and influences people. He was a master salesman, and he had a repertoire of endless amusing anecdotes with which to beguile customers. He reputedly made a million dollars in the lumber business, lost it all; started all over from scratch, made another million, lost that; and started in the boat business.

Higgins naturally knew the lumber business upside down and backwards, and he believed in using this knowledge in the boat business. He was one of the first to import Philippine mahogany, or luan, as it is more correctly called, and he had no shortage of long leaf yellow pine, African and Honduras mahogany, and cypress.

He evolved a series of power boats which were widely used by the oil companies and many others, including the Coast Guard. The midship section consisted of a Vee-bottom, with moderate deadrise, a hard chine, and straight topsides, slightly flared out. Forward, the bottom and the chines curved upward, almost to the deck. The sides curved in to a straight stem line, 1-2 feet wide. Keel, chines, planking, deck clamp and shelf, and deck all met in a huge block of solid long leaf yellow pine, rabbeted and notched to secure them all. Even on the smaller boats, this block was at least 12 by 12. Needless to say, it was very rugged construction, as Mr Higgins was quick to point out to anyone within earshot of his powerful, gravely voice. Aft, the Vee-bottom changed to about half a tunnel, resulting in very shallow draft, good protection for the propeller, and surprisingly good performance in the menacing water hyacinth, which constantly encroached on the bayous and other waterways in the area. Needless to say, these boats were called Higgins Boats.

In the late thirties, the Navy became interested in boats which could land marines on beaches or rocky shores. They asked each of several boat builders to submit a sample of his conception of the best boat for the job. The year before I arrived, Mr. Higgins got his crew to put together their best effort to meet the Navy requirements, hastily, without any plans. While I was there that very boat, along with various other contenders, was with the fleet in the Pacific, being tested.

One day an official telegram arrived from the Navy, announcing that Higgins had won the contest and calling for copies, in sextuplicate (or more) of all the plans. The fact that there were no plans whatsoever didn't faze Mr. Higgins one iota. He merely ordered me, in his stentorian voice, to draw them up. I protested that no one in the company knew less about the boat than I, but there was no arguing with Mr. Higgins. I went around to all of the men in the shop, begging them to try to recall the frame spacing, planking thickness, floor timber construction, etc., and devised plans from my copious notes.

During World War II the allies used thousands of small landing boats, which were universally referred to as Higgins Boats. Actually, although Higgins built many of them, they bore little resemblance to the ones I had drawn up with so much difficulty. Instead of spoon bows, they had bow ramps, which proved to be much more efficient. I went out on trial trips of many of them, characteristically refusing to wear the life vests on which the Navy insisted.

One day Mr. Higgins invited me for Sunday lunch (dinner here in Maine) at his house, with his wife and two daughters. Dawn Gloria Higgins, the youngest at 8 or 9, played the accordion very well and was quite charming. After lunch, Mr. Higgins took us all on a tour of the area. We stopped at the remains of a rusty old building on a bayou, which I believe had been used during World War I. Mr. Higgins told me that some day he was going to have the world's largest boatbuilding plant there. I thought to myself, this guy is crazy. How wrong I was! It happened just about as he had prophesied, only a few years later.

Next we stopped at the yacht club, just as a big yacht was approaching. Mr. Higgins asked me what kind of a boat it was: "Elco 50, sir," I replied. "That's where you're wrong, Martin," he admonished. "If you want to be a naval architect, you should get to know the different boats." Just then a deckhand jumped ashore with the bow line. "What kind of a boat is that, son?" asked Mr. Higgins. "Elco 50, sir," replied the sailor. The subject was promptly dropped.

The Army Engineers were good customers, the Higgins Boats being very handy in controlling the unruly Mississippi. I was given the job of designing a conventional 50-foot "inspection" boat. I was almost finished with the plans of what I thought would be a suitable vessel when Mr. Higgins escorted a Colonel Crawford, who seemed to be in charge, into the drafting room. Amid much loud laughter, they agreed that my plans were completely unsatisfactory. I had allowed no space for the bar, the women, or the fishing gear. Back to the drawing board, and another valuable lesson in naval architecture.

One weekend Mr. Higgins' youngest son and I delivered a large old yacht far down the Bayou Barataria, a euphonious name which I never forgot. We ran aground several times, but here were none of our Maine rocks, and no damage was done. I was fascinated by the bayou country, and the Cajun people we met along the way. One, named Roosevelt Cheramie, let me paddle his pirogue. These boats, though crudely hacked out of a solid log, have surprisingly good lines. There is one here on the island, carefully preserved. The pirogue is extraordinarily unstable, as I soon found out, but fast to paddle, and the local fishermen can really make them talk. It is fascinating to see how many really fine designs have evolved from the fertile minds of a succession of practical people, unfettered by book wisdom, rules, or laws, to fit the circumstances of the local area, wherever on the globe it may be located.

Higgins Industries was building a 50-foot steel tug for the Army Engineers that summer. I was scheduled to be part of the crew running it to Baltimore, promising an interesting trip and a free ride more than half way home. But as the summer wore on, it became obvious that it would never be finished in time for me to make the opening classes of my final year at Webb, let alone any cherished time at the Shoals. Neither Mr. Higgins nor any of his people knew anything about steel construction, nor the complicated engineering of a tugboat.

During World War II, President Roosevelt, on one of his non-political trips, stopped in New Orleans. All the national media showed him riding down Canal Street in an open limo, waving to the crowds lining the sidewalks. Sitting beside him was none other than the great salesman, Andrew Jackson Higgins. A few days later we all learned what had been sold.

Higgins had mysteriously landed the largest contract in the country for cargo ships. At the time many established shipyards were launching these Victory ships at a furious pace in a desperate effort to keep one step ahead of Hitler, whose submarines were sinking them at an alarming rate. Henry Kaiser became a national hero because of the speed with which he was building them, but Bethlehem and several others were doing almost equally well. There was a critical shortage of steel, but shipbuilding had a high priority.

Higgins offered a proposal which was so preposterous it would have been ludicrous were it not for the seriousness of the situation. He had no suitable place to launch ships, no experienced labor, no experienced supervision, and no experience himself. He proposed to put up huge buildings, just one of which would require 38,000 tons of precious steel, employ some of the largest cranes ever to be built, and put the ships together on an assembly line, like Henry Ford's, but magnified thousands of times. Admiral Land, and others responsible for war production, were horrified, but it seemed that the commander-in-chief could be neither persuaded nor overruled. Fortunately, common sense eventually prevailed, and the whole project was dropped in the early stages. The cranes, which had already been completed, were put to good use at Bethlehem-Hingham Shipyard. I often thought of my experiences with Higgins as I walked by them.

AEM in tipping chair, with Sport, son of Princess. Photo: Franklin Martin.

14 • *Graduation*

*a*s my days at Webb were drawing to a close, I was once again summoned to the Admiral's office. To the best of my memory, the conversation went something like this:

AR (Admiral Rock):"Well, Martin,(hrumph hrumph) you will soon be graduating, and I see that all of your classmates have lined up jobs."

AM (ye scribe): "Yes, sir."

AR: "You don't seem to have found a job."

AM: "No, sir."

AR: "I think I could still get you a job in a shipyard or one of the Navy yards. It is far too late, but I will try."

AM: "No thank you, sir."

AR: "Well, what are you going to do?"

AM: "I'm going out to the Isles of Shoals."

AR: "That's near the Portsmouth Naval Shipyard. I have been there many times when I was in the Bureau of Ships. It is a good yard and a good place for you to start working."

AM: "But I am not going to work there."

AR: "(hrumph) What are you going to do then?"

AM: "I'm going to catch lobsters."

AR: "(hrumph hrumph) That's not much of a challenge for a graduate naval architect, but I guess you could make a living at it, if you sell enough."

AM: "But I'm not going to sell them, I'm going to eat them."

With that I thought the poor admiral would really expire on the spot, but he survived this final confrontation, and so did I.

As the day of commencement ceremonies approached, the final rankings were given out. I was thirteenth, which is extremely good for Harvard or the Naval Academy. For Webb, with only 13 in the graduating class (of the original fifteen, one had flunked out, and one had transferred to West Point), this was not quite such a sensational achievement. Our class had quite a sense of humor, and I was elected to give the valedictory address, in contradiction of the usual procedure.

I chose as my subject our founder and benefactor, whom I greatly admired, William H. Webb. Along with enumerating some of his many achievements, I managed to work in the fact that he stood for freedom, private enterprise, and individual initiative, and was sometimes hampered by Navy red tape. I was somewhat ambivalent about this speech, sometimes fearing that the point would be lost, and at others fearing that it would be only too well understood.

As I look back on it, I realize that Admiral Rock was a good man, extremely conscientious, a hard worker, and one to go by the book, without questioning it. I hadn't learned to accept authority and still haven't.

Now a full-fledged naval architect, and free to do what I wanted, I made plans to go to the Shoals, this time by myself. Actually, I did not plan to survive on lobster alone. I made a deal with V.D. Harrington, the manager of the Oceanic Hotel, that I would tie up and help unload the *Sightseer*, and do occasional repairs at the hotel. In exchange, I would have lunch and supper with the "Pelicans," the waitresses and bellboys, and also receive $10 per month. I also made a deal with my Uncle Jack that I would take his hunting dog, "Shot," a cross between a pointer and a setter, with me as long as he gave me sufficient funds for dog food. Shot did very well on fish and lobster, and scraps brought over from the hotel, but he never had any dog food, and I derived some extra income.

With this arrangement, I made at least two or more daily trips back and forth between Star and Appledore in the peapod, which suited me just fine. I usually stayed over at Star after supper to participate in dances. They had an all-girl trio for classical music during the day, and Gracia Harrington substituted the drums for her 'cello at dances. I talked my way into playing the drums, but Mr. Harrington felt that I was making too much noise for a religious conference, and my services were no longer required in the music department. The only activity other than dancing was known as rocking. To participate, a young man would go to a wood building, known as "the shack" to the South of the hotel and whistle. By prearrangement, one of the waitresses, who all lived there, would appear at the head of the outside stairs, carrying a blanket. It was very romantic on a high rocky ledge, looking at the shimmering path of the moonlight on the dark water below.

Despite the pleasures of the evening, I always enjoyed the row back to Appledore in the peapod, all by myself. I am constantly surprised to hear of a rowing enthusiast who has never rowed at night. There is nothing in this world quite like it. The boat seems to go much faster, with less effort. The phosphorescence is like a string of pearls, far more brilliant than anything one could buy, suspended from each side of a well designed bow. The oar blades make swirls of fire, and a chain of platinum streams from the sharp stern. It is very peaceful and quiet, and I often pity all those who choose instead a crowded, noisy, smoky, night club.

Upon reaching Appledore, I would tie the peapod to the outhaul, pull it out, and climb up the rocks and steps to the back porch. There I would invariably hear the thump thump thump of Shot's tail on the kitchen floor. He never barked, or even got up, but his quiet way of confirming his presence was enough for me. He was a magnificent dog, referred to by my father as "The people's choice." By day, he would often wade into the water at the Half Tide Ledges until he spotted a crab. Then he would stay there and bark for as long as the crab could stand it. He never caught one, but that did not seem to bother him. He was a great companion.

Toward the end of the summer, the rest of the family arrived to share the lobster. I saw an ad in Yachting, seeking a young naval architect to work at Greenport Basin and Construction Company. I had completed my education and enjoyed a most satisfying vacation to reward myself for four years of what was, for me, very difficult work. Now I was ready to see what I could do with all that knowledge. So I answered the ad, giving as salary required forty dollars per week. I received a telegram from Marshall E. Tulloch, Treasurer, saying "Salary you suggest tentatively satisfactory. Report as soon as possible." I pulled up my lobster traps and headed for Long Island.

15 • Greenport

*W*hen I arrived in Greenport, I received an early lesson in business, to add to my education. My salary was not forty but thirty dollars per week. I was somewhat upset by this kind of dealing, but it was too late to return to the Shoals, and I liked the area and the yard, if not the double-dealing Mr. Tulloch.

Greenport is almost at the end of the north fork of Long Island, near the New London ferry dock at Orient Point. It is hard to believe that this clean, sparsely populated rural area is on the same island as Brooklyn and Queens. Outside of boatbuilding, oysters were the principal product, which I soon learned to acquire without cost and consume in huge quantities.

The yard had just completed a big Sea Sled for the Navy. It had four Hall-Scott Invader engines, with five and one-half by seven bore and stroke, developing 275 horsepower each, driving four surface propellers. It was designed by Albert Hickman himself, and it made more than 40 knots. They said it pounded so savagely that it broke limbs of crew members, unless Hickman himself was at the helm. I had ridden in a Sea Sled previously, enjoying the huge rooster tail sent up by the surface propeller, and I much admired the design. With Hickman's subtle refinements, such as the cut-away chines, it was most efficient, and when I applied George Crouch's speed formula, it came up with the highest coefficient I had encountered. Actually, the design was somewhat like a Tripoliss bow turned inside out. Whereas the Tripoliss threw the water out to the sides, the Sea Sled trapped it, along with air bubbles, in the middle, increasing the lift and adding to the speed, but also, unfortunately, increasing the pounding.

The Navy had ordered a Sea Sled previously, having sent out several requests for bids. My old friend, Alfred E. Luders, came up with the lowest bid, thanks in part by cutting Mr. Hickman out of the pattern, to avoid patent fees. The Navy had specified a speed of 40 knots, with a penalty for each knot below that, and a stipulation that the boat would not be accepted if the speed did not reach a specified minimum. On trials, the finished boat could not get above 28 knots and graced the space outside the Luders shops for several years.

The boats under construction when I arrived were five patrol boats for the Venezuelan Coast Guard, powered by eight-cylinder Superior Diesels. These boats had a very good design feature for which Greenport was noted. They had nicely flared round bottoms forward, but hard chines and V-bottoms aft. This gave them good speed and rolling characteristics. An American Coast Guard inspector named Schoffield was engaged to keep an eye on construction quality. He traveled to and from the yard by Coast Guard boat, one of which was a captured rumrunner. I was intrigued by this boat, and couldn't resist a thorough inspection of the engine room, which contained two Liberty aircraft engines on each shaft, giving it 1,800 horsepower, quite a lot for those days. When they started it up, they advised me not to stand directly between two engines, for these powerful *prima donnas* had a habit of throwing connecting rods out through the casings when starting up. The elegant sound was worth the risk.

Harold Vanderbilt's big yacht, *Vara*, was tied up there for the winter, and I stayed at a boarding house run by a Mrs. Hedges, the sister of George Monson, the paid captain. The latter took himself quite seriously and made sure that everyone was aware of his importance, although it was said that Vanderbilt handled all navigational matters on any of his boats. When the five new patrol boats were ready to be run in to the pier in New York, the good captain assumed command. He spent the best part of a day in our drafting room, working over charts of Long Island Sound with dividers and parallel rules, much to our amusement. It was a clear and mild day for the trip, but the lead boat went ashore at Port Jefferson.

While I was there, we received a contract to build five airplane rescue boats for the Army Air Force. These were 72 feet long with a very good hull design, round forward and vee aft, and a streamlined superstructure, which appealed to me. They were powered by twin six-hundred-horsepower Hall Scott Defenders, the then new V-12 engines composed essentially of two Invader blocks. Greenport had built a previous prototype, but it had had Wright Typhoon engines. Old Mr. Brigham, who was president of the company, and basically a very fine and honest man, was afraid that the new engines would not deliver as much power, and he might be penalized for not making the specified speed. Mr. Tulloch had put money into the yard to keep it going. A somewhat devious plan was hatched.

The Army inspector, named McCullom, was a very pleasant little man from the South. He had a great sense of humor, especially when he had had a few drinks. He often joined a group of us in sessions with old John Barleycorn, where he was the life of the party. But he knew practically nothing about boats.

It was reasoned that such a man would never think of putting a micrometer to a steel bulkhead, so these were reduced considerably in thickness, assuring a lighter weight, to maintain the specified speed. It so happened that some of the men were disgruntled because of differences with the management over pay. They also enjoyed drinking sessions with Mr. McCullom, and did not hesitate to tell him about the lighter metal. As they say, the rest is history. Despite the considerable fuss over the bulkheads, the boats performed beautifully, they made their speed with some to spare, and the Army accepted them.

The launching of the first of these boats was quite an occasion. I quote from a letter I wrote to my parents:

"The first boat went down the ways yesterday in the midst of a most incredible pandemonium. As her great 33" by 41" propellers hit the water, the wife of a major general broke a ribboned bottle of Rheims Pere et Fils over the bow, being supported on the bow (the sponsor) by the none too steady arm of Mr. Tulloch, in a new gray gaberdine suit. Back aft were me and a girl and all of Mr. Tulloch's kids. He had tried to kick us all off, but while he and Mr. Brigham were arguing about it, they took away the gangway and the boat started to go down the ways. Later in the day Mr. Tulloch was to be found behind the improvised bar, kissing a Mrs. Meany from New Jersey.

"Meanwhile Mrs. Tulloch had maneuvered the Army inspector into a corner and was proceeding to admonish him with her tongue and her fat fists for finding fault with the boats. He, thoroughly wedged into the corner, continued to smile like a chipmunk and call everyone a bastard. The wife of the assistant secretary was crying and screaming and throwing champagne, glass and all, at a tall, cynical individual who had called her a hick.

"Some time later a great line of cars could be seen parading up the main street at about five miles an hour. At the head of the line was the City of Skinflint (my 1938 Ford coupe), with the aforementioned girl at the helm. And in front of that was I, on her bicycle, pointing an imaginary gun at everyone, and yelling 'Hi Ho Silver.'

"After several more fights, the day ended for most of the merry-makers. But not for that amiable little group, the Tullochs. They evidently kept it up all night, for there are reports of Mrs. Tulloch hanging onto a post outside the waterfront gin mill, trying to be sick into Gardiner's Bay instead of down her front, and asking an unsympathetic group of bystanders where Mr. Tulloch and the children were. This morning, while the good people of Greenport were walking to church, Mr. Tulloch drove into the shipyard in his great green La Salle with white wall tires and a freshly smashed up front which was not there yesterday. He unloaded a fishing rod and a case of liquor and proceeded down to the dock to go fishing in the company speed boat. To his surprise, no doubt, he found the speed boat leading a serpentine course around the bay, with all of his progeny aboard and Mrs. Tulloch at the wheel. That may give you some idea of what a launching is like out here".

It was at this time that the Soviets attacked Finland, in one of their earlier efforts toward conquering the world. The desperate Finns needed PT boats and sent over a young naval architect to negotiate purchases with American boat builders. We were one of the ones being considered. This was a great opportunity for me to figure displacements, speeds, and cruising radii, as various alternative lengths, armaments, crew requirements, etc. were considered. In addition to the Crouch formula, I had accumulated constants from every boat on which I could collect data, including tank tests of a PT model made by Richards Miller (later Captain, U.S.N., and a proud owner of a wood Appledore 16) in the class below me at Webb. I knew that all the pirates in the business would be giving unrealistically optimistic estimates of performance to secure the order, but I kept all of my forecasts on the conservative side. I thought this was creating a favorable impression on the prospective buyer, and that was confirmed when he asked Mr. Brigham and Mr. Tulloch to bring their final proposal to Washington. I worked feverishly to get everything in order for their scheduled departure.

The next day they called me from Washington in a panic. Our friend from Finland had changed the specifications but was still very interested. They asked me to take the next train for the Capital, bringing my slide rule and all my data. I was tempted to say that I would leave as soon as they paid me the promised salary, but I was too excited about the prospect of being on center stage in Washington. When I arrived, I immediately delved into the new requirements and worked all day on the various calculations. They invited our visitor for dinner, and the four of us had what was for me a most luxurious dinner, ironically including blue mussels at seventy-five cents apiece, the very same mussels that we obtained free from our mooring at the Shoals.

During dinner, our guest told an interesting anecdote from World War I. His family owned a boat yard, and they obtained a contract to make oars for the Russian Navy. No matter how hard they tried to assure quality, the Russian inspector always rejected a great many of them. Then one night, at his suggestion, they all played poker, and it happened that the Russian won. The next day there were no rejections. They arranged more poker games, which they contrived to lose. There were no further rejections.

After our friend from Finland had left, Mr. Brigham asked me what I made of the little anecdote. I replied that he came from a well-to-do family and appeared to be extremely honest and very patriotic. I thought he told the story to lead them into a bribery attempt, and I said I thought that such an attempt would warn him to have nothing further to do with us. They exchanged knowing glances and suggested that I get some sleep after my arduous duties. Whatever happened after that I know not, but there was no further communication concerning the anticipated order, which was placed elsewhere.

At Greenport I was exposed to many kinds of boatbuilding wood. In addition to the usual white oak, long leaf yellow pine, mahogany, cedar, and teak, there were greenheart, rosewood, lignum vitae, and osage orange, among others. I brought little samples of each home to my father. He had learned from Mr. Brewster how to knit the net heads for lobster traps. This required a special flat needle, about a foot in length and an inch wide, with an internal spindle and a notch at the back on which to wind the twine. The needles were carved out of wood, and my father developed a great interest in making them, even after he had made enough for every lobsterman at the Shoals, and then some. He would carve out a needle from each piece of wood I brought him, sand it, oil it, and polish it, and tie a little tag to it, giving the kind of wood and the date. After he died, they were divided among his four children, and mine grace our living room wall to this day.

One of our courses at Webb consisted of designing a small boat. I chose to try my hand at designing a V-bottom double-ender (what else) for rowing and sailing. There was a certain amount of plagiarism in this, as in so many boat designs. Milt Hall, another of the loved and respected lobstermen at the Shoals, not only took good care of all his boats, he built them. He had built a rowing boat with the same concept as my design. I was impressed with its stability, without too much sacrifice in speed. It is here in Kittery Point, still in commission after half a century, named after the builder. I did not know if mine would be as good, or if it would sail, and there seemed to be little prospect of its ever being built, but I kept the plans anyway.

Mr. Brigham, though somewhat penurious when it came to my salary, was more than generous in letting me use the shop and power tools at night. So I started to build the little boat I had designed. Rabbetting the stem and stern was like whittling, and came easily, but otherwise I did not have the patience to become a good craftsman. Furthermore, I had to chose between neglecting the night boatbuilding project or neglecting the young ladies of Greenport. The choice was not an easy one, but the keel, stem and stern, and sawn frames, looking like the forlorn carcass of a long dead animal on the desert, gave mute testimony to my decision. When some Webb students arrived for summer work, I turned the project over to them. They completed the little boat in good order and sailed it down Long Island Sound in a northeast storm, reporting that it performed admirably. I never did have a chance to go out in it, although I did see it once at the old alma mater.

As summer approached, I yearned to be back at the Shoals, and I did not see much future for me at Greenport Basin, which was showing signs of financial clouds on the horizon. Consequently, I left in June of 1940 to head once more for the magic islands.

The U.S.S. Massachusetts. *AEM did various calculations including some of the critical launching data. Photo: U.S. Navy.*

16 • *Bethlehem*

*M*y father accompanied me to the Shoals after I left Greenport. The summer was much the same as the previous one,
with one exception. The submarine *Squalus* had gone down in 1939
southwest of the islands, bringing many good men to a tragic and horrible death. Rescue operations were only partially successful, but work
was continued until finally the sub was brought to the surface and
repaired. She returned to the Shoals the following year, under a new
name, as good as new. She was anchored about a mile off Appledore
one night, and I rowed the peapod out there. An interest added to the
joy of rowing at night.

My father had always been intrigued with Morse code, and he
was quite adept at sending and receiving audible messages. Blinking
by Morse code was a fascinating new hobby for him, and he was always
looking for someone with whom to communicate by this challenging
method. When I reached the side of the submarine, I chatted with
some of the crew who were on deck. They were blinking in Morse
code, and wondered who it could be blinking very slowly and poorly
on Appledore. I proudly announced that it was my father.

I had a habit of tipping back in my chair, which could undoubtedly be harmful to the health of the average chair, designed to have
all four legs on the floor. My father's most brilliant sarcasm failed to
break me of this habit. He finally solved the problem by building me
what he called a tipping chair. The vertical members consisted of the
looms of ash oars, the blades of which had long since seen better days.
These sturdy members were securely fastened to the framework of a
seat. Lobster pot warp (wop) was woven into a seat and back. It was
surprisingly comfortable for tipping, and practically indestructible.

The Soviets and Nazis had by this time started World War II,
marching into Poland and dividing that hapless country between

them. Neither of the two partners in crime had yet double-crossed the other. The Nazis had conquered France and the low countries, and their submarines were decimating the cargo ships attempting to supply the British. The Kellogg-Briand Treaty limiting warship construction had compromised our ability to defend ourselves at sea. How foolish to believe that limiting heavy cruisers (those carrying eight-inch guns) to ten thousand tons would have the slightest deterrent effect on a tyrant determined to conquer the world. History repeats.

But with the war all but lost, we were waking up, and it was apparent that there was a desperate need for ships. A similar need for small boats was to arise later, but I saw little evidence of it at the time. It seemed that I should devote whatever talent I had accumulated to the shipbuilding effort. Consequently, I joined the Central Technical Department of the Shipbuilding Division of Bethlehem Steel Company, in Quincy, Massachusetts.

When I first came to work at Bethlehem, I lived in a boarding house known as the Miller Stile Inn. I bought Arrow shirts for $2 rather than attempting to make arrangements for washing the ones I already had. I got my meals at the first restaurant Howard Johnson ever started. He would invite the owners of other franchised restaurants to dinner meetings there, charging them full price for dinner, but coercing the owner of that restaurant to provide the dinners without charge. Having nothing else to do, I watched these procedures with interest, and acquired a superficial acquaintance with the principals.

My brother Bill, who was in the cavalry at Fort Devens at the time, occasionally joined me in Quincy whenever he could get away from his arduous duties learning how to fight World War II on horseback. One day we drove down to Cohasset, and when I saw that beautiful waterfront and the endless Atlantic stretching to the far horizon, it was love at first sight, and I vowed that some day I would get married and live in Cohasset. But for the immediate future, I made other living arrangements.

A family who lived in a big house in Hingham experienced a devastating tragedy when one of the members committed suicide by wrist-slitting in the bathtub. None of the family wished to continue living there, and so they put it up for rent at a very modest fee. An enterprising group of young bachelors, most of whom worked for Bethlehem,

Deadwood. For young bachelors: luxury at $20 per week. Photo: Marjorie Martin.

got together and rented the house, and employed a couple to serve as cook, maid, butler, and purchasing agents for luxurious food and drink. The cost of this high living came to $20 per week per young man. Satisfying though this arrangement was, one by one the young men were lured away to try matrimony. This called for replacements from time to time, and I became one of these. There I heard many tales of a very interesting former member: Phil Le Boutillier, Jr.

My tenancy at "Deadwood," the name given to our luxurious abode, was short lived, for I soon left to get married and, as quickly as possible, to move to Cohasset.

There I met a man named Max Savage, who was about to move away. He said he had a kayak for which he had no further use. I offered him $10 for it on the spot, the same price I had received for my old kayak at Webb. When he accepted, I was delighted to discover that it was a sister ship of *Cynthia*, and in reasonably good condition. Although I suppose it would not last there one night today, I kept my new little ship just above high tide at Sandy Beach, all summer, for all of the war years. I paddled all up and down that beautiful coastline, and into Cohasset Harbor, and up the reversing rapids at the end of the harbor into the Gulf, a completely protected stretch of salt water, winding through marsh surrounded by trees and rocky cliffs for more than a mile. Many a mackerel became a victim of my jig, trolled Isles of Shoals fashion, for I still had not accepted the rod and reel. I took my children out in my new ship, one by one, as they arrived on the scene, as soon as they showed an interest in going out on the water instead of just playing on the beach. When my father came up to visit us, he immediately took to the kayak. I recall his accompanying me out fishing one day in a mild northeast (notheast) storm, when, just after he pulled his line up, there was a huge swirl, obviously made by considerably more of a fish than we were prepared to deal with. Though nearly seventy, he seemed completely unphased by the incident, and went right on fishing. The kayak was a great boat for those days. My shipbuilding job allowed little time for recreation, and the military took a dim view of bigger pleasure boats going outside, where target practice for airplanes took precedence. While the war kept many boat owners ashore, the little kayak kept me in my chosen element whenever time permitted.

Designing a mighty battleship sounds like a fascinating challenge. Actually, so many individuals are involved, and so much time is required, that there is little opportunity for the lower echelon technicians to exert much influence on the basic design strategy. All of the millions of details of armor, armament, machinery, wiring, piping, living quarters, and hull structure are important, but once the process is understood, each increment of design becomes repetitive and boring. I was trained to do any and all of these jobs, so there was little challenge. Instead of being the eager young naval architect, I soon became a clock-watcher, performing routine tasks. One of these was calculating tank capacities, so that when a tank was sounded,i.e. when the depth of liquid in the tank was measured, anyone could read from a curve on a graph the amount in the tank. At the Fore River (Quincy) yard we were building the battleship *Massachusetts*, among other ships, at the time. She had hundreds of compartments, the better to sustain damage from bombs or torpedoes without sinking. This meant that many of them were on the outside of the hull, where one surface was curved in two planes. Consequently, calculating the capacity at any depth was similar to calculating the displacement of a boat at any waterline. Very interesting the first time, but the novelty wears off after the first thirty or forty tanks.

I was paid the same $30 per week that I had earned at Greenport, except that overtime brought it to $39. This was far less than they were paying untrained draftsman, and when I found that my official title was "learner draftsman" I was furious. As a result of my outspoken ire, Jimmy Hunter, the head naval architect, did give me several raises, but he said I had a chip on my shoulder, which was true. Long after he died, his daughter bought one of our Oarmasters to put in a Gloucester Gull dory that her husband had built.

Despite the boredom, the low pay, and the stodgy atmosphere, I succeeded in finding interesting projects. One job that I liked was doing launching calculations. There is nothing quite like the excitement of participating in an end launching of a big ship. The exacting calculations must start before the keel is laid. The angle of declivity must be determined, so each bulkhead is built to this angle rather than being plumb. The launchways are designed for the weight of the ship and consist of twelve-by-twelve long leaf yellow pine timbers, side by side, in numbers sufficient to carry the entire launching weight of the ship, without excessive pressure anywhere. The ways are curved along their length so that the slope becomes greater as the ship moves down. This curve usually has a 40,000 to 70,000- foot radius. The fixed ways are greased with a thick base coat which is ironed on, topped with a less solid slip coat. Then bars of steel, as thick as the grease, are inserted, and they take the weight of the sliding ways and the cradle while the ship is being built. If the design of the ways, the greasing, and all of the other ramifications are not right, the ship might stick on the ways, or start down after the turn of the tide, breaking in half because of excessive pressure at the end of the ways. All of these calculations must be revised according to expected tide height on the scheduled day of launch, total weight estimate at day of launch, etc.

Getting the ship safely in the water is only half the battle. It hits its element at tremendous speed, and it must be stopped, neither too soon nor too late. Professor Henry H.W. Keith, of M.I.T., worked out a

technique with the Bethlehem naval architects which was very successful. Since it did not require human beings to chop manilla lines at
precisely the right moment, it was much more reliable than the older
system of dropping anchors. One or more heavy cables were attached
to pads welded to either side of the bow. Each cable was led back
toward the stern, supported by manilla stops, and then led forward to
a pile of old anchor chain, arranged in the shape of a horseshoe, the
open end toward the water.

The day of the launch, the excitement started to build with the
removal, early in the morning , of the grease irons, allowing the
weight of the sliding ways to be taken by the grease, for the first time.
The grease irons were hung on a numbered board, with a place for
each one. One neglected grease iron could ruin the whole day. Then
a gang of men would pound in wedges between the cradle and the
sliding ways, starting the process of gradually transferring the huge
weight of the ship to the launching cradle. One by one, in a carefully
timed order, the shores, bilge cribs, and keel blocks would be
removed, until finally the great mass of the ship stood entirely unsup-
ported save for the cradle. Then two oxy-acetaline burners, one on
each side, would start to burn through the steel plates holding the
cradle. There were a series of holes, as in a postage stamp, in the middle of each plate. The plates were designed to break when the two
solid outsides were burned through, and half of the numbered holes
were connected by burning. The leader would give the order "burn
one," and then after a pause for compliance, "burn two," etc. Hopefully, there would be a loud report slightly before or after burning
through half the holes, and the ship would be on its way, to the
cheers of the crowd and the profound relief of everyone responsible
for the launching. If all of the holes were burned through and the
ship refused to move, a lot of gray hair and sweat resulted. Hydraulic
jacks, already in place, were a last resort, but after that, if the ship
didn't start, there was real danger. The ship could still start at any
time, but, because of the falling tide, could break its back in the process. Any attempt to secure it with blocking could result in damage to
the ship and loss of life if it suddenly decided to head for its element.
All of these disasters happened at one time or another, but never at
Bethlehem while I was there.

The light cruiser San Diego. *AEM figured out chain drags to stop her two and one-half feet from the middle of Fore River after her launching. Photo: U.S. Navy*

Best of all I liked making the calculations to determine the weight and placement of the chain drags, as they were called. My immediate boss, Harry Andrews, very kindly catered to my preferences and allowed me to do all of the chain drag calculations. We had received a contract for two light cruisers, the *San Diego* and *San Juan.* All of the ways suitable for launching big ships were occupied with airplane carriers or cruisers, and the only two open ones faced a very narrow section of Fore River.

I made an exact diagram of the river, with the *San Diego* right in the middle, and there was only 85 feet from the stern to the further bank and only 85 feet from the bow to the end of the ways. I set about doing some rather complicated calculations. There were a number of factors which had to be taken into account. There were constants such as the weight of the ship and the coefficient of friction of the ways. But the slope of the ways changed with every foot of travel, due to their curvature. As the stern hit the water, it would offer resistance which would tend to slow the ship down. But the resistance would vary according to the speed, which was constantly changing. With each foot of travel, more of the stern would be in the water, to offer more resistance, and the huge propellers, securely locked with welded plates, would have an added effect. As the ship pivoted, due to the stern rising above the ways, the effect of gravity would be decreased.

When I completed these lengthy calculations, they were thoroughly checked by Harry Andrews, Jimmy Hunter, and Professor Keith, but not a single change was made. I had called for 540 tons of old chain, more than had ever before been used, since even much bigger ships had so much more room to stop. The day of the launching, I was tense and excited, as I watched the ship accelerating down the ways, as though it were so anxious to join its element it would never stop.

There was a mighty splash as the stern hit the water, and the cables began snapping the manilla stops with a series of pistol shots. Finally the ship was entirely in the water, traveling at an alarming speed, when the cables began to drag the huge piles of chain down into the water. I breathed a sigh of relief as it stopped. A wire attached to the bow ran to a reel on an instrument called a chronograph which recorded time and distance. The ship had stopped exactly two and one-half feet from the very middle of the river.

Among the many requirements for Navy ships were minesweepers built of wood to thwart magnetic mines. My old friend, George F. Crouch, received a contract to design a class of these ships, one hundred and thirty-six feet long. He asked me to be his second in command for this project. I was faced with a decision which seemed difficult at the time. but with 20-20 hindsight, would be only too easy today, and would certainly be a different one.

I took the bull by the horns, and hastened to the New York office of Arthur B. Homer, Bethlehem's vice president in charge of shipbuilding, as well as the enthusiastic owner-skipper of *Salmagal,* an auxiliary sailboat which he claimed to have designed "with John Alden looking over my shoulder." He was most generous in devoting so much time to the problems of such an insignificant member of the vast organization over which he presided. He made no effort to persuade me, one way or the other, and showed empathy for my love of small boats, which somewhat paralleled his own. He pointed out that each of us has a level of achievement which one tends to reach, regardless of external circumstances. This appeared to be wise advice, but had I been more perspicacious, I might have guessed that I would never reach a very high level at Bethlehem or any other large company. My outspoken contempt for company politics and company politicians would surely militate against advancement in any organization where "playing the game" counted for more than creative ability. But I had yet to figure this all out, and I made the fateful decision to stay with Bethlehem.

Without my assistance, George Crouch proceeded with the design of the minesweepers, gradually supplying all of the blueprints required by the Navy. But not quite all. He received a stern letter which I attempt to reproduce below, taking the liberty of improvising names and details which I never knew, or have long since forgotten:

Department of the Navy   April 1, 1941
Bureau of Ships
Washington D.C.

To: George F. Crouch, Design Contractor
Henry Nevins & Company
City Island, New York
Subject: 136-foot minesweepers, plans and specifications
Petty officers' washroom, location of toilet paper holders.

   You are hereby notified that subject plans have omitted subject location of toilet paper holders. According to Navy Regulations 1776-4Q-Section D, Paragraph 13, contract plans cannot be approved until all requirements have been met.
   Acknowledge and comply at once.

Signed _____
Pomp N. Circumstance
Rear Admiral USN

To this rather impressive and threatening missive, George replied more or less as follows:

George F. Crouch, Design Contractor April 5, 1941
Henry Nevins & Company
City Island, New York

To: Pomp N. Circumstance Rear Admiral USN
Department of the Navy
Bureau of Ships
Washington, D.C.
Subject: 136-foot minesweepers, plans and specifications
Petty officers' washroom, location of toilet paper holders.

> *Your letter of April; 1, 1941, received.*
> *You are hereby advised that the Design Contractor will furnish, in sextuplicate, plans for location of subject toilet paper holders immediately following notification by your office as to whether subject petty officers intend to use the one-finger, two-finger, or three-finger wipe.*
> *Respectfully submitted,*
> *George F. Crouch*

Lest anyone conclude that all past and present naval officers are anathema to me, I hasten to point out that such is not the case, and there are many whom I admire, both as friends and distant figures about whom I have only read. One such was Admiral William Brockett, the youngest man ever to become head of the Bureau of Ships. He resigned when he concluded that the infamous Robert McNamara was wrecking the Navy with his heavy computer and light brain. Bill later became head of Webb Institute, where I met him. He was as different from Admiral Rock as day is from night. He was completely unassuming, but no amount of modesty or consideration for less-gifted subordinates could conceal his brilliant mind. He very kindly researched the naval architecture education programs in Denmark to facilitate procurement of U.S. citizenship for Ib Ladefoged, a talented designer at the John Alden Company and good friend of mine. The present administrator of Webb, Admiral Stabile, retired from the Coast Guard, impressed me in a similar way, though my only contact with him was at the fiftieth reunion of our class at Webb.

After Pearl Harbor the shipbuilding program became more critical. Hitler's submarines became more numerous and more successful, and it appeared that our construction of sophisticated destroyers was taking so much time that we were not keeping up with losses. Consequently, the Navy embarked on a program of building destroyer escorts, or DEs. It was announced in hushed tones that Bethlehem was to build a great number of these ships, to a new and top secret design. The Navy was to send us the basic plans as soon as they were completed, and we were to be responsible for completing the design, building a completely new yard in Hingham, and delivering great numbers of these final answers to the submarine menace as fast as possible.

I awaited the arrival of the secret plans with great anticipation, trying to guess what innovations in design were to take the Germans by surprise. When the plans finally arrived, I was more than disappointed. The hull was the same old round-bottom transom stern design of which the Navy brass seemed so enamored. To my astonishment, the design called for three-inch guns. To fight Nazi submarines with five-inch guns? I went immediately to Jimmy Hunter's office to protest what I considered a drastic mistake. He calmly advised me that our job was to build what the Navy wanted. No one, I least of all, tells the Navy what to do. The ships had bad rolling problems, taking in salt water through the stacks, which could never be corrected, but the guns were eventually changed to five-inch.

One interesting assignment was the inclining experiment on the battleship *Massachusetts*. Anyone who has had any exposure to the water has some idea of stability, exemplified by the familiar admonishment, "Don't stand up in a canoe," and the common knowledge that stability is increased by increasing the beam. A complete understanding of metacentric height, and the ability to calculate it, requires technical training.

There is a story, the veracity of which I cannot guarantee, concerning the procurement of naval vessels by the Japanese, many years ago. They would ask the British to quote on building a ship, submitting complete plans and specifications along with the bid. Then, having this valuable information in hand, they would proceed to build the ship themselves. The British, not to be deceived again, submitted their next bid with plans for a destroyer which deliberately did not comply with the stability characteristics which the unforgiving sea requires. As expected, the Japanese went ahead and built the ship according to the plans, and sent it down the ways, only to see, to their dismay, their new creation capsize and sink.

No such fate awaited the *Massachusetts*, however, for many naval architects had made endless stability calculations before the keel was laid, and every item, from the steam turbines to the smallest instruments, was weighed as it went aboard. The inclining experiment would enable the naval architects to correct their weight estimates and establish the true vertical center of gravity.

The metacenter, though quite complex and difficult to calculate, can be explained so that anyone interested can understand it. If you draw a midship section of any ship or boat, with a vertical line in the middle, you will have a diagram showing all the possible locations for the metacenter. It must be somewhere along that vertical line, unless the two sides of the boat are not the same. If you also draw a horizontal line at a height above the keel equal to the draft, you will have the load waterline. Now draw another waterline through the intersection of the centerline and the load waterline, at a slight angle with the original waterline. This line represents the waterline when the boat is slightly inclined. You will see that at the new waterline, a little wedge of the midship section has come out of the water on one side, while a similar wedge, like a piece of pie, has gone down into the water on the other. Because of this shift in the two wedges of buoyancy, the entire center of buoyancy has shifted slightly. If you knew where this new center of buoyancy was, and drew a line through it perpendicular to the new waterline, this would intersect the original centerline. The point of intersection of the two centerlines is the metacenter.

The calculation of the location of the metacenter is quite complicated, and beyond the scope of this chronicle. The important point to remember is that if you could calculate the position of the metacenter, it would come out as a distance in relation to the center of buoyancy. This means that the lower the center of buoyancy, the lower the metacenter. If you draw a midship section of a round bottom boat, and a flat bottom boat of the same beam and displacement, you will see at a glance that the round bottom boat has a lower center of buoyancy, and therefore a lower metacenter. This explains why a flat bottom boat is more stable than a round bottom boat.

If you cut off a short piece of a round closet pole, or otherwise acquire a wood cylinder, you can put it in the water and see some interesting phenomena. The cylinder will sink into the water to a depth which depends on its density, or weight. Regardless of where it floats, if you tip it slightly, it will have no tendency to return to its original position. If you push the top smartly to one side, it will spin over and over, stopping at random, upside down, or on its side, or wherever the friction of the water stops it. This shows you that the metacenter is at the center of the cylinder, as is also the center of gravity. That is why it has no tendency to return to its original position. If you attach a lead weight to some point on the circumference, it will always return to the point where the weight is on the bottom. It could be said that a cylinder has no form stability and depends entirely on ballasting to lower the center of gravity. A piece of a two-by-four, on the other hand, has a strong tendency to stay upright, even with a small weight on top. I hope the above sheds some light on the vital subject of stability, so that the inclining experiment is better understood. Also, the reader can understand that any small boat, designed by someone completely lacking in technical training, nevertheless has a metacenter and a center of gravity, and if the boat is not a radical departure from previous successful boats of a similar shape, its performance may be quite satisfactory. A naval architect, on the other hand, automatically keeps in mind all of the factors which affect stability, and even though no stability calculations are performed on a given design, the performance of the boat reflects years of training and experience. With the *Massachusetts* no guesswork could be tolerated, even by the best naval architects. Everything had to be calculated, checked, and double-checked.

The day of the inclining experiment on the *Massachusetts*, all of the troops from the Central Technical Department were called out, to be joined by the civilians in the Navy Department, and sufficient naval officers to take command as the situation might require. My duty was to assist in recording the draft aft. This required a detail to put to sea in a rowing skiff, suitably armed with accurate measuring equipment, including a glass tube to nullify the effect of the ripples. The stalwart crew consisted of a worker from the rigging department, who manned the oars, a Navy civilian, a Navy officer, and myself. I never feel comfortable in any kind of a rowing boat unless I am at the oars. In this case, there was nothing I could do about it, for there was a certain protocol that had to be followed. Render unto Caesar etc.

We finally reached the stern of the *Massachusetts*, despite the very un-Shoals-like rowing, completely lacking in feathering. There we manned the instruments to the best of our ability. Considerable arguing ensued over the final thirty-second or sixty-fourth of an inch, but at last agreement was reached after several more readings. Then the commanding officer wrote down the figure in the official report. Unfortunately, he was not too familiar with the details of battleships and assumed that the single digit marked on the stern indicated the actual draft in feet. I had to remind him that a battleship was unlikely to draw less than ten feet. With this correction duly noted, our job was completed. I asked the oarsman to let me off at the handholds welded to the stern and proceeded to climb up toward the deck.

The naval officer called out to me that I couldn't do that , since the draft had already been taken. I suggested, not without a hint of my father's well known sarcasm, that he read the draft again, and see how much difference my modest hundred and forty pounds made in the draft of a 35,000-ton battleship. Following that exchange, I gained the deck and watched with interest as several huge billets of steel were transferred across the deck by overhead cranes, while the very slight angle of heel was recorded by a very sensitive instrument. Figuring backwards from the angle of heel, the weight and distance moved, the calculated metacenter, and the calculated displacement at that draft, the vertical position of the center of gravity was established.

Despite such interesting experiences, the work in the Central Technical Department seemed dull and repetitive. Working away hour after hour at the calculating machines, which were primitive predecessors of computers, or at a drafting table became boring to me, and I longed to do something more challenging and more people-oriented. I surmised that the proposed new shipyard at Hingham would require a resident naval architect, and I believed that I was qualified for the job. I expressed my wishes to Jimmy Hunter, who replied that it was too soon to make such decisions, but he promised to keep me in mind when it was time to select personnel for the new yard, the ground for which was just being broken. I followed progress of the yard with great anticipation and high hopes, while I worked on the comparatively simple launching arrangements for the proposed DEs.

Douglas and Lorna in the kayak at Cohasset. This kayak was a sister-ship of Cynthia. *Photo: Franklin Martin.*

17 • *Hingham*

*a*t last the Bethlehem-Hingham Shipyard was ready to open and start production of vitally needed ships, although construction of buildings and facilities was yet to be completed. I was offered the job of head of the technical section for launching. This would give me a chance to work with the various departments concerned with launching, such as carpenters to build ways and cradles, riggers, outside machinists, shipfitters, and others. I accepted immediately, and looked forward to a chance to deal more with people, and less with a drafting board and slide rule.

But there was one aspect of the new assignment which I could never bring myself to accept. My job as a supervisor of launching, with two or three people working for me, came under the jurisdiction of the Naval Architect of Bethlehem-Hingham Shipyard, named Bill Viden. He was a decent enough older man, and a capable draftsman, with many years of experience. But he was not a naval architect. It was my strong conviction, and still is, that no one can confer the title of naval architect on some one who is not qualified. If someone poses as a doctor or lawyer without proper credentials, he may find himself practicing behind bars, like our friend the self-styled brain surgeon at the Shoals. I worked hard for my degree, and I doubt if there is anything in a course in medicine or law more challenging than in the brutal higher mathematics of naval architecture. In short, I was qualified for the title of naval architect at Hingham; no one else at the new yard was.

Since I had never been one to conceal my beliefs in the name of hypocrisy, sometimes referred to as diplomacy, friction developed almost immediately between Mr. Viden and myself. Nevertheless, I did my job to the best of my ability, finding it quite challenging to explain all of the vital details of launching to people who had no prior knowledge of the subject. At the Quincy yard, hundreds of people, from superintendents on down, had long experience in the yard work connected with launching, and thousands of important details were attended to automatically, with little, if any, help from the Central Technical Department. At Hingham, I had to try to keep one jump ahead of the yard people, figuring out procedures that I had not been involved in at Quincy so that I in turn could explain them to inexperienced yard people.

Although the yard was planned for building DEs, over three hundred feet long, LCIs (landing ship infantry), little more than half as long, suddenly received a higher priority, and they were the first to be launched. They were built two to a launchway , one in front of the other. The first to be launched had only a short distance to go before hitting the water, but the second had a run like a bobsled, and hit the water with a most exciting commotion. These ships were driven by multiple small diesels connected to two shafts. Rather than employing reverse gears, these ships had reversible-pitch propellers, operated by racks inside the shafts. The propellers were rights and lefts.

One of my jobs was to check each ship before it was launched, to make sure that the propellers were securely welded, to prevent spinning when they hit the water. This was particularly important with the upper boats, as the force of the water attempting to rotate the propellers was awesome. The locking devices fitted on one side of the starboard propellers and the other side of the port ones in accordance with the direction of rotation of the propellers. This became a smoothly running routine, but nevertheless, I checked each one carefully. One day I noticed that the propeller locking devices were reversed, which could have been disastrous. But a further check revealed that the propellers were also reversed, so that the locking devices would work as well as ever. I reported to Roger Adair, the engineering superintendent, this state of affairs, suggesting that either specifications had been changed for some reason, and rotation reversal was planned and known to all concerned, except for myself, or one of his departments had made a horrible mistake, and another of his departments discovered it and installed the locking devices correctly, with the idea of letting the first department suffer for their error, while saving their own skin by preventing any propeller spinning. Mr.

Adair was very soft spoken, calm, slow-talking, and oblivious to all the politicking and back-biting that were a way of life in that and all other shipyards with which I have had experience. He assured me that there was no problem, and the ship slid down the ways without a hitch, to be picked up by the tugs *Venus* and *Luna*, as usual.

Later, when outfitting of this particular LCI had been completed, and the Navy acceptance trials were imminent, I was at home in Cohasset, it being Sunday morning. Suddenly the telephone rang. It was Sam Wakeman, General Manager of the Yard. He explained that one of the LCIs had the propellers switched, which I already knew. He said that they did not want to get the Navy all upset by taking the ship to the nearest dry dock to effect the change. They thought they could ballast the bow, and pick up the stern with a railroad crane high enough so that men could work safely underneath. He said that Bill Viden was there, along with many others, and there were all kinds of guesses. He emphasized that he did not want a crane tipping over with men under the ship, and he was not going to allow the unusual procedure on the basis of guesswork. He asked if I could calculate the force necessary to lift the stern, and if so, how long it would take. I replied that I could do it and estimated that it would take a couple of hours. Then, at his request, I rushed over to the yard and went to work with my slide rule. The resulting calculations revealed that it could be done safely, and before the day was over, the mistake had been corrected, and the ship was safely back in normal trim.

Perhaps as a result of this episode, I began to take exception more and more to orders from Mr. Viden. The old aversion to orders by the dumb rearing its ugly head once more. I finally told him off in no uncertain terms, informing him that as a naval architect he was a sorry mess. This ill-considered outburst naturally resulted in his firing me on the spot.

I wound up in General Manager Sam Wakeman's office. He was very calm and quite friendly and even, if I read between the lines correctly, not unsympathetic toward my position. I came to know him much better in later years, racing in the International 210s, as commodore of the Cohasset Yacht Club, and as one of the early owners of an Alden Ocean Shell. His untimely death was a great loss to all of us privileged to know him. On this occasion, he said that I could work anywhere I wanted in the yard, and he would make all the necessary arrangements. I chose the testing department, to give me some practical experience to go with my marine engineering training. Little did I suspect that it was to give me something else, many years later.

Following my unceremonious departure from the naval architecture department, I went to work as a so-called deck leader in the testing department. My boss was George Gammons, a jovial maverick who had been sent to Hingham from Fore River. He had worked there in the testing department as a deck leader, and his promotion to test supervisor at Hingham could be construed as less of a reward and more of a subtle way of removing him from Fore River. He was quite tall, and, although not fat, he had an impressive pot belly. He had a loud voice, an infectious laugh, and a most entertaining and disrespectful sense of humor. He was well known and well liked by all of his contemporaries at Fore River, but he was the bane of existence of the upper management. One of his many exploits in the test department at Fore River concerned the testing of the ice cream making machine on the battleship *Massachusetts*. A test of such equipment called for testing the electric circuits with a megameter to check for grounds or short circuits. Then the electric motors would be run, and the R.P.M. and ampere draw would be duly noted and recorded. To George, this seemed like a somewhat inadequate test of ice cream making equipment. He therefore took it upon himself to order some very expensive ingredients and proceeded to make eighty gallons of ice cream, which he generously shared with his many friends in the yard. This generosity was not appreciated by his boss, Outfitting Superintendent Jim Landis, a parsimonious Scotchman.

Needless to say, I thoroughly enjoyed working for George, but before long he left, for reasons I do not remember, and I eventually became test supervisor. The tests were a critical part of production. A ship could not head out to sea until it had successfully completed dock trials with all propulsion and other machinery running. It could not be scheduled for dock trials until everything had been tested and approved by a Navy inspector. The function of my department was to check progress of construction of every single item, from lifelines to stowages, to pumps and motors, to LCVPs (Higgins Boats), to boilers and turbines, noting work remaining to be done, persuading the vari-

A destroyer escort (D.E.) built by Bethlehem-Hingham Shipyard. Testing machinery in the fire rooms and engine rooms of these ships resulted in exposure to asbestos used for pipe covering. One of these ships was launched four and one-half days after keel-laying, and steamed out of the harbor in twenty-five. Photo: U.S.Navy.

ous trades to complete or correct their work, scheduling a preliminary test, and finally calling a Navy inspector to attend the official test. If the test did not merit the signatures of the Navy inspectors concerned, i.e. electrical, mechanical, hull, the faulty items had to be corrected and the test repeated.

Joe Townsend was the general superintendent. He was a big, rugged man whose hobby was boxing. He had a very direct, no-nonsense manner, and he was most intolerant of any delay in production. He started as hull superintendent, and soon proved that he could launch ships faster than the engineering and outfitting departments could complete them. He launched a DE four and one-half days after laying the keel. He was promoted to general superintendent with the idea of applying his drive to the entire operation. The ships were desperately needed.

The people who worked at Hingham were a varied lot. The experienced shipbuilders had long since been hired by the old, established yards. Management had to turn to anyone and everyone they could get. There were service station attendants, baseball players, circus freaks, and lawyers dodging the draft while at the same time trying to drum up business among other employees. There were purveyors of liquor, and bookies. The riggers had a rowing skiff for various waterfront duties, and this proved valuable in getting in and out of the yard without encountering the guards at the gates, and a staunch rowing skiff could carry plenty of booze with ease. Bookies could get the latest race results at outside telephones. These were the days of Rosie the Riveter, and the fair sex was well represented at Hingham. Welding took the place of riveting, and not all of the ladies practiced such trades exclusively. The DEs had two propellers, two engine rooms, and two fire rooms, in tandem, so that the ship could sustain considerable damage without losing all power. The port main electric motor, being close to its propeller, was right in the bottom. The starboard shaft, at the same angle, attained considerable elevation by the time it reached its drive motor in the forward engine room. One enterprising lady set up a mattress under this motor and worked at a profession considerably older than shipbuilding.

Supervision likewise left something to be desired. Some were good at their trade but given more authority than they were ready for. Others were short on knowledge of the business but good at promoting themselves with upper management. Any shipyard is so vast and complicated that it is hard to pin down responsibility. The world is full of people who seek authority without responsibility, and a shipyard ranks close to the government as a haven for these types. They play politics to the hilt, constantly jockeying for status and position, ruthlessly employing any methods, fair or foul, to eliminate anyone who threatens their power. Such a one was a huge man named Batchelder, who was foreman of the outside machinists. It was his department that brought about the propeller drama with the LCI.

Roger Adair, the engineering superintendent, called me into his office one day and, in his quiet way, explained a problem of major proportions. The starboard motor of the DEs, already high by design (not in anticipation of the commercial possibilities below it), had to be raised several more inches above the foundation in order to line up with the shaft. Roger asked me to check through the whole procedure, from establishing the shaft line with a transit, to boring the stern tube, to lining up the shaft and the motor. This I proceeded to do, step by step. Before long Mr. Batchelder got wind of what I was up to, and threatened to throw me overboard. The extreme difference in size and weight made me somewhat apprehensive, but I continued and found that they were not taking into account the fact that the shaft sags of its own weight between bearings, making each pair of flanges open a few thousandths at the top when the true shaft line is followed. Without allowing for this opening, the angle of each section of shaft was increased, resulting in the necessity of raising the motor. I found a sag diagram among some neglected plans, explained its use to the men, and the problem ended, without my having an unscheduled swim in the frigid waters of Hingham.

The problems with Mr. Batchelder continued, however. It appeared that no one had the courage to reprimand him. Until the day that Joe Townsend officially became general superintendent. His first act in his new job was to walk into Mr. Batchelder's office, hand him a termination slip, and tell him to get out of the yard immediately. The big bully took one look at Joe Townsend's muscular form poised in front of him and meekly left.

Joe very quickly grasped the fact that the tests were the key to production and initiated frequent test meetings. All of the outfitting and engineering foremen were required to attend—or else. Joe would have a master list of all the tests, and after giving the hull number of the next ship in line, he would read out the name of the test, such as anchor windlass, auxiliary turbo-generators, etc. I would reply "passed by the Navy," "failed because of a piping leak," or "not ready for test." He would then turn to the foreman of the department involved and extract a promise as to when the necessary work would be completed. There were many tense moments as various people tried to pass the buck, while Joe pinned them down in no uncertain terms. One test which never seemed to be completed, ship after ship, was the searchlight on the LSTs (Landing Ship, Tanks, just over three hundred feet long). Joe would read out "searchlight," and I would answer "not tested." He would practically snarl, "Why not?" "Not cut in," I would reply. The electrical foreman would sometimes give an excuse or say the wires had been connected, but the fact remained that the test of the very uncomplicated searchlight caused more delay than the main propulsion units or the bow doors on the LSTs. Finally one day the searchlight performance was repeated once too often for Joe Townsend. He ordered the entire meeting to repair to the bridge of the ship and see for themselves who was telling the truth. I had anticipated just such an occurrence and had gone down to the ship just before the meeting to make sure that the wiring was not complete. Nevertheless, I had butterflies in my stomach as we walked down to the pier. Could someone have cut in the searchlight during the meeting? Fortunately for me, nothing had changed, for I was most anxious not to fail Joe Townsend. The foreman learned his lesson, and the searchlights gave no further trouble.

I spent a great deal of time in the engine rooms and fire rooms of the DEs during my days as test supervisor. Pipe coverers would be slopping soggy masses of asbestos on the pipes overhead while we were running tests. Much of this would fall to the platform below, to be swept up when dry by the cleaning crew. None of us suspected the lethal properties of asbestos at the time.

The Navy decided to have a sea trial of the first Hingham DE. There were already other classes of DEs, diesel, and geared turbine, but the Hingham ones were the first of their class of turbo-electric ships. The regular Navy crew, young and inexperienced, were required to run the ship and fire the guns, while there was a mad scramble among the shipyard personnel to be included in what promised to be a very exciting cruise. Some were necessary to assist the Navy in running the unfamiliar equipment, while others were required to make any repairs which might prove necessary. I was included because of my job, but various company politicians were able to go along for the ride. As we left the pier, to the tune of loud cheering and shouting, it became obvious that the occasion was not being celebrated without the added stimulus of alcohol.

We had two blimps for escort. There was the remote possibility that the Nazis, having submarines just off the coast, might pick the occasion to score a great moral victory by sinking the first of the very ships highly touted to be the great secret weapon against them. After some speed runs off Provincetown, we began the live ammunition tests by dropping some depth charges, set to go off at a minimum depth. There was a mighty geyser of water and a deafening sound, like two automobiles hitting each other. I was sure the entire stern would fall off, knowing the quality of some of the welding. To my amazement, it didn't. Next came the twenty millimeters, which make quite a staccato noise, followed by the much louder forty millimeters. At this point, I went below, to enjoy the sumptuous lunch someone had had the foresight to provide. I was sitting next to a young enlisted man, who was obviously somewhat nervous about the whole performance. He was a little timid about the guns and after venturing an opinion that at last the shooting was over, raised a forkfull of steak to his mouth. Just then the three-inch gun went off, and he jammed the fork up through the roof of his mouth.

Meanwhile great excitement and controversy erupted all over the ship. One of the blimps had picked up an echo of a vessel below the surface. The people from the yard were raring to go after the German submarine, while the Navy people were reluctant to engage in combat with all those civilians aboard. The matter was solved when it was learned that the returned ping came from a ship, so recently sunk that its whereabouts had not yet been released.

As D-day approached, we were all in ignorance about when the action would take place. Secretary Forrestal came to Hingham in the spring, and said that while he couldn't give out any reasons, the Navy desperately needed all the LSTs it could possibly get from Hingham in the next few months. He said that nothing should stand in the way of production. Costs, protocol, union job classifications, and red tape were all to go out the window. The only thing that mattered was how many LSTs left the harbor under their own power, manned by their inexperienced young crews.

There were endless problems with the three-cylinder General Motors diesel generator sets. We ran the same two-hour tests at a 25% overload that all of the earlier Superior diesel sets, though rated for less horsepower, had passed successfully. After much arguing in the upper echelons of management and Navy, and tests of fuel, exhaust system, and installation demanded by General Motors, the test require-

A Landing Ship, Tanks (L.S.T.) as built at Hingham. As D-day approached, all-out efforts were made to increase production of these ships. Bethlehem-Hingham led all other yards for speedy production and quality. Photo: U.S. Navy.

ments were lowered, first to 15% overload, then 10%, and finally no overload. General Motors was well represented in Washington.

The bow doors and ramps were a most ingenious design. Open, they presented a huge aperture instead of a bow, with a ramp on which tanks could rumble swiftly down to a beach under their own power. Closed, the doors formed a bluff but adequate bow, with the strength to withstand wave action, but they were by no means watertight. The ramp, raised and pulled up tight against a rubber gasket, kept the tank deck dry. I was fascinated by the sensation of climbing down between the doors and the ramp while the ungainly ship was ploughing through some moderate seas on the way to Boston. The water was sloshing around in the bottom of the compartment, while gallons and gallons more poured in with the thunder of each wave, only to drain out through many openings when it reached the crest. The stresses in a real storm were hard for me to imagine, but I always thought of them as we strove to get yet another pair of bow doors completed properly and tested.

Because of the complete abandonment of the usual regulations, I did not hesitate to work on bow doors myself. I recall one afternoon going down to a ship which obviously was not ready for dock trials the following day. The bow doors were the bottleneck, and much work remained to be done. I borrowed tools from the machinist on the job, the pipefitter and welder cooperated fully, and I went to work. Before I knew it, the machinist asked for his tools. It was the end of the day shift. In a few minutes the machinist on the second shift showed up, and I borrowed his tools. Things began to shape up as the hours went by, but all too soon the machinist was asking for his tools. When the third shift machinist appeared, the performance was repeated, but at break of dawn the doors were working perfectly, and I was able to locate a very knowledgeable and cooperative Navy inspector named McSwiggin to sign off the official test. When Joe Townsend arrived, I went into his office. He seemed dejected, for he hated to postpone a dock trial, and yet, based on his best information, that is what he would have to do. When I told him the tests were complete, he seemed incredulous, and he fired back "Not the bow doors." When I showed him the card with the official Navy sign-off signature, he burst into a broad grin which turned into a loud laugh of pleasure. Joe was a great man to work for, and he inspired others, including me, to do their best.

Hingham delivered LSTs faster and of better quality than any of the other shipyards, most of which had more experienced help and supervision. Despite our lack of skilled personnel, the many unproductive things that went on in the yard, and the many bureaucrats and company politicians who took refuge there, the yard had something going for it besides Joe Townsend's inspiring leadership. I think that without doubt, it was the Bethlehem bonus system.

A time study was made of every job, on the basis of which time would be assigned to a contract for the job. If the worker completed the job in those hours, or took longer, he received only his regular hourly pay. But if he could think of a way to do it faster, Bethlehem would pay for whatever tooling or equipment it required, and the cost savings of the reduced man-hours would be divided between the worker and the company. The old-time shipbuilders knew all the things you could not do in building a ship. The ingenious young garage mechanics at Hingham did not. They went ahead and designed jigs and fixtures that saved untold hours and put extra money in their pockets and Bethlehem's as well. Some managements look upon labor as numbered bodies, to be paid as little as possible, whose brains are expected to be turned off as they enter the gate. Many labor leaders, for their part, look upon the company as a source of unlimited ill-gotten wealth, to be bullied into giving it away or wasting it on foolish work restrictions which do no one any good. Fortunately, foreign competition has forced labor and management to cooperate for their own survival. But a great deal more can be done. For my own part, I have always profited by the knowledge that the man on the job often knows more about it than I do, despite my diploma, and I am never too proud to change a plan to conform to a suggestion from a craftsman who has thought out an unquestioned improvement.

The older naval officers at Hingham were, for the most part, pretty fine men, having the practical common sense acquired in business as civilians. One of these was Lieutenant Commander Smith, who had graduated from Webb years before my time. He could grasp a problem and help to find a solution, rather than treating all non-Navy people with suspicion and contempt. A pompous young lieutenant named Pratt was just the opposite. He never hesitated to hold up the delivery of a desperately needed ship to correct an insignificant detail, such as a sloppy paint job in an almost inaccessible corner, while failing to notice that the boat davits were unworkable. The day after the yachting trip of the first DE, which we all enjoyed so much, he was wearing a ribbon for the Atlantic Theater of Operations.

Commander Smith arranged for me to accompany him on the trial trip of a frigate built in Rhode Island. This was most interesting to me for two reasons. The hull was a British design, having a much more subtle shape than our DEs, and therefore more sea kindly. It was propelled by reciprocating steam engines, said to turn at the highest revolutions ever for such an installation. They were lubricated by hand, which took a lot of agility, for the huge piston rods, crank rods, and crankshafts were flying around so fast that it was hard to see them, let alone to squirt in oil without being clobbered. The engine room was blue with smoke and permeated by the aroma of steam and lubricating oil. At cruising speed it was impossible to set a coffee cup down on the bridge, the whole ship vibrated so violently. Nevertheless, these ships performed their duty admirably, and steam engines, like sails, are easy to understand and repair. I had a great trip, and retain a nostalgia for the quiet, graceful days of steam, which I first learned to appreciate on the *Sightseer* at the Shoals.

During the war there was a strong feeling among most people that they should be actively involved. Because of my training and position, I was deferred in the draft. I was not particularly enthusiastic about being shot at or bombed by the Germans or Japanese, but Navy ships, like all floating vessels, had a great appeal to me. On the other hand, if I volunteered for the Navy, I might be put right back into the shipbuilding program, just where I was already, but with a difference. Because of my age, I would be a mere ensign, and likely an errand boy for lieutenants, whereas at Hingham I was dealing with Navy people at the lieutenant commander level. I decided to apply anyway, but only for sea duty. Lieutenant Commander Smith wrote a very flattering letter of recommendation, repeating my thoughts about sea duty. In due course, the Navy replied, stating that under no circumstances would they waste a naval architect on sea duty. Toward the end of the war, I had the satisfaction of learning that their policy had belatedly changed.

When a big ship was damaged by bombs or torpedoes, the crew was remarkably adept at extinguishing the fire, ballasting the ship to put it on an even keel, and getting it running again. But no one was able to appraise just how much the damage had done to the structural integrity of the ship. Suspended between two waves, a ship is like a huge beam structure, which would break in half if not properly designed. After surviving severe battle damage, that is exactly what happened to several good ships when they encountered waves far from the scene of enemy action. The Navy began putting naval architects, as soon as they graduated, on capital ships. Had they thought of this strategy sooner, I might not have been exposed to so much asbestos, but on the other hand, I might have been at the bottom of the Pacific Ocean for the past forty-five years. Despite our best efforts to control our destinies, much remains in the hands of fate.

With the Japanese surrender, the need for Bethlehem-Hingham Shipyard and its impressive production of ships evaporated overnight. Many applied for transfers to other Bethlehem yards, and I added my name to the list. A written summary of my qualifications would have made impressive reading. I had a most respected degree in both naval architecture and marine engineering. I had had considerable practical experience in all three major divisions of shipbuilding: hull, engineering, and outfitting. I had had very successful experience with all the trades, the people who actually do the work. As I looked around, I could see no one who could match such diversified qualifications. On the other hand, I was outspoken, opinionated, independent, and contemptuous of the goal of most politicians and bureaucrats: authority without responsibility. It was not unreasonable to assume that such an ornery cuss from the Isles of Shoals would be likely to rock the boat in one way or another. It was not surprising that management could find no use for my talents other than in the Central Technical Department, to which I had vowed never to return. So my days with Bethlehem ended, for better or worse, and I found myself unemployed,but it was not to be for long.

18 • *Ray Hunt*

$\mathcal{W}$hen we first moved to Cohasset, one of our nearest neighbors was Ray Hunt. His sons, James Henry and Josh, who were very young children at the time, frequently visited our house. Ray was involved with boats almost to the point of obsession and had little time for the usual social activities. I had heard about his accomplishments but had scarcely more than a nodding acquaintance with him. Until the Japanese surrender, most of my time had been spent at Bethlehem.

It was quite a coincidence that a mutual friend, Bob Catlin, was working with Ray on a little pram with a propeller, powered by pedaling like a bicycle. As I was later to confirm so often, Ray was far ahead of his times. Bob Catlin, knowing my background, wanted me to see the novel craft, and thus it was that both Ray and I were invited to a cocktail party at the Catlins. That was the first time I ever had a chance to talk to him at length. He had a perpetual deep tan, from endless hours on the water most of the year and skiing in the winter. He had a ready wit and a hearty laugh, which was quite contagious. The most outstanding quality I noticed, however, was his tremendous enthusiasm as soon as he began to talk about boats. It was immediately obvious that his mind was fully occupied with the subject, and while he certainly had other interests, one would have to be completely oblivious to boats to come away from a conversation with Ray without absorbing some of his irrepressible enthusiasm for anything that floated. I soon began to discuss the pedal boat with Ray, and that led to his spirited description of the other boats on which he was working. When I replied to his question about the upcoming closing down of the Bethlehem-Hingham Yard, he suddenly asked if I would like to work for him, starting the following Monday. Thus began an association which I will always treasure, and regard as a rare opportunity to

Ray Hunt, probably the most innovative designer of the century. Photo: The Rosenfeld Collection. All rights reserved, the Rosenfield Collection, Mystic Seaport Museum, Inc.

work with the man whom I, along with many others in and out of the industry, consider the most innovative designer of his day.

Ray had grown up in boats, not little rowing boats such as I enjoyed so much but all kinds of sailboats. Starting with the Duxbury Ducks, he had sailed and raced in Star Boats, Q-boats, and many others, almost always coming in first or at the top of the fleet. He sailed in the afterguard of the J-boat *Yankee*, with the great Charles Francis Adams, even taking the helm occasionally. A race between Harold Vanderbilt, Dennis Conner, and Ray Hunt, in equal J-boats would be an interesting contest, if we could recall those who are no longer with us. I would bet my money on Ray Hunt.

Ray's extraordinary success in racing sailboats would have been impossible had he not had a very thorough knowledge of how a boat went through the water, what design factors reduced its resistance, most effective sail shapes, optimum spacing of center of effort and center of lateral resistance, and the many other factors which influence performance and play such a big part in determining the winner. Although Ray never received a formal education in naval architecture, he effectively filled the gap with his constant and never-ending observations of nautical phenomena, references to Skene's Elements of Yacht Design, and picking up valuable information from naval architects with whom he associated. A formal technical education would doubtless have been a great advantage, but even without it, he could never be considered in the same class as the many people who aspire to design boats without any of the necessary qualifications, and his many works of design placed him far ahead of most highly trained practitioners of the art.

His first effort was a small keel double-ender. He and his boyhood friend, Dick Fisher, later of Boston Whaler fame, put together the prototype in the latter's barn in Duxbury. The final design became the International 110, built in substantial numbers by George Lawley and Sons, in Neponset, Massachusetts, and later by The Hagerty Company in Cohasset, and others. The 110, with its plumb stem and stern, and arc bottom, does not appeal to everyone aesthetically, but to many enthusiastic owners, sitting down on the floorboards in the bottom, tiller over one shoulder, watching the water rush by, only inches away, it has no equal. It is challenging to race, in that the

Invader II, *Doug's International 110. Many famous racing sailors gained experience in these exciting boats. The Martin offspring had two of them. Photo: Marjorie Martin.*

fin keel does not have enough lateral plane to keep it from sideslipping unless it has enough forward speed to develop lift, like an airplane wing. Graduates of 110s have made notable records racing all kinds of larger boats. My children were to become the proud owners of two of them, which were passed down from the older ones to the younger ones as they became eligible to race them. I served as crew many times, and in one 110 race in Cohasset, our family could not have lost, as one of us was in every single boat in the race.

In addition to the 110s, Ray had designed many other successful boats before I came to work for him. A larger version of the 110 concept was the 225, of which five were built by Lawley. Ray believed that people ready, willing, and able to pay for such a relatively more expensive boat would not by happy with the plumb stem and stern. After experimenting with prototypes, made at considerable expense by Cape Cod Shipbuilding Company, Hagerty Company, and Graves of Marblehead, the design of the International 210 was about to be finalized when I arrived on the scene. He had found that the plywood construction, as used in the 110s, need not preclude a graceful curve in the stem and stern. The 210 was to have a beautiful profile, despite the plywood construction which L.Francis Herreshoff, and many lesser authorities, looked upon with such scorn. Once he solved the appearance problem, he could have gone into production on one of the later prototypes. But Ray could always think of ways to improve any design, and he was reluctant to start production if he thought better performance could be achieved.

Ray had worked with Waldo Howland in the Concordia Company for several years, best described in Waldo's book, *A Life In Boats, Parts 1 and 2,* and also Elizabeth Meyer's beautiful book on the Concordias yawls. He had drawn the lines of these now-famous yachts, of which three had been built before the war. There had also been a very successful schooner. But Ray Hunt's active mind could never be confined to sailboats alone. He never observed any kind of a floating vessel without trying to think of a way to improve its performance.

Lobster boats, such as Mr. Brewster's, evolved, mostly by trial and error, to be sea kindly and efficient at the displacement speeds their small engines could power. With more powerful automobile engines readily available, the torpedo stern of the early Frost boats gave way to a wider transom stern. The resulting boats became semi-planing, but the bow wave rose up to the deck, adding the drag of unnecessary wetted surface, and making them very wet in a blow. After giving this matter much thought, Ray came up with a semi-planing design which was superior in many ways. The bow had a round bottom at the keel, but then it flared out to a hard chine, sometimes described as a bell bottom, the bell being upside down. Unlike a typical V-bottom of that time, with a very low chine, submerged almost to the stem, Ray's design had a chine which intersected the waterline almost amidships. This design gave good lift at moderate speeds, a well cushioned but dry action in head seas, and stability much improved over that of the round bottom design. To test out his theory, Ray had a lobster boat built according to his plans, and used it himself for lobstering in the worst weather in the winter. Outside of the fact that Josh fell overboard in Cohasset Harbor and went straight to the bottom, where Ray had the presence of mind to dive after him, the boat was very successful. It demonstrated dramatically that a boat could be driven safely, economically, and swiftly far offshore in the worst conditions, adding considerably to the potential for catching lobsters. Two of the native lobstermen, although known for a belligerent attitude toward any additional competition, became friendly with Ray Hunt, and each bought boats of his design.

The old round-bottom design of destroyers did not escape the notice of the young designer. Although their speed-length ratios were in the range of semi-planing, their lines ignored everything except wetted surface, the important part of resistance at lower speeds. Ray tried to sell his idea, which had worked so well in lobster boats, to the Navy, but despite his great talent as a salesman, he got nowhere. However, his racing prowess had earned him the friendship and admiration of former Secretary of the Navy Charles Francis Adams. Mr. Adams arranged for a 20-foot model of Ray's destroyer design to be tested at the David W. Taylor Towing tank at Annapolis. The people at the model basin were ecstatic over the results. They said the tests indicated that they could add ten feet to the beam without sacrificing speed, giving space for the additional firepower that the war had proved necessary. The added dynamic stability would add to the safety and comfort of the crew, as well as giving a more stable platform for firing the guns. But that was not the way of the Navy, and the promising new design was cast aside in the interest of tradition.

Undaunted by his lack of success with the Navy, Ray went ahead with plans to incorporate his revolutionary new design concept in pleasure boats, and the first stock boat, a twenty-eight-footer, was already in the works when I joined his firm. A thirty-seven and a half-footer and a twenty-one footer were soon to follow. Figuring out speeds and propeller sizes for these power boats, with various engines, was right up my alley, and, thanks to George Crouch's formulas and data which I constantly collected, we could predict performance pretty accurately. I also drew up plans for these boats with various arrangements to suit the owners. Ray's primary interest was in hull shape and performance, and he was impatient with the details of the interior. Unfortunately, I was somewhat similarly inclined, so that in retrospect I think I was a poor choice for this kind of work.

The thirty-seven and one-half-footers occupied a lot of my drawing time. The high chine of all these boats made a graceful sweep up toward the bow but then reversed before reaching the stem. Ray liked to have the shear parallel this line, thereby reversing the shear at the bow. This gave better visibility when the bow lifted at speed. But I have never liked reverse shear, following the old traditions whereby the top of the stem always had the greatest freeboard. When green water comes over the stem, a boat can no longer be considered seaworthy, even though watertight decks and superstructure may enable it to survive. From the Viking ships to Maine peapods and dories, and almost all of the really seaworthy boats in between, the shear determines how steep and high a wave a boat can encounter without burying its bow. Obviously, other factors such as flair also play an important part. But the unseaworthiness of many racing sailboats designed to the International Offshore Rule is well documented. One feature of these boats is a perfectly straight shear, with the stern giving the appearance of being higher than the bow. One such boat, depicted in a series of photographs in *Yachting*, is shown burying its bow right up to the mast, thereby gybing and throwing some of the crew overboard. As for motor yachts, burying the bow in rough water is a common, though frightening occurrence for some of the few who venture too far from the marina. For rowing boats, foam and watertight decks may save the boat, even though hypothermia or exhaustion claims the occupant.

The seaworthiness of all the Huntform boats, as they were called, was remarkably good and more than well tested and proved. Still, I did not like the reverse shear, and Ray did, good-naturedly, accuse me of taking out some of the reverse shear in the 37s. Whether or not there was any truth to the suggestion, I always preferred the 37s to the 28s. I saw one recently, and years of neglect could not obscure the lean, graceful look, so lacking in the popular power boats of today. I recall one customer who wanted to have one built with a sedan cabin, all the comforts of home, and tremendous headroom everywhere. I was anything but enthusiastic about putting it down on paper, but following the old axiom of the customer always being right, we went ahead, even though it almost made me sick to see how our beautiful boat had been ruined by my pencil. Whenever it appeared, we looked the other way, hoping that no one would take it for one of ours. The same mistake is repeated over and over. Someone observes a Maine lobster boat performing beautifully in rough water and decides to opt for a similar boat to be used for pleasure, rather than a great big box, slightly pointed at one end, containing two huge fuel-guzzling engines and all the shoreside accommodations and amenities of a house, regarded by current wisdom as a motor yacht. But he insists on dragging in the same creature comforts that make the other choice so lacking in the grace and sea-kindliness he seeks. The result is that the poor lobster boat is submerged far below its designed waterline, and its performance is all but totally destroyed.

One of the most interesting projects I worked on was the International 510. This was similar to a 210, but 45 feet long instead of just under 30. It had a proportionately narrower beam, and greater freeboard. The keel, which I drew up, was similar to that of a 210, but it was fabricated instead of cast out of iron. It had a steel fin, with a streamlined lead bulb at the bottom.

The mast, borrowed from an inactive 6-meter, was altered according to plans which I drew. Ray was bubbling over with enthusiasm for this new creation and couldn't wait to try it out, even though 1945 was rapidly drawing to a frigid close. Selman Graves, who was building it in his yard in Marblehead, was pestered, on a daily basis, to hurry up construction. Finally, on Christmas Eve, launching took place, in a typical winter northwester. Naturally, Ray had to take it right out and sail it, though the wind velocity was not what most people would select for the first trial of a new design. Rod Stephens, never one to pass up a challenging trip on the water, was also aboard, while I watched from the warmth and safety of one of the buildings.
The performance seemed sensational to me, and Ray was obviously pleased, demonstrating even more than his usual enthusiasm.

Later Linc Davis, one of the most famous and winningest racing skippers in Marblehead, took it out and asked me to act as crew. For all my technical training and small boat experience at the Shoals, I had never sailed in a boat with a genoa jib and winches. I was mortified when Linc pointed out, in no uncertain terms, that I had

Gregg Bemis in Alar, *leads a fleet of International 210s in National Championships. AEM did some of the detail drawings, and raced one of these classic boats for many years. Photo: The Rosenfield Collection.*

put the jib sheet around the winch the wrong way. It was somewhat incongruous for me, without any racing experience, to be drawing up plans of deck fitting locations on the 210s, sail plans, and designs of other equipment with which I had had virtually no experience. Ray persuaded me, against little opposition, to buy a 210, so that I would be more familiar with what was going on. Once ordered, the acquisition of my own 210 became a matter of the greatest urgency. Unfortunately, demand far exceeded the supply that first year, and I watched with envy as 210 after 210 sailed out of Marblehead Harbor, a happy new owner at the helm. My boat had a low priority.

We exhibited a 210 at the New England Sportsman's Show in Boston in February 1946. Ray had all the qualities of a great salesman, not the least of which was the enthusiasm which was obviously so genuine. Additionally, his fame in racing circles put him on a first name basis with most of the best sailors in New England and all over the country. It was therefore not surprising that we were able to post a chart at the show, giving an impressive list of owners of these revolutionary new boats that hardly anyone had ever sailed. The list was headed by Charles Francis Adams and included Linc Davis, Gregg Bemis, Phil Benson, Sam Wakeman, and many others. I was completely unknown to most of these prominent yachtsmen, and I still had had no personal experience with the boats we were trying to sell. My efforts at the show seemed all in vain, much as I wanted to be able to sell a 210.

But one night Ray went out to dinner, leaving me in charge of the booth. Before long, a friend of mine, Bob Meyer, from Plymouth, wandered in with his father. The latter was a big power on Wall Street, and he never made any effort to conceal the fact. He was used to having people jump when he spoke, and I was somewhat intimidated by the questions he asked about the boats. He asked if we could make a 210 with a shallower draft for sailing in Duxbury Bay. I quickly guessed that we could design a shallower keel, with a heavier bulb, and a centerboard inside it. Suddenly he commanded me to come down to his office the following day, and he would give me a check and an order for two. I could hardly wait to tell Ray the good news of my first sale. It would have been quite a story, had it then ended happily. It didn't.

As the season approached, customers wanted their boats. Unfortunately, there was a severe bottleneck in rigging. Not only was there a shortage of stainless steel wire, but the Graves credit rating left something to be desired. I would sometimes go to Merriman Brothers, the supplier, with a personal check from Ray Hunt, which I was instructed to hand over to the vice president in exchange for one or two sets of rigging. Ray never liked details, and whenever a decision on some matter outside of design came up, he would brush it off with "That's a detail." As a result, the records of 210 orders became somewhat sketchy, resulting in confusion over color, extra equipment, payments, etc. Consequently, I took it upon myself to make up a sheet for each order, giving the date of the order, and complete information about everything on the order. I tried to arrange the ever more critical delivery on the basis of the chronological sequence of the actual purchases. But Ray would have none of that. As well known skippers, such as George O'Day, ordered boats just before the season, he would put them ahead of less famous would-be owners who had been waiting patiently. There is no doubt that this strategy resulted in the impressive numbers of prominent racing people who brought fame to the new class in its first season. But it did not ingratiate the ones waiting on the shore. Particularly Mr. Meyer. I accepted the fact that as a member of the firm, I would have to wait until the season was almost over to have my first sail in my new boat. Mr. Meyer had no such restrictions, and he was not one to accept no for an answer. He called up frequently about his boats, always asking to speak to me because I was the one who sold them to him. I used successively every excuse I could think of: it took time to design and build the keel centerboard (although this was not the bottleneck), rigging was hard to procure, the yard was very busy at the beginning of the season, etc. With each call, Mr. Meyer became more irritated, and I became more intimidated, dreading each ring of the telephone. He threatened to put the matter in the hands of his lawyer and, as a final showdown, announced that he was coming to Marblehead the following Saturday. Whether by happenstance or design, I was not to be in Marblehead that day. I told Ray that since he had gotten us into what promised to be a most unpleasant confrontation, he alone would have to face the music. The following Monday, I asked him, not without a touch of malice, how he had made out with Mr. Meyer. "Fine," he replied, with his usual smile, "he bought a special twin-screw 37-foot power boat." This incredible piece of salesmanship solved the problem for the time being, but we were to let Mr. Meyer down once more.

The first of the special 210s was launched shortly thereafter, and I took my three-year-old son, Douglas, to Marblehead to give it its first sea trial. As we left the dock, we ghosted along in one of those light and variable winds for which Marblehead is famous. When we got out-side, however, it turned into a hard southwester. I was somewhat apprehensive about just what the boat would do, I still had had little experience with a 210, and I was well aware that the heavier keel might be too much for the foam flotation in the event of a knock-down. Douglas, however, his inability to swim notwithstanding, was laughing and having the time of his life, reveling in the excitement of suddenly heeling over. The boats were successful, and faster on some points of sailing than the standard 210s.

Work on the power boat proceeded rapidly at Graves' other yard. Built of mahogany, finished bright, it looked every bit the part of the gold-plater she was. The day of the launching, I was riding up to Mar-blehead with Ray when he calmly announced that he would be meet-ing Mr. Meyer and Mr. George Nichols, the son-in-law of J.P.Morgan, and a prominent owner of all kinds of yachts, including a 12-meter, and therefore I was to bring the new power boat down through Mar-blehead Harbor to the float where the anxious owner, Mr. Nichols, and Ray would be waiting. Me? I had taken the wheel of my father's Elco in the open ocean more than once, but other than that, my expe-rience had been limited to sail, oar, and paddle, where I felt at home. My stomach filled with butterflies at the prospect of suddenly being responsible for the first voyage of such a costly vessel.

I climbed aboard the sleeping monster on the launchways, my hands shaking with fright. I started up the two Chrysler Royal engines and gave Sam, the manager of the yard, the signal to let her go imme-diately, for the engines could not be deprived of cooling water for long. With rocks and boats on all sides, there was no chance to check anything out, and I gingerly threaded my way through the crowded harbor toward the dock. As I approached the float, with its distin-guished audience waiting expectantly, I throttled both engines down to idle, with the thought that if it crashed into the float, at least it would be a gentle contact.

Graves had had a contract to build a number of Sea Sleds for the Navy during the war. These had steering wheels which incorporated throttles for two engines, each throttle sliding on a sleeve on the steer-ing wheel shaft. When the war ended, Graves was left with a surplus of these wheels, which were stored in an open shed for the next 20 years.

Never one to pass up an opportunity to save some money, Selman Graves decided to use one of these old steering wheel assemblies in Mr. Meyer's gold-plater.

As I carefully approached the float, I turned the wheel to starboard. All of a sudden the port engine raced ahead, straight for the assembled company. Mr. Meyer's face turned ashen, and Ray looked daggers at me. I quickly throttled back the port engine, and succeeded in backing off for another try. This time, the starboard engine flared up, and we almost hit the float again. I finally figured out that the old throttles were sticking to the steering column, suddenly speeding up with each turn of the wheel, and somehow got the boat to the float without further motion of the steering wheel. I breathed a sigh of relief to be on terra firma again with no further responsibilities, and we all went out to lunch. Mr. Graves assured us that he would take care of the steering wheel problem while we were having lunch so that the boat would be ready for Mr. Meyer and his sons to take it to Plymouth in the afternoon. But after lunch, Mr. Meyer allowed as how I knew more about the boat than they did, and would I run it to Plymouth with them? I felt like saying "That's what you think," but decided against it, and, finding no ready excuse, acquiesced, praying that Graves really would have the steering wheel fixed. But as I took the wheel, with only a little more confidence, the same thing happened. It was too late to make any more repairs and still get to Plymouth at a reasonable hour, so we continued on, with hope on my part that I would be able to make a landing at the destination without smashing into anything.

Many of the calculations I did were beyond the scope of Ray Hunt's knowledge. But all too often, when I proudly presented the results of some complex figuring, Ray would say, "I'm sure you know what you are doing, but that answer doesn't look right." I would go back over my figures to make sure, only to find an obvious mistake. He had an uncanny way of making a hasty estimate in his head and coming up with an approximate answer. I found this to be a great asset in many later situations. Much as I defend the engineering approach, there is nothing like a little common sense thrown in with it. The classic example is the laborious calculations some engineers made to prove that a bumble bee cannot fly. The bee, however, being unable to comprehend these figures, goes ahead and flies.

I enjoyed arguing with Ray about theories of boat design. He never took it personally and only seemed to be searching for further truths about the motion of boats through the water. I found myself eating humble pie many times, as a theory of Ray's proved to be correct. There was one occasion where I was correct, and it stands out because of its rarity.

The 510 was a truly sensational boat. With its long, beautiful lines, and its nicely rounded trunk cabin of bright mahogany, it was a sight to behold. Because of its proportions, its arc bottom was less inclined to pound than that of the 210s. It was entered in the New York Yacht Club Cruise more than once, where it astonished one and all by its speed, especially when it beat the great 72-foot *Baruna*, boat for boat. The crew of the larger boat couldn't believe that the little plywood cigar box was overtaking them and looked in vain for some drastic impediment in the rigging or the keel. But under the rule, the 510 suffered from its long waterline and fin keel. Ray decided to substitute a wide, wood keel, with lead on the bottom. Because of the reduced girth the wetted area would be decreased. Ray was very enthusiastic about improving the performance in this way and asked Graves to make the change as fast as possible, regardless of the cost or interference with production of our various other boats. I was aghast at the idea, always conscious of the fact that at the higher speeds, the wave-making, or residual resistance, becomes more important than the frictional resistance which is purely a function of wetted area. Also, on a shallow draft boat, such as the 110s, 210s, and the 510, the top of the keel gets into the interface between air and water, and a shape which would be ideal on the bulb of the keel, or an atomic submarine, completely submerged, is not likely to be the optimum. My arguments were all in vain, however, and Graves' capabilities were pressed to the limit to get the altered boat ready for the New York Yacht Club Cruise.

The work was finally completed one night, allowing little extra time to sail to the starting line. Ray and his wife, Barbara, set out on the first leg of the journey, arriving at Cohasset at two o'clock in the morning. Ray let Barbara off at the Cohasset Yacht Club, and sailed alone back to Marblehead. He had noticed an ominous quarter-wave, lacking with the original keel, and as soon as the yard opened in the morning, the first order of business was to reinstall the old keel.

The 510 was always a favorite of mine, and in later years I sailed on it many times, first under the ownership of Bob Pierce, Dick Fisher's partner in Fisher-Pierce, and then when Bob Meyer owned it. I was fortunate to be in the crew for a race from Marblehead to Scituate. A northeast storm had just ended, and the surviving waves were both large and steep. Although there was hardly a breath of air, boats were rocking and pitching as they struggled to stay near the starting line prior to the gun. George Crocker's 8-meter *Tango* was taking green water over the bow and the stern. Other long-ended boats were suffering equally, and there was real danger that all that motion, without steerageway, would cause a damaging collision.

As soon as the starting gun went off, the 510, with its long waterline, started ghosting toward Scituate. We were at least a mile away before the next boat was able to cross the line, and we were first to arrive in Scituate. Today, long overhangs are out, but other features, designed to beat the I.O.R. rule, are in, to the detriment, I think, of ocean racing.

During the course of my association with Ray Hunt, it was inevitable that I would hear tales of the thirty-nine-foot Concordia yawls. I had never seen one, let alone sailed on one, and, with all of the other boats with which we were concerned, it appeared that I would remain in ignorance. But a man named George Parson, from Brooklin, Maine, expressed an interest in acquiring one. This brought Ray and his former partner, Waldo Howland, together again, to go over plans and specifications and find a builder. Major Casey, of Fairhaven, Massachusetts, submitted a bid in accordance with the wishes of the prospective owner, and the comparatively minor changes that were made. I drew up a new mast plan, incorporating Ray's latest thinking, and we presented the whole proposal to Mr. Parson for his decision on whether or not to spend $16,000, which seemed astronomical to me but is far below the going price for an old Concordia today. Actually, the later boats, built to much higher standards by Abeking and Rasmussen in Germany, cost far less. Whatever the economics of the situation, Mr. Parson decided to go ahead, and we celebrated the sale of the first post-war Concordia in what we called the State Street Trust, a little bar close to the original Hunt office at 53 State Street in Boston.

I was assigned the job of riding herd on Major Casey to see that specifications for hull and rigging were met. One of the best parts of this duty was the chance to work with Waldo Howland. He was, and is, one of the finest people I have ever met. Friendly and agreeable, his outstanding quality, in my opinion, is his complete honesty, a character trait I had learned to admire, above almost all others, by the example of my father. Owners of Concordias and other boats stored at the Concordia yard soon found that they could trust Waldo for anything and gave him carte blanche for winter repairs, a dangerous practice almost anywhere else. Insurance companies took his word for estimates of repairs to damaged boats.

Waldo was an ideal partner for Ray Hunt. Whereas the latter was almost oblivious to details, the former was very exacting and precise. Waldo worked out all of the little details of the interior of the Concordias, as well as hatches, stanchions, and the like. One of the most striking features of the Concordias is the ample evidence of the thought behind each part, however insignificant it might at first appear.

Since only minor changes were to be made in the first post-war Concordia, the part I played in the design was insignificant. But I was given the job of checking, periodically, construction at the Casey yard. I was often accompanied on these trips by Waldo, whom I would meet first at the Concordia Company in Padenarum. While I checked out the mold loft work, and hull measurements at each stage of construction, Waldo saw to it that each of the myriad items required for completion was of good quality and properly installed.

I would gaze out over the big Casey shop, where a number of boats, in addition to the Concordia, were under construction. They were Alden yawls and ketches, and Major Casey's own designs, which bore a remarkable resemblance to the Aldens nearby. I was familiar with these boats from my trip from City Island to the Isles of Shoals. As I surveyed the lines of all of these boats, it seemed to me that the Concordia appeared like a racehorse in a stable of truckhorses. I often asked myself what made the Concordia so strikingly different. The perfect curve of her shear, so low and unbroken. The graceful arc of the bow, later straightened somewhat by Ray Hunt himself in the later Concordia 41s, and thereby losing something of the aesthetic value. The dainty little transom, ending the lines with a touch of elegance.

But in my opinion, the real secret of the success of the Concordias is the subtlety of the lines in the water. The unusually hard bilges spell form stability, as opposed to the slack, rounded shapes that depend so much on beam and ballast. When a sudden gust hits a Concordia, there is a solid feeling of security, rather than the well justified panic that one associates with some of the current rule beaters. All of this was conjecture on my part, for I had yet to sail in one of the famous boats.

The hard bilges, which made the Concordias such a dream to sail, created a nightmare for builders. There are limits to how much an oak frame can be bent without fracturing, even with thorough steaming. The Concordia's ribs came close to these limits. Perfect oak, with a very straight grain, is a must.

The Casey crew broke many frames in their first attempts to follow the battens which had been set up on the forms. Major Casey asked me if they couldn't ease the bilges a little, like the other boats. "Not a sixteenth of an inch," I replied, visualizing the scene when Ray Hunt's eagle eye would discover such a detriment to his lines.

Long after I had left the Hunt organization, Drayton Cochrane, of Oyster Bay, initiated a Concordia building program unparalleled in the entire boating industry. He ordered a Concordia to be built by the world-famous firm of Abeking and Rasmussen in Germany. Their superb knowledge and workmanship, together with attention to detail to rival Waldo's, were responsible for delivering nearly one hundred of these magnificent cruising boats, almost all of which are still going strong today. Drayton Cochrane later bought several of our Alden Ocean Shells from my brother Bill, who sold them on Long Island. I had the privilege of meeting Drayton just before he died, when we stopped in Oyster Bay in the Energy 48. With his keen interest in all kinds of boats, he was anxious to go out in the unusual craft, even though he already showed signs of failing health. I was only too happy to oblige.

It was a little frustrating to have such a close affiliation with the Concordias without once having sailed in one. This paradox was resolved when my lifelong friend, Fran Loutrel, acquired *Starlight*. He very generously allowed me to clutter up his spotless foredeck with an Alden single, and I was at last allowed to confirm my speculations

The Concordia 39 Starlight, owned by Fran Loutrel. Photo: Francis Loutrel.

about the performance of these famous yawls, without losing any precious rowing time. Throughout many miles along the New England coast, in all kinds of weather, *Starlight* never disappointed me. Being able to row the Alden in light weather, or after the hook went down, added frosting to the cake. The experience was well worth waiting for.

In expanding his operations, Ray hired a young war veteran named Charlie Pickering under the G.I. bill for on-the-job training. Charlie was a great sailor, having sailed and raced all kinds of boats in Beverly and Marblehead. It was my job to teach him the basics of naval architecture to fulfill our side of the bargain with Uncle Sam. There was so much to be done in boats, making deliveries, serving as crew for famous people in races, etc., that very little time was left over for the study of naval architecture. Charlie did not object too strenuously to this arrangement, and he was always ready to take off, with or without any of his many sailing friends, on any kind of a nautical adventure. He used to sail the 510, single-handed, down through the Cape Cod Canal for the New York Yacht Club Cruise. She had no engine at all. Charlie had no trouble sailing in the tricky current and shifting winds of the canal, but the law required power there. When the authorities came alongside to demand that the engine be turned on, Charlie went below and banged some pots and pans together, poked his head out of the companionway, and said he was working on the engine. After they left, he continued sailing.

Ray and Dick Fisher had collaborated on the prototype 110 and later had joint ownership of one of the production boats. The partnership was resumed when they ordered a 210. Meanwhile, all the very competitive racing had developed various gimmicks to make the boats go faster. Despite the fact that the 210s seemed very well balanced when day-sailed, it developed that there was a little too much helm for the optimum speed in racing. People began to carry loose backstays, held tight with elastic, so that the top of the mast could be moved forward with a crank on the jibstay. Linc Davis persuaded me to design a movable mast step for a more sophisticated way of moving the center of effort forward. I came up with a design and ordered two from Graves, one for Linc and one for myself. They were inordinately expensive, and I was ashamed to discover that the design was totally inadequate. I was saved from utter disgrace when the class ruled them out.

As a result of all the experimenting with the center of effort, Ray decided to try the other approach and move the center of lateral resistance aft. Consequently, he had the new Hunt-Fisher boat, named *Et Tu*, built with the keel four inches further aft. The day it was launched, Ray raced it at Marblehead, in a big fleet of 210s, sailed by some of the best. He came in far ahead of the second boat to finish and decided there and then to build all future boats with the new keel location, regardless of the consequences to the numerous present owners. I was elected to work out a procedure for altering the existing boats without the cranes and other sophisticated equipment of a boatyard. I made a deal with Martin Grassie, the steward at the Cohasset Yacht Club, and Charlie Antoine, the groundskeeper on the William C. Cox estate, where I stored my 210, whereby they would work with me, using my boat as a guinea pig, to perfect a procedure, and then they would make the change on other boats for a fixed price. Their work was so satisfactory that they altered not only all the Cohasset boats but many more besides.

Charlie Pickering was given the job of towing *Et Tu* to Cohasset from Marblehead, using Ray's own 37-footer, *Dianna* (named for his beautiful daughter) to pull it. This boat had a Hall-Scott Invader engine with 275 horsepower, far more than the usual 141-horsepower Chrysler Royal engines. Charlie hitched up the 210 and headed for Cohasset at full throttle, against a moderate southwester. As he neared his destination, he happened to notice that the 210 was remarkably low in the water. In fact, speed alone held the bow above the waves. There was nothing for it but to continue, hoping to reach the railway at the yacht club soon enough. By dint of very good seamanship, and excellent cooperation, this was done, and expensive repairs were made. The arc bottom had experienced stresses for which it was never designed.

One day Charlie was scheduled to head for New York in *Dianna*, towing several 210s and a Herreshoff S-boat which we had agreed to deliver for Sparkman and Stephens. Dawn was greeted by a raging northeast storm. Charlie and several of his friends, Ray, and I were having lunch with the inevitable beers, lamenting the fact that the trip would obviously have to be postponed. Some one suggested that we sail all the boats to Cohasset, thus covering at least part of the distance. In retrospect, such a venture does not seem to be an acceptable risk, but no one in that crowd dared to be the one to chicken out. So we headed out into the storm, one man in each boat, with two in a couple of them, and Ray in *Dianna*. We used just the mainsails, which had no reefpoints. Some of the one-man boats had pumps, but it would have been difficult to use them without someone at the helm. A batten soon ripped out on the boat I was sailing, but there was no turning back for that. We followed Ray in the power boat, heading above the rhumb line for a better point of sailing. All of the boats began to take in water, but we were making good speed, and the distance was only fourteen miles. As expected, the Herreschoff did well on this point of sailing, having no trouble keeping up with the 210s. When we got to the Boston Lightship, we changed course for Cohasset, running before the wind. The 210s surfed down the big waves, gaining frightening speed. I watched nervously as the bow of my boat plunged into the troughs. I could see the bow wave approaching the deck, but the bow never buried. The Herreschoff was no match for the 210s in these conditions, rapidly falling behind, but experiencing no difficulties. In what seemed like no time at all, we were safely behind the breakwater in Cohasset, and all of the shivering crew repaired to Ray Hunt's house to warm up, internally as well as externally.

Ray was always extremely performance oriented. He was more than well aware that pounds per horsepower is always an important factor in determining speed and always tried to keep weights down. Construction details held little of his interest, and he left a great deal up to the builder. The 210s, as originally built, had bent frames, in three laminations, held together with bronze screws. Conventional wood construction, much as it appeals to so many people, including myself, has a serious weakness as compared to gluing with epoxy, as in the WEST® system, or welded joints in steel or aluminum. If a boat calls for a certain thickness of planking for strength, it is weakened by the countersunk or counterbored holes for the screws, in the same way that postage stamps tear easily along the lines of holes. Likewise, the frames are weakened by the same screws. The solution is to have heavier planking and frames. But this calls for bigger fastenings and therefore bigger holes, and the added weight calls for heavier construction all around, and so on in a vicious circle. Welding and gluing, on the other hand, add to the strength of the members they join.

The shrouds of the 210s come through the decks and the threaded ends pass through bronze castings fastened to wood blocks between two frames, where they can be adjusted with wing nuts. The wood blocks were fastened to the laminated frames with long screws. Before many 210s entered their element, these blocks began to pull out, usually resulting in the loss of the mast. This was a serious threat to the new class, and grist for the mill of detractors, such as L.Francis Herreshoff. I wanted to make a study of the situation and come up with a design which would end the failures once and for all while there were still a limited number of boats to be retrofitted. Ray, however, accepted Selman's assurance that he could correct the problem very easily. He began putting bolts through the plywood planking, but without adequate framing to hold the planking there were more failures and more I-told-you-sos from critics. A second attempt was made to strengthen the area, this time by means of sawn frames from chine to deck, fastened only to the plywood planking.

Shortly after this alteration had been made, at great expense, to all the boats, I was acting as crew on a visiting 210 in the Manhasset Bay Challenge Cup races off Cohasset. I was lying on the windward rail, watching the water racing by, when I suddenly saw the whole side of the boat caving inboard. I shouted to the skipper to come about, and we saved the mast, later limping in with a Rube Goldberg support of the side. I decided to correct my own boat at least. Jack Bishop, a delightful member of the Cohasset fleet, had a big oak plank which he had used to hold the camber in his wooden skiis. I cut this in half, and made a support under the deck, running from one side to the other. It not only held both shroud anchorage blocks firmly in place, but also, by means of a threaded rod, supported the mast step against the mast compression which had been pushing the bottom down alarmingly. Though it added too much unwanted weight, it worked perfectly on my boat and the identical one worked equally well on Jack Bishop's. Graves finally got the message and began installing oak and spruce arches, which accomplished the same thing, without so much added weight, in all the boats.

With all of the interesting design and building going on, I should have been satisfied. But I felt that something was missing. It was one thing to carry out the details of Ray Hunt's designs and quite another to have a chance to complete a design of my own from start to finish. Besides, despite my absorbing interest in sail and power boats, rowing boats remained in first place in all my thoughts. I missed the peapod, now rotting away at the Shoals and wondered if I would ever be able to design its equal. I brought up the subject of peapods with several of our better customers, and, while no Ray Hunt as a salesman, I did manage to drum up some interest. I pestered Ray to let me go ahead and design a peapod. For a long time he resisted these entreaties, but finally, to my delight, he gave in. But first, at his insistence, we took measurements of several peapods said to be good performers. Armed with this data and some measurements I had taken from our old peapod, I went ahead, with great enthusiasm and excitement.

After completing the lines and offsets, I did a construction plan which was remarkably complete. Drawing in all the frames, seats, inwales, etc., remembering to draw exactly what one would see of each, looking outboard from the centerline, a process which I usually found boring and time consuming, I seemed to derive extra energy from the fact that this was my own creation. I made wooden patterns for bronze breasthooks in the shape of an A, the round crossbar to serve as an excellent fitting for the painter.

The boats were to be built in Cohasset by Mr. Ellsworth, an old-timer who knew more about boatbuilding than I would ever learn. He would not touch the white cedar for planking until he was satisfied that the moisture content was low enough. I was impatient with the delay but wanted nothing but the best for these boats.

I was not around the day the first boat was launched, so Ray Hunt took it out. He was horrified at the lack of stability, and immediately instructed Mr. Ellsworth to increase the waterline beam on subsequent boats. Ray was absolutely right. I had blown my big opportunity completely. Perhaps I confused myself with all of the dimensions from other boats. Certainly I was overly concerned with having a narrow waterline. Peapods had originally been built in Maine to haul lobster traps. Getting a heavy lobster trap, with four bricks for ballast, up over the gunwale called for all possible stability. Very hard bilges were the answer, just as they were in the Concordias. The lighthouse keepers at the Shoals had such a boat, which I had rowed many times. Its stability was tremendous compared to our peapod, but it was much harder and slower to row. I had a fixed idea that by narrowing the waterline beam amidships it would be faster. This was by no means a new idea, pursued by many before and since. It was a good idea, considered alone, but I certainly should have been aware of the other factors it influenced. In addition to reducing the stability beyond acceptable limits for this type of boat, it reduced displacement in the middle of the boat, forcing the ends to be deeper in the water. This submerged the nice hollow load waterline at the bow, presenting a blunter entrance which made a bow wave too far forward and at too low a speed. Even with the change that Ray had made, I could see that the boat was not what I intended. It was a bitter pill to swallow, but everyone makes mistakes, and one has to pick up the pieces and go on, vowing not to repeat the same mistakes when hard work or good fortune presents another opportunity. Actually, the boat, as amended, was not all that bad, and was certainly seaworthy as well as sea kindly and easier rowing than most boats, as I was to find out later from years of personal experience with one of them.

Although it sometimes seemed that my own 210 would never be finished, it finally joined its element. I sailed it morning, noon, and night, relishing the way it sliced through the water on the wind. When heeled over smartly, one side and the bottom formed a V, with the sharp chine acting like the blade of a knife. The action in waves when in this mode was very smooth and satisfying, and the great stability allowed the sails to take full advantage of a fresh breeze. Racing against the top competitors who had joined the class was very challenging. As already mentioned, experience with my own boat gave me a better understanding of structural problems and owner requirements.

We offered a choice of nylon sails made by Wilson and Silsby in Boston or the old reliable cotton sails made by Ratsey in New York. Nylon sails were a recent development, but Stan Hayes of Wilson and Silsby had learned how to deal with the new material, and, outside of the fact that the bolt ropes had a tendency to shrink, the sails were durable and quite satisfactory.

One day Ray Hunt told me that he had been talking to a young man who wanted to be in the sail business and had some good ideas. He wanted to try his hand at making sails for the 210s, and Ray was inclined to give him a chance. I was very much against it, arguing that we already had two of the best sailmakers, and it would be foolish to experiment with an unknown. Ray ignored my advice, and thanks to his irresistible salesmanship, he talked me into getting one of the very first of the experimental sails, made out of another new material, Orlon. Racing with this new sail was almost like driving a motorboat through the fleet, and I did so well in the Cohasset fleet that I got into the National Championships. My unfair advantage was short lived, however, for 210 owners soon flocked to buy the new sails. The young sailmaker: Ted Hood.

Ray had working for him an older draftsman named Skip Bezanson, who had worked for Nathanael Herreshoff. Skip told interesting tales of events at the famous yard in Bristol. One that I remember involved a J-boat designed by Starling Burgess, nearing completion in the water. Mr. Burgess was checking some rigging details on the towering mast and had hauled himself up in a bos'n's chair, using the steel wire main halyard. The higher he got, the less of the heavy steel wire was on his side of the sheave. Suddenly this weight, together with his own weight and the weight of the chair, was exceeded by the weight of the cable on the other side, and he found himself heading for the very top of the mast, at ever increasing speed. When he reached the top, he shouted frantically for help. One of the workers went to Mr. Herreshoff's office in a panic, to report the alarming event. Mr. Herreshoff calmly walked outside where he could see Mr. Burgess waving and shouting, and hanging on for dear life. "Let him stay there until he cools off," said the Wizard of Bristol, as he returned to his office.

Lindsay Lord, a naval architect from Falmouth Foreside, Maine, had written a book called The Naval Architecture of Planing Hulls. Ray bought a copy and was most enthusiastic about its contents. Perhaps out of professional jealousy, I was somewhat critical and enjoyed arguing with Ray over the subject matter, neither of us taking it personally. Mr. Lord pointed out the effect of beam on a planing boat and even went so far as to suggest that speed-length ratio be abandoned in favor of speed-beam ratio. I had learned years earlier from George Crouch, and various technical papers, that the dynamic pressure on a planing surface was by far the greatest near the leading edge. It was certainly common knowledge that wing span is more effective in generating lift than wing area, and high aspect sails are more effective going to windward. Today our Douglas oars generate more lift and less drag by their short and wide design. But applying this general knowledge to the design of a planing boat is something else again. There are many more factors to be considered, and the inordinately wide power boats of today lack something in the way of seaworthiness and sea kindliness.

The book also stressed the undesirability of what the author referred to as a warped bottom, giving the impression that such a boat, like all V-bottom boats of that era, was akin to a person having a warped mind. What Mr. Lord meant was that the bottom, aft of the midship section, presented a decreasing dihedral angle toward the almost flat bottom at the transom. This gave a different angle of attack to the buttock lines. According to Mr. Lord, this unfavorable situation could be corrected by what he called a monohedron hull, having a constant dihedral, or angle of the Vee, aft of amidships. Actually, this design concept was something of a detriment to speed, but, with the right angle and some other subtleties of design, resulted in one of the greatest breakthroughs in seaworthiness for motorboats. It took the genius of Ray Hunt to put it all together years later when he created the revolutionary deep-V design. I was to meet Lindsay Lord much later at Jewel Island in Casco Bay, he in a beautiful old traditional yacht, finished in bright mahogany, and I in the Energy 48.

One of Ray's most interesting and revolutionary designs was the Shoaler. This was a double-ended cruising boat with a centerboard instead of a keel. Nothing is ever entirely new in the boat business, and certainly there had been plenty of catboats, sharpies, bugeyes, and other boats built without keels. But the Shoaler had subtle lines, giving form stability and speed without sacrificing seakindliness. The first Shoaler 32 was built with strip planking, without the benefit of the epoxy glue which is such a boon to that type of construction today. The water permeated the strips, and when they swelled up, it squeezed the opening in the bottom of the centerboard well, making it impossible to move the board up or down. Despite this problem, which was later corrected, the Shoalers were a great success, and Phil Benson's Shoaler 38, *Reaper*, won many races. Others followed Ray's lead, the best known being *Finisterre*, designed by Sparkman and Stephens.

Selling our various boats was becoming the most interesting part of the business, as well as the obvious solution to the ever worrisome financial situation. I enjoyed selling boats in which I believed, and I learned a great deal from Ray Hunt. One day we both had a lesson to learn, one that I have never forgotten. A man walked into our Marblehead office inquiring about a used 210. I guess we were brought up on the elder J.P. Morgan's philosophy that if you have to ask the price of a boat, you can't afford one. Ray had other things on his mind and turned the apparently poor prospect over to me. I had other things to do, and since the good natured and ever obliging Charlie Pickering was spending one of his rare days ashore, I neatly brushed off the gentleman to his care.

Charlie obligingly took the intruder through the manufacturing operations at the Graves yard. As they came to the mold over which the boats were built, the prospect noticed that the one under construction was being made with mahogany plywood instead of the standard fir. After Charlie explained that this was an option which cost considerably more money, the man allowed as how that is what he wanted. When they came to a compass being mounted in a drawer under the stern deck, he said that was no good because you had to turn around to see it, and that would interfere with racing. Charlie suggested that they could install the compass in the deck beside the cockpit. "That would be fine on one tack, but no good on the other. I want one on each side," said the prospect, talking more and more like an owner. So it went, to the conclusion of an order for the most gold plated of all the 210s we ever sold.

As time went on, my family increased in number and size. Looking ahead, I could see a rising demand for little boats in addition to the usual paraphernalia of growing children. Despite the brilliance of the Hunt designs, I could not see a viable and financially rewarding business developing. The money to be made in the boat business went then, as it does today, to the astute businessmen who are more concerned with the bottom line than the merits of the lines of the product. Ray Hunt could never bring himself to think this way, and, on reflection, neither could I. I would rather take a job completely divorced from the boating industry in order to support my family than to work in that part of the industry where there was money to be made, but out of boats of which I would be ashamed.

With most of the major designs complete, and the need for speed calculations decreased, there was not much left to do in my favorite field. Although Ray never mentioned the subject, it was obvious to me that for routine drafting work, I was neither enthusiastic nor particularly effective. All things being considered, it was time for me to leave, by mutual consent. Fortunately, it was not the end of my association with Ray Hunt.

19 • *On The Beach*

i had finally learned that selling Ray Hunt's boats had more appeal for me than making drawings of them. I enjoyed meeting the people who shared my interest in good boats. I found that getting an order for what I considered a good boat was more interesting and exciting than working out the little details of construction. If this were the case, why not try pure selling of an industrial product I could believe in?

Pursuing this line of thought, I ended up taking a job with a small company having the unlikely title of Lee H. Long Associates, in Boston. The name suggests a Chinese laundry, but actually the Lee originated from parental respect for the Confederate general, and the business was local selling of materials handling equipment, primarily fork lift trucks manufactured by Yale & Towne. Before taking the job, I assured myself that the infant materials handling technology had a promising future in American industry, and the products I sold would be the best. To this end, I contacted my father's cousin, Bob Struthers of Wood, Struthers, a director of Yale & Towne. He arranged for me to meet Calvert Carey, the president, Sam Gibb, the sales manager, and Charlie Schroeder, the chief engineer. I was particularly impressed with the latter, whom I immediately sized up as a genius in his field. His many innovations in fork truck design are now standard practice on all such products, including those made in Japan. At the time, however, Yale was far ahead of all the competition, and I was satisfied that I would be selling the best.

During the next several years I was to learn the answers to many questions, most of which I had never thought to ask, and others which, unsuspected at the time, were to prove highly relevant in future activities. How did they make forgings for aircraft and jet engines, paper, textile machinery, castings, stampings, beer, wire, abrasives, and numerous other products? How did a successful small business operate? An unsuccessful one? How did company politics affect big businesses? How did nepotism affect small family businesses? How did multi-layered management affect efficiency? I was exposed to answers on a daily basis, at the same time that I was learning to sell in a professional manner for the benefit of my customers, myself, and my family.

I found that my interest and experience in boats opened many doors to executive offices, for most men have unfulfilled aspirations towards a more satisfying life around the water. My own engineering background was beneficial in working out solutions to problems of materials handling efficiency, while at the same time I was storing away information on various manufacturing techniques, fiscal policies, and sales techniques.

My vague ideas about big business and company politics gradually became crystalized. What I had observed at Bethlehem was repeated in various forms in companies with whom I dealt, particularly Yale & Towne and International Harvester.

A company usually starts with owner management, the principals risking their own or borrowed money. Their dominant motivation is that the company must succeed. They do not hesitate to hire the best available brains, even those that exceed their own abilities. As owners, their position is not threatened, and every success of subordinates helps them to attain their goals. As a company achieves success and growth, ownership becomes more diverse. Stockholders' primary interest is in dividends and quick appreciation, while outside raiders seek greenmail or stock manipulation for quick profit at the expense of the health of the company. Executives fight for power and money, often to the detriment of the company which predecessors have worked so hard to build up. Subordinates are selected more on the basis of loyalty than ability, and the organization becomes infested with mediocre managers who might otherwise be government bureaucrats.

I saw this happening at Yale & Towne, under the machinations of vice president Elmer Twyman. John Baldinger, his chosen general manager, had no discernable ability other than a talent for laughing at the jokes of his benefactor. Production became such a shambles that it was impossible to forecast shipping dates, and more and more good customers were becoming furious at receiving endless broken promises. I became concerned that the great company I represented was headed for oblivion. I had worked hard to make an enviable sales record. I considered myself a creative sales engineer, working out solutions to the problems of my many valued customers. I believed that most of them considered me a helpful friend and man of integrity. Now I was in a position of passing along delivery promises I knew from bitter experience would never be kept. I couldn't stand deceiving my good customers any longer.

I was desperate to resolve my dilemma. I was looking for some sign that the top management would do something to reverse the trend before it was too late. Otherwise, my conscience advised leaving the company.

I had read a thrilling account of Hurricane Carol at the Shoals, in *Yachting*. The author and his wife had been there in a cruising sailboat, anchored in Gosport Harbor behind the breakwater. As the storm intensified, and the tide came up, the waves began to come up over the breakwater. I have been at the Shoals in lesser storms and watched in awe as spray began to be visible over the tops of the islands. But that was nothing compared to the sudden realization that there is no real shelter for any boat at the Isles of Shoals in extreme conditions. For the hapless yachtsman there was no alternative but to go out into the teeth of the hurricane. A big breaking wave washed his wife overboard, where death seemed inevitable, but another wave washed her back on board. The name of the author was William Mathers, Secretary of Yale and Towne.

Although I had never met him and had no business to contact him, I decided to take a chance that our mutual interests would grant me an audience and set out for the Chrysler Building. He was most cordial, and after discussing the Shoals, boats, and his harrowing experience, I came right to the point and told him of my concern for what was happening to Yale and Towne. To my astonishment and great pleasure, he agreed completely with me and said that he planned to correct the situation. I left in high spirits, but I learned shortly that he had been fired. The forces of evil had won again.

Yale continued downhill. Finally the financial figures confirmed the tragedy, and the consulting firm of McKinsey was hired, at great expense, to study the entire operation and make recommendations. When the lengthy study was completed, the advice was exactly what I could have given them for nothing far earlier: fire Twyman and Baldinger. But it was too late. The great company, like a giant blue whale, was taken over, dismembered as divisions were split off, and to all intents and purposes, the famous name became extinct.

In a brief experience selling earth-moving equipment for International Harvester, I witnessed a replay of the same plot, more obvious, if anything. Clyde Everett, who owned the dealership for which I worked, used to say that if you were sitting at a bar with several International executives, and asked one of them what he thought the weather was going to do, he would look right and left to see if anyone in the company who outranked him chose to answer. Only if all of them declined would he dare to open his mouth.

The price list for farm tractors and related equipment rivaled a congressional continuing resolution for size, and changes were so numerous and frequent that it was a full-time job to keep it up to date. One of the top executives announced that he wished to purchase some equipment for his gentleman's farm. Naturally everyone jumped to attention to curry favor with the big boss. But it took four days to arrive at a price. Mr. Everett asked me to purchase a truck we needed, suggesting that we get it from our cousins in International. A salesman came first thing in the morning, and I gave him the specifications and the stipulation that we would have to have it by a certain date or it would be cancelled. He asked for space to sit down and work out a price, so I ushered him into a vacant office. He emerged late in the afternoon with a price and refusal to be pinned down on delivery. "Go tell them to fry their ass," said Clyde Everett. I called up Ford, got a price almost immediately over the phone, ordered the truck, and it was delivered ahead of schedule.

Clyde Everett had lost over a million dollars in just one day, auctioning off used equipment. None of the salesmen bothered too much to sell it, but always begged for higher trade-in offers in order to sell new ones. As sales manager, I worked out a system of ratios for used equipment whereby the salesmen made more money selling it, and they all competed for the opportunity. Clyde Everett made fun of my slide rule efforts, but the fact was that we began to show a profit for the first time in several years. Clyde was getting on in years, and wanted to retire to his native Nova Scotia. I worked with a brilliant financial wizard named Walter Hungerford to take over the dealership. He had arranged the family sale of Welsh's Grape Juice, to the great tax advantage of the family and the consternation of the I.R.S., which tried in vain to find something wrong with what he had done. He had also been treasurer of American Locomotive and CBS Hytron. With the combination of our abilities, and the huge tax loss carryover, prospects for success appeared favorable. But the company politicians at International succeeded in blocking the plan, making it a company branch, which managed to lose huge sums of money. When International Harvester went into bankruptcy later, it was no surprise to me.

I had tried to take over the bankrupt Yale dealership under somewhat similar circumstances and received a verbal promise from the man in charge, right in my own living room in Cohasset, that the deal would go through in 48 hours. But it was more than six months, after many letters and phone calls, including one to the president of Yale and Towne, before I was able to ascertain that company politics had won yet another victory. In retrospect, it is hard to avoid the stigma of sour grapes in these two bitter defeats. But, had I succeeded in either one, I would not have gone back into the boat business, and today there would be no Alden Ocean Shell or the sport of recreational rowing. The sum of all my business experience convinced me of one thing. I wanted no more part of big business, and I was later to find the ultimate satisfaction in my own small business, where success, as in lobstering, depends almost entirely on effort and merit.

While my business experience during these years was unrelated to boats or rowing, my leisure hours were not. My land in Cohasset was only 37 steps from the nearest land of the Cohasset Yacht Club. I had the 210, which I raced for 16 years. Racing these boats, in the distinguished company of the members of the Cohasset fleet, was an experience I recall with a great deal of pleasure.

The grand old man of the fleet was Charles Francis Adams. He had raced various boats at Marblehead for years, sailing across from Cohasset single-handed, picking up a young crew for the race, and sailing back alone, arriving after dark if the wind was light. After he celebrated his eightieth birthday, his family insisted that he stay closer to home; hence the 210. He studied the new boat endlessly, sailing around by himself, adjusting sails, getting the feel of the tiller, and adding to his already impressive knowledge of local windshifts and currents. He could make a 210 go to windward as well as anyone, with the possible exception of Ray Hunt. Looking out from under his old sailor hat, with the brim turned down almost over his eyes, he looked like an eagle, and if he was passing you, you felt like one of the prey of those cold, piercing eyes. He never paid you the compliment of looking back if you were astern of him, for he really didn't expect you to pass him.

One day, when spinnakers had just become available, it was blowing very hard from the southwest the day of the race. Phil Benson, who later invented the turtle to facilitate spinnaker handling, felt that we should agree not to carry spinnakers that day. Gregg Bemis felt otherwise and succeeded in persuading a slim majority to vote for spinnakers. Mr. Adams, living out in the isolation of the Glades, was not a party to the discussion. As we jockeyed around at the starting line, mainsails shaking and flapping like a flock of angry seagulls, each with two, three, or four to handle the sails in the high winds, there was Mr. Adams, with no one but a little kid in a life jacket (the former was said to keep a supply of pebbles aboard, the better to enforce orders to young crew members, such as the latter). When we reached the weather mark, and some started struggling frantically to get their spinnakers flying, while others chickened out and settled for the slower but safer genoas, a huge spinnaker, full and pulling like a team of horses, appeared on *Harpoon*, as Mr. Adams had named his 210.

He thought nothing of sailing this boat, under bare poles, to get it in to the safety of the harbor from the exposed mooring at the Glades, right in the middle of a severe storm.

As he got older, Mr. Adams tended to forget some of the racing rules, and sometimes went around marks the wrong way, which no one dared to protest. In one race he hit the stern of Phil Benson's boat, inflicting some damage. I was chairman of the Cohasset fleet and had the unhappy responsibility for doing something about it. I dreaded a confrontation, and put off initiating any action, although it was obvious to all that Mr. Adams was in the wrong. Then one night my telephone rang. When I said hello, the following terse conversation followed: "This is Charles Francis Adams. Tell Phil Benson I will pay for the damage to his boat. Goodnight."

The Cohasset fleet had a series of team races with Marblehead, Western Long Island Sound, and the Pequot Yacht Club of Southport,

Connecticut. While Marblehead had many good 210 skippers, they seemed to have difficulty with a team effort, and we beat them so soundly that the contests were discontinued. The other races continued for many years, and were a source of great fun and a challenging change from individual racing. There were four boats on each team and we always arranged to have all the boats hauled the previous day and the bottoms scrubbed. Then we made up two groups of boats, as evenly matched as possible based on fleet standings, and offered the visitors first choice of boats for the first race, alternating them thereafter. This extreme fairness was largely the work of Gregg Bemis, whose exceptional objectivity as a judge is admired all over the world. Would that others would follow his example and not abuse power for personal advantage. Honesty seems to be an endangered species.

Ray Hunt was a skipper in one team race off Cohasset. As we tacked back and forth toward the windward mark near Boston, ominous hard-edged clouds moved in from the west. As they advanced, they darkened, until the whole scene became very black and the seagulls and white boats became very vivid. As to be expected, Ray Hunt was the first to reach the weather mark. After rounding, he immediately lowered both sails, unhanked the jib, removed the mainsail from the tracks on mast and boom, and stowed both sails in their bags under the bow deck. To me, this seemed like a dramatic illustration of superb seamanship. All too often, the competitive spirit is so overwhelming that prudence is forgotten, and foolish chances are taken. In rowing, I clearly remember a newspaper photograph of a college crew racing in choppy water. All eight oarsmen are pulling their hearts out, perfectly synchronized, while the coxswain is shouting for still more power. Meanwhile, the 62-foot splinter of a boat has filled with water, up to the seat tracks, and is obviously just about to swamp completely, which it did only seconds later. Phil Le Boutillier, was captain of a Princeton crew which was the only one of many crews racing on Lake Cayouga to reach the starting line in a seaworthy condition. Rescue boats took care of all the disabled boats, but the seaworthy Princeton crew was completely forgotten in the resulting confusion. To avoid further exposure to the increasing chop, they landed on a rocky shore, thus saving themselves and their expensive shell. Good seamanship is always a great asset in any kind of a boat.

When Ray Hunt stowed his sails, the race was obviously over, and even the most competitive among us followed suit. His daughter, Dianna, was on one of the other boats, and perhaps this influenced his wise decision. A few minutes later all thoughts of the race were suddenly forgotten. A white wall of spray advanced upon us with the speed of an express train, and we were enveloped in an awesome maelstrom. It is always surprising how quickly menacing waves can spring up under the influence of such a wind. I cautioned the crew to stay in the cockpit no matter what, for the boat was picking up speed in a horrifying way, under completely bare poles, and there was only one direction it was going to go. If anyone went overboard, there was nothing that any human could have done. We rigged a bucket to a long piece of line and trailed it over the stern, but it had little effect on the speed of the boat. Judging from the wave formation, we were certainly at hull speed, which is quite impressive in a 210, having such a long effective waterline. The squall ended as suddenly as it had begun, and what might have been a disaster ended as an uneventful routine.

One 210 race in Marblehead was blessed with a summer northeaster instead of the usual light and variable winds. As we jockeyed for position after the warning gun, I misjudged the surfing effect of the waves. I thought I had allowed plenty of space between my boat and Eileen Shields, daughter and inheritor of the racing skills of Cornelious Shields. But as she came surfing down, my bow hit her backstay, fracturing the turnbuckle, and put her boat out of commission. Although my boat was undamaged, I reluctantly withdrew from the race, without crossing the starting line. Rules are to be followed and not misused for the acquisition of silverware after winning legal battles.

At the start of the same race, Bobby Coulson, one of the coolest and most naturally talented of skippers, as well as possessing quite a sense of humor, threw a cherry bomb at Clint McKim's 210. The bomb landed in the water adjacent to the side of McKim's boat and exploded under water. With the incompressible water for leverage, the concussion blew a hole in the plywood, just above the chine.

Graves had put Styrofoam blocks under the bow and stern decks, guessing that this would be sufficient to float the 1200-pound keel. We had confirmed this by having Charlie Pickering (later to provide practically the only good music on Boston airwaves on Station WJIB) fill a

210 with water and stand in the swamped but still floating boat for a photograph which we showed to nervous prospects. Unfortunately, air trapped under the decks held the test boat up. It did not hold up Clint McKim's *Mons Meg III* which went right down so that only the top of the mast was available for surface salvage. Needless to say, Styrofoam flotation was increased forthwith. The lesson from this little episode is that one cannot be too careful in testing flotation.

The tender for my 210 was an 8-foot pram made by Graves. This was a very clever design, in that the bottom, though made out of a single sheet of plywood, had a remarkably effective shape. Plywood cannot be bent in two directions at once, into a compound curve. But these little boats had a perfectly flat bottom at the midship section, allowing the plywood to be bent upwards for considerable rocker. At the ends, however, it became straight in profile, allowing it to be bent transversely into an arc. With the arc bottom at the ends, it was much more sea kindly, as well as faster. With its light weight, it was easy to row, but with such a short length, its maximum speed was limited. Even with the best of lines, such a short boat cannot provide very satisfactory speed, regardless of minimum weight and maximum human power. A compromise between this boat and a twenty-six and one-half-foot racing single scull suggests itself.

Ray Hunt was using one of the ill-designed and partially corrected peapods as a tender. It was unsuited for stowing aboard a bigger boat, which he often had occasion to do, and he was anxious to have a Graves pram. I, on the other hand, would much prefer the peapod, despite the nuances of design of which I was so painfully aware. We therefore exchanged boats, in addition to which I gave him twenty-five dollars, for the peapod had cost far more to build.

I soon became accustomed to its faults, the way a parent accepts imperfections in a child. Actually, its performance was not all that bad. It was certainly seaworthy enough and so sea kindly that it was always a pleasure to take it out in waves. It was big enough for the entire family, including by this time five children. They all liked to ride in the peapod, towing their model boats, just as I had done so many years before. Voyages were short, mostly just across the channel, from the yacht club to the flats, where there were sand castles to be built, minnows stranded in tidal pools to catch, wading or swimming whenever the spirit moved, and plenty of clams to be dug. We shared this paradise with a few other residents, most of whom we knew. Today, as many as one hundred power boats from out of town frequent the place, polluting the water with gasoline and oil, shattering the peace with loud rock music, and often operating the boats to endanger, thanks to drugs or alcohol, or under age drivers. In later years I saw a friend's little child, standing in shallow water, almost get cut to pieces by an outboard motor. I am grateful for the peace we enjoyed, and the simple, unregimented activities my children thought up for themselves to give them a lifelong appreciation for living by the edge of the sea.

I rowed many miles along the beautiful coastline of Cohasset in the peapod, enjoying the exercise and relaxation after the tensions of work and racing in the 210. The kayak was long gone, a victim of old age and the accompanying rot of wood and canvas. There are many advantages to rowing, but there are also many advantages to kayaking. Having enjoyed both for many years, I try to avoid futile arguments about which is best. As much as I delighted in rowing my first peapod, I missed the kayak.

One rainy morning, as I left the house for work, I noticed a crowd of people at the yacht club. This aroused my curiosity, for I couldn't imagine why they would congregate there so early on such an unpleasant day. So I went in and soon learned the reason. The rain was the overture to Hurricane Carol, and people were hastening to put out chafing gear and extra anchors. Thinking only of my precious 210, I went out in the peapod to set the anchor with plenty of scope to the southeast, the direction from which a freshening wind was already blowing. I added chafing gear for both the mooring pennant and the anchor rode before rowing ashore. My business suit and tie looked like a wrinkled old-fashioned bathing suit, and I was drenched to the skin, but the 210 was as safe as I could make her.

Perhaps Admiral Rock's words about the work ethic had finally sunk in, for I foolishly changed into dry clothing and set out once more to try for a sale of materials handling equipment. By this time the wind had increased alarmingly, and branches were beginning to come down. I drove on, heedless of the circumstances, until I reached the factory which was my first target. There I was informed by a watchman that everyone had gone home because of the storm. I repeated this futile performance several more times, until someone suggested that I had better get home while it was still possible. At this eleventh hour, I finally gave in and headed for Cohasset. It was almost too late, for fallen trees had already blocked my usual route, and I had to turn back and seek an alternate path several times, like being in a maize with many dead ends and only one circuitous route to the goal.

When I arrived in Cohasset, I changed to some clothing more suitable for the occasion and returned to the yacht club to enjoy the spectacle with fascination mixed with horror. Although Cohasset Harbor is almost completely landlocked, it was receiving the full brunt of the fierce winds. It was astonishing to see the vicious little breaking waves that were building up in such a short distance. My 210 and her sisters were wrenching at their moorings, heeling over and sailing off at an angle, only to come about and try the same thing on the other tack. None had any sails aboard, much less rigged on mast or boom. Some of the larger cruising boats were not so fortunate.

When one lets go of the halyard, the mainsail comes sliding down of its own weight. It is difficult to imagine a sail going up the mast without any help from a halyard which has been unshackled and secured elsewhere. But that is just what can happen in a hurricane. The boat heels over under bare poles, and the head of the sail breaks loose and is blown a little way up the mast. Even a hankerchief-sized sail greatly increases the heeling, allowing the wind to exert greater pressure on the remaining furled sail. As the sail area increases, the forces far exceed the strength of any stops, and the result is that the entire sail, or what is left of it, goes up the mast, and the ultimate result is disaster.

Nelson Hartstone, a lawyer who later represented Ray Hunt in his unsuccessful legal battles to protect his interests in his deep-V design for power boats, had a very good cruising boat known as a Galaxy, designed by the famous Bill Tripp. I had sailed on this boat, and marveled at its windward performance, enhanced by its hollow waterline at the bow, reflecting the Nat Herreshoff technology. As he watched helplessly from the dock, Nelson saw the stop holding the head of his furled mainsail work loose. The sail started up the mast, starting the vicious cycle of more heeling, more determined sailing back and forth, more strain on the remaining stops, which were already beginning to fail, one by one, and more chafing of the mooring pennant.

In those days, there was no fleet of Boston Whalers or other high-powered outboards. It was something of a challenge to row out to a boat on a mooring, especially in a hurricane. Nelson asked me if I would row him out to his boat in the peapod. This was an opportunity I could not turn down. Nelson crouched in the stern, as near the bottom as possible, to reduce windage and give us the maximum stability, while I rowed in the bow position. The boat took the waves easily and smoothly, but there was no shortage of spray. I put everything I had into the 9-foot ash oars, but in the gusts, we lost ground. There is nothing worse than the realization that one's maximum power is not enough to prevail against the forces of nature. It was reassuring then, as it has often been since, to know that terra firma lay directly to leeward (louard). All too often, people set out in small boats without giving a thought to "what if" and become panic stricken when they discover that they are unable to make it back to shore against the wind. A sliding seat releases the big leg muscles to help out, more than doubling the available power, but it doesn't eliminate all the "what if's."

Between the severest gusts we were able to inch ahead to gain back the lost ground and gain a little more besides. Eventually, we reached the thrashing sailboat and stood off waiting for it to stay in irons long enough to land. The wildly flapping mainsail was quieted down with a long piece of heavy nylon line, wrapped around and around the boom. The weakened mooring pennant was assisted by another heavy line, well protected against chafing. The return to the dock was nothing if not speedy. The peapod had certainly proved itself.

I returned to the house when the wind died down and went up on the roof with a saw to cut up a tree which had blown against the house, forgetting that after the calm passage of the eye, the wind suddenly returns in the opposite direction. I was caught unaware by the hasty departure of the tree, fortunately without any part of me in its clutches.

Professor George Owens, who taught naval architecture at M.I.T., also designed many fine boats. One of these was the *Ski Bum*, a double-ended auxiliary sailboat. On a calm and clear night, the sea and sky were brightly illuminated by the funeral pyre of this beautiful boat. There were no casualties, and I never heard any explanation for the fire, other than the suggestion that the owners might have needed an insurance settlement more than a yacht. Whatever the circumstances, as the flames reached the waterline, it was obvious that her sailing days were over. The charred remains washed ashore near Cohasset, and I undertook the task of towing them into the harbor. The oars got a good workout that day, for progress was unbelievably slow and arduous. All that remained in a usable condition was a small area of the solid teak deck planking at the stern and small pieces of mahogany planking, painted the red of the boot top, and the green of the bottom. Not to waste the object of my back-breaking row, I made a heavy little tray out of these remains, with the teak king plank and adjacent planks just as they were in the boat, and mahogany handles showing just a touch of the original red and green. It has been a prized possession ever since, serving various alcoholic beverages to many a sailor and a few landlubbers as well.

The Cohasset Yacht Club and the Beverly Yacht Club in Marion, Massachusetts, had long ago bought fleets of little sailboats, called Rookies, from a builder named Perry, whose name was burned into the bow deck of each boat. They were used in the sailing program at Cohasset, where many a famous sailor first grasped a tiller. What I liked especially about these boats was that they could be rowed as well as sailed, making the young skippers completely self-sufficient, providing the adults left them alone. The boats were only eight feet long, with Marconi mainsails. They had flat bottoms, with rocker, and topsides made out of a single plank. One of the secrets of their success was their very full bows, giving them a great deal more stability than one would expect. Later attempts to duplicate them failed miserably because the builder bent the topside plank in an easy curve, resulting in far less stability, and a number of capsizes not deserved by capable young skippers. Still later I found myself in charge of having some built by Junie Butman, of Cohasset. He was well able to understand my admonitions concerning the bow lines, and his boats were the equal of the original ones.

One of these boats would belong to a family and be passed down from child to child, in the order of age, until the youngest outgrew it. As Douglas, my oldest, approached the Rookie age, I bought one of the originals, *Silver Moon*, from Gregg Bemis, whose two offspring had grown up. After all five of my children had gone on to other boats, I sold it back again for the Bemis grandchildren. It took all of my patience to keep the little boat in the barn until Douglas learned to swim. But I firmly believe, as my parents before me believed, that all

A fleet of Rookies racing off Cohasset. A child could sail or row one of these little boats, or pull it up on a beach, thus learning to become independent around the water. The Martins had two of them. Photo: F. Gregg Bemis.

children should learn to swim, and pass a test, before being allowed out in a boat without an adult. I am always appalled by the sight of one or two children, wearing life jackets, being towed out to the starting line of a race before they know how to swim.

After Douglas learned to swim, he was allowed to use his boat, but the mast and sail remained ashore. He had a full year of rowing, exploring, testing his skill and strength against wind and current, learning to be independent and self-sufficient in a boat without so much organization and regimentation that there would be no time to notice the beauty of the environment. The same rules applied to the other four, and as they followed so closely in age, we had to acquire another Rookie, which we named *Palomino* in deference to Lorna's interest, shared with most young girls, in owning a horse. After proving more than adequate ability in rowing, each one was allowed to sail, but not race until they demonstrated a good understanding of the rudiments of sailing. It happened that all five of our children took to sailing and won numerous prizes racing. Parents would ask me how I was able to generate such interest in racing in all of my offspring. I would patiently explain that the way to generate interest is to hold back the exciting experiences until they are deserved and the necessary preliminary skills acquired. They would invariably explain that their children were exceptionally gifted and could learn to race right away. Later I would see junior, crying and slamming his tiller back and forth, behind the starting line, while the other boats were rounding the first mark.

On the Fourth of July and Labor Day there would be rowing races for Rookies. My offspring did so well in these races that it was almost embarrassing. Except for one time. Rod and Charlie were racing each other, neck and neck, for the first mark, while the rest of the fleet were far behind. As they neared the mark, each one tried to cut inside the other and the boats collided. There ensued a naval battle to rival Trafalgar, while the rest of the fleet went by, and the rowing Martins finished last and next to last.

I became chairman of the Junior Activities Committee at the yacht club and attempted to bring the Rookie program, which had been suffering for lack of interest, back to life. I was able to inflict my family rules about rowing and sailing on all the children. As expected, there was opposition from some of the parents, but the children ate it up. If a sudden high wind were to come up during a race, what would happen to all of those little boats? How could one or two supervisors handle two dozen or more capsized boats? I initiated a program whereby I could give a signal by whistling four times (I have a very loud whistle, unaided by artificial means). At the sound of this whistle, all racers were to take down their sails and row to the committee boat. I practiced this procedure several times in moderate weather, giving a prize to the skipper to reach the committee boat first. The response to this procedure was so fast that I felt confident that one person could safely handle many boats.

Each year, the big event for the Rookies was the Rookie Cruise to a distant deserted beach, there to cook supper and spend the night under the stars. In years past, this had been quite an adventure for the young skippers, but it had gradually degenerated to the point where fewer and fewer bothered to participate. Boats were towed over to the beach, hauled up by adults, supper was brought over in cars, and cooked by parents, and more and more grown-ups gathered for one more occasion for drinking, an activity in which the Cohasset population was extremely proficient. Some of the older people were worried that the yacht club was going down hill.

I made various qualifications mandatory for going on the Rookie cruise. The children, as expected, worked hard for the privilege of going, instead of enjoying their parents' consternation when no form of bribery could persuade them to participate. When the fleet set out from the dock, I knew that, for the most part, they were well qualified and enthusiastic, and looking forward to cooking their own meals, taking care of their boats, and performing, on their own, all the chores that would be necessary.

They all arrived safely and helped each other to pull all the boats up far above high tide. The next morning was bright and brisk, and after breakfast all the boats were launched, and forty-five little sails were hoisted. I was rowing in the peapod, where I could easily reach anyone in trouble, even in shallow water, should the need arise, and my trusty whistle could furl all the sails in less than a minute. The venerable Pat Reid, one of the saltiest of the old-timers, was a little further offshore in his classic open motorboat, *Shag*, keeping an eagle eye on the forty-five young skippers. As we passed by the houses on the shore, people came out and waved to the fleet, and I was gratified to hear several comments later about how good it was to see such a glorious event. Unfortunately, after I left, the Junior Activities Committee invested in several escort boats and instructors to run them, and tow the Rookies out to the starting line and back to the harbor, making sure that no young skipper was given an opportunity to show any initiative. The fleet dwindled in size, and enthusiasm waned. The gallant little Rookies remain in my memory as the perfect boats for young people to find out for themselves what life on the water is all about and to learn to be completely self-sufficient.

The Huntform power boats, particularly the 37-footers, had been very successful in their day. They went very smoothly and efficiently with moderate power (141 horsepower in the 37-footers). They cruised in a semi-planing mode, which still seems fast enough for me. But, because of their relatively flat sections aft, they would pound when driven into big head seas. Buyers of motorboats, encouraged and seduced by the high-pressure advertising and promotion of boat and engine manufacturers, were seeking ever more powerful and faster boats. The graceful motion of the Huntforms, along with that of many another good boat of that time, was forsaken for the allure of power and speed. Ray Hunt, rather than deploring the trend, applied his fertile mind to the problems it introduced. There is no way that the typical low-chine V-bottom boats, with their almost flat bottoms aft of amidships, could be driven hard in rough water without severe pounding and dangerous plunging of the bow. Ray solved the problem with the deep-V.

One day he appeared in Cohasset with the prototype. This was a wood boat, and in addition to the high deadrise running right back to the transom, and the multiple spray strips, it had an opening in the bottom of the transom, so that the entire bottom below the cockpit sole filled with water. This was an ingenious use of water ballast. It lowered the boat in the water to increase the effective beam at rest and at low speeds, but all the water ran out as soon as the boat began to plane.

Ray later experimented with a way of adding water ballast after a boat was fully planing, improving control and motion in some wave conditions, without requiring extra power to initiate planing. Water ballast had been used for years in ships for the same purpose. Even today, tankers add salt water to empty oil tanks when caught in severe storms. Connected tanks on each side of a ship served to reduce rolling, and our friend and neighbor, Fran Stokes, recently used ballast tanks to provide movable weight on the windward side of a sailboat to win a single-handed transatlantic race. The naval architects who design ships have usually been far ahead of small boat designers, but Ray Hunt was right there with them, despite his limited technical background, and sometimes he was ahead. As far as I know, he was the first to suggest bow thrusters to help maneuver ships.

It was late fall, there was a strong northwest wind, and when Ray invited me to go out in the radical new boat, I could hardly refuse such an invitation. Before we left the yacht club, Ray put on a life jacket and offered me one. Whether from more confidence in the boat than the designer, or just stubbornness, I declined. As we got outside the harbor, the full force of the wind and waves became apparent. I was astonished to see how easily the bow lifted over the waves, going to windward, landing in the troughs with the same satisfying whoosh of a well designed displacement hull at much lower speed. As speed was increased, we became completely airborne, even going down before the wind, landing sometimes in such a way that the stern hit the water first. But there was no real pounding, such as I would expect in any other planing boat. There was no doubt that Ray's triumphant laugh was more than justified.

Later Ray designed the 12-meter *Easterner,* In which Chandler Hovey and his family raced to determine who would defend the America's Cup. I understand that of the several new 12s racing that year, *Easterner* was the one that Olin Stephens considered a threat to his position as designer of all of the successful cup defenders. But fast as the bright mahogany challenger from Marblehead appeared to be, 12-meter racing is serious business, requiring more than a family cruise, and she was eliminated from the fierce competition. Although she made quite an impression, her tender, the unique new deep-V, dashing back and forth regardless of the sea conditions, made even more of an impression, particularly on one of the crew of another contender. His name: Richard Bertram. He evidently thought the radical new design was good enough to manufacture and sell in quantity.

Eric Olson, a good friend in the boating fraternity whom we see frequently at boat shows, related the following sequel: Dick Bertram had a prototype of his proposed deep-V constructed and launched in Florida. As he walked down on the dock to board it for the first trials, who should appear but Ray Hunt. Recovering quickly from his surprise and consternation, Dick initiated a conversation, the gist of which follows:

Dick Bertram: "Hello, Ray, would you like to come for a spin in the new boat?"

Ray Hunt: "No, thanks."

D.B.: "Why not?"

R.H.: "Because it won't work. The design is wrong."

D.B.: "Would you design one which will work?"

R.H.: "Yes."

There followed one of the most successful partnerships in the boating industry. Ray designed and Dick had built the original *Moppie,* which astounded the entire power boat world with its sustained high speed in winning the Miami-Nassau race in very rough water. *Moppie* was the forerunner of the famous Bertram 31s, still outstandingly distinctive among all of the thousands of would-be copies afloat today. As far as I know, Dick Bertram paid Ray a fair royalty on every deep-V he sold, as long as he owned the company.

There was no question but that the deep-V was a real breakthrough in hull design, and was certainly patentable. Nelson Hartstone, who handled all of the legal hurdles on Ray's behalf, succeeded in forcing, one by one, some of the many who sought to profit by stealing the idea, to pay just royalties. Unfortunately, it came to light that a little over a year before the patent was applied for, Ray, with his usual enthusiasm, had described the new design to an enquiring writer, who later published an article about it. This constituted public disclosure, making the patent void. Ray had to pay damages to some who had been restrained by the patent. One more example of the difference between law and justice. It is interesting to speculate about just what would have happened had the legal effort been as successful as the design effort. My own opinion is that Ray would not have driven around in a Cadillac, nor indulged in other ostentatious displays of wealth, but would have gone right on cogitating, designing, and experimenting in a ceaseless effort to improve the performance of all kinds of boats.

In some respects, I was like a fish out of water selling industrial equipment. Despite my many marine activities during leisure hours, as far as work was concerned I was "on the beach." There was, however, one small exception. Our company represented, in addition to Yale & Towne fork lift trucks and other industrial equipment, the Marine Travelift. This innovative machine, designed by my classmate and good friend, Dick Stearn, revolutionized the boat hauling business. Moving out over the water with two of its widely spaced wheels on one pier, and the other two on a second pier many feet away, it could straddle a boat in the water and pick it up with two slings. Then it could deposit it anywhere in the yard without having to move any other boats. Naturally I was happy to be on the fringe of the boat business again and gave boat yards more than their share of attention.

Barnacle II, *the Greenwich 24 which went on many cruises to the Isles of Shoals from Cohasset. Photo: Ann Grinnell.*

I also arranged to man the Travelift booth at the New York Boat Show. I would walk down the aisles, surrounded by endless sailboats, to get a beer or a sandwich. There was a dismal sameness about the slick, shiny boats, almost all too wide, lacking in shear, underwater shape, or the grace that I had come to associate with good traditional designs. I could walk among them looking neither right nor left, like a loving mate walking along a line of chorus girls. One day an entirely different boat caught my eye. It was a Greenwich 24, designed by George Stadel and built by Allied Yachts. Nothing was further from my mind than buying a cruising sailboat, but the beautiful little craft was suddenly sweeping me off my feet. I talked to the Allied people and got complete specifications and prices. I was a little skeptical about the fiberglass construction, particularly the balsa sandwich construction of the decks. They introduced me to Robin Graham, the teenage boy who was in the process of sailing single-handed around the world.

He was very quiet and modest, but his words carried the conviction of one whose knowledge is based on first-hand experience and an analytical mind. The boat in which he started the voyage developed severe leaking at the deck and had to be abandoned, postponing the completion of the trip pending the delivery of a new replacement from Allied. He pointed out to me the many quarter-inch stainless steel bolts connecting the deck to the hull and gave me a section of the fiberglass sandwich. Convinced of the soundness of construction, and more than optimistic about the performance, based on eyeing the lines from all angles instead of actually sailing it, I ordered one then and there, naming it *Barnacle II*. She never disappointed me during several years of cruising from Cohasset to the Isles of Shoals (where else?), usually towing one or two kayaks and later Alden Ocean Shells. Even in the worst conditions, she always gave a feeling of solid security, and her graceful motion through the water was always a joy to experience. When I sold her to buy a lobster boat, more practical for carrying shells long distances, it was not without some moisture in the eyes. She had added considerably to my enjoyment of the years I was divorced from the boat business.

AEM in the original Alden Ocean Shell (now at Mystic Seaport) followed by Marjorie in the second one, which was later used as a plug for the first production boats made by Tillotson-Pearson. Note short oars and poor rowing strokes. Edwin Hills photo.

20 • *Birth of the Alden*

*W*hile all of our family's boats were of wood, fiberglass began to rear its head, which some would characterize as ugly. I was not prejudiced, for a change, having little knowledge of the new material. Now that I have had some experience with it, I still retain my objectivity, and although I take great pleasure in the wood out of which some of our boats are made, I am happy to accept the advantages which fiberglass offers. Just because a boat is constructed of fiberglass does not mean that it has to be a poor design. *Barnacle II* was an excellent example.

One day Dick Fisher invited me over to see a new material with which he was experimenting. It was epoxy resin. The early fiberglass boats, like most production boats today, were made with much cheaper and faster curing polyester resin. Dick had made a miniature Sea Sled for his son, Dickie, and a boat similar to a Sunfish, with a modified Sea Sled, or one-piece catamaran hull. He had shaped these boats out of Styrofoam, and covered them with fiberglass and epoxy resin. Polyester resin dissolves Styrofoam, but epoxy does not, making an ideal combination for building one-of-a-kind or experimental boats.

I could hardly believe what I saw demonstrated so conclusively. Styrofoam could be cut with an ordinary hand saw, a couple of inches or more per stroke. It could be shaped with a file or rasp, or coarse sandpaper. This process immediately captured my imagination, and I told Dick that I would procure some materials forthwith, and design and build a kayak. It would be for Douglas, who had become too old for his Rookie, but not quite ready for a 110. One part for Douglas; two parts for me.

Mark Hollingsworth, who owned a paper company, gave me a roll of heavy paper from which I unrolled a considerable length on the living room floor. I procured a long length of clear white pine to use for a batten. The usual mold loft procedure calls for driving nails in the floor to hold the batten. Since such a process would be unlikely to add to the value of the house, I had to improvise other methods. After striking in a centerline, and the half-breadth at the midship section, I rounded up the five children and instructed them each to hold the batten in both hands, spread far apart. I squinted along the resulting tentative shape of the deck at side, trying to visualize a shape full enough to allow for some flair at the bow, but sharp enough for such a narrow boat. To get it fair, I gave a series of commands, such as, "Douglas move your left hand out a little," "Lorna move your right hand in a little," "Rod, let go with your left hand, let the batten move where it wants to, and put your hand back." When I was satisfied, I drew a line along the batten, trying to avoid little fingers along the way. It was easy to make a mirror image of the line for the other side, and the shear and stem and stern profiles were done the same way, while the bottom was a straight line.

Next, I glued several blocks of Styrofoam together with epoxy to form one big solid block. Placing the paper on top of the block, I punched a series of holes through it with a pencil, spaced roughly an eighth of an inch apart, thus leaving the deck line clearly visible on the Styrofoam. Rough cutting with a hand saw was as quick and easy as I had expected, but it was difficult to avoid cutting off too much. For final fairing to the line, I used a coarse belt from a floor sander, cut and nailed to a long 2-by-8 with rounded ends and a handle. The same was done for the shear, and then I was on my own, free to improvise the shape as I saw fit, without the constraints of drawings, offsets, or templates, or preconceived ideas of what a kayak should look like. It was perhaps a little incongruous for a trained naval architect to be designing and building a boat exactly the way primitives build log canoes or pirogues out of solid logs. But all of the factors that influence performance, when once calculated and understood, are never forgotten. Besides, whether out of laziness or the impatience to see the results, learned from Ray Hunt, the idea of seeing my ideas take shape so quickly and easily appealed to me.

Meanwhile, Dick Fisher had asked me the dimensions of my new creation and decided to follow them in making his own kayak. He, however, was interested in the process of making a plug from which to make a mold, which could then produce any number of kayaks quickly and easily. He first drew the lines, using a dinner plate for round sections, and then made an upside-down plug, covered with a clear plastic, PVA, as a parting agent.

It took a lot of time to cover my Styrofoam hull with fiberglass. The neat little metering pumps which we now use to mix the epoxy and the hardener were not available. I made a little balance out of wood, with paper cups supported by thread at each end. I placed a few pennies in one cup, and a multiple number, corresponding to the mixing ratio by weight, in the other, and positioned a fulcrum point where they would balance. Then I dumped the pennies out of one cup and replaced them with the resin to balance the pennies in the other cup, finally dumping out the remaining pennies and balancing the epoxy with the hardener. This was a long process, but it served the purpose, and eventually the hull was covered with fiberglass saturated with epoxy. Then the foam deck was covered the same way, except for the small area of the cockpit.

For the cockpit, I partially hollowed out the Styrofoam, leaving a nice Styrofoam raised seat and enough foam remaining under the legs and feet to stiffen the light layup of fiberglass in the bottom. With great anticipation and excitement, we launched the new creation at the yacht club in November.

I was the first to try it out and immediately discovered to my chagrin that it was incredibly unstable, although I somehow managed to avoid capsizing. I have to point out here that in all my years of paddling or rowing narrow boats, from *Barnacle*, to canoes, to kayaks, to pirogues, to racing singles, I have never capsized, except deliberately for testing or demonstrating. The same does not apply to sailboats or white water kayaks in rapids. Douglas, who was neither a skilled nor enthusiastic swimmer, especially in the winter, tried it next and landed in the water.

Something had to be done. Once more I had made a classic error. The kayak was thirteen and one-half feet long, and only nineteen inches wide. Even though it had the flat bottom of an ocean liner, resulting in a higher metacenter than had the round-bottom white water kayaks, it was rendered excessively unstable by unduly raising the center of gravity of the paddler, who would always far outweigh the boat. I hastened to scoop out all of the remaining Styrofoam from the cockpit, and added some more fiberglass in the area, to strengthen the bottom. This lesson was not forgotten in the design of future narrow boats. Not only did the lower center of gravity make the stability tolerable, the single, strengthened, but flexible bottom proved very tough in resisting the inevitable contact with rocks and other obstructions. At the bow and stern, the fiberglass was stiffened by the Styrofoam, and was punctured several times. Repairs were difficult and added excess weight. With this experience sharply etched in memory, we were never to make a boat with an inner liner, despite the big savings in manufacturing costs. To avoid sitting on the cold bottom, we used a thin cushion of closed cell neoprene, named Armstrong Armaflex, readily available at the time at the Braintree dump, which was adjacent to the Armstrong plant.

Dick Fisher and I paddled the two boats around Cohasset waters all that winter, often breaking through skim ice. We exchanged boats back and forth, comparing various characteristics. There seemed to be agreement that while his mold was far superior for making more boats, with far less labor and wasted material, the hull shape of mine was superior.

The Fisher experiments ultimately led up to the design of the Boston Whaler. The first prototypes were shaped like the Sea Sleds of the past. The Sea Sled trapped air, spray, and solid water between the two sides of the bow, getting dynamic lift from all three. This gave it remarkable speed characteristics, the best ratio of speed to pounds of displacement per horsepower of any boat for which I had made calculations. There was one problem, however. All that trapped air went down to the propeller, causing ventilation and cavitation. Albert Hickman had solved the problem by the invention of the surface propeller. The hub of this propeller was above the bottom of the transom, and the blades hit the frothy mixture of air and water a resounding slap with each revolution. Thus the propeller blades, instead of "flying" through the solid water, getting "lift," like an airplane wing, were getting thrust by the dynamic action of rapidly hitting the mixture of water and air. I recall riding in my Aunt Sabina Bartow's Sea Sled when I was only ten years old and delighting to see the huge rooster tail thrown up by the surface propeller. A similar principle applies to the unlimited hydroplanes of today, riding on the tips of the sponsons at the bow, and held up at the stern, as well as being rapidly propelled, by the tips of the propeller blades, slapping the water at a furious rate, due to the step-up gear in place of the usual reduction gear.

The Boston Whaler was designed to be driven by an outboard motor, precluding the surface propeller solution. Dick called on his old friend and colleague, Ray Hunt, to help with the problem. Cavitation was always anathema to Ray, and he jumped at the challenge with his usual enthusiasm. I had nothing to do with the design of the Whaler, but I was a fascinated spectator as the design progressed. I recall riding in a transparent prototype, watching the air bubbles rushing by under the bottom, heading straight for the propeller. The ultimate result of these and other experiments was the original Boston Whaler, with its now familiar central hull, allowing the propeller to run in solid water.

Having finalized a most efficient and seaworthy hull shape, Dick set about working out a fiberglass and foam sandwich construction which would provide adequate flotation under almost any disastrous circumstances, but would also be as durable as his perfectionism could make it. One day he showed me several apparently perfect Whalers in the shop at his company, Sigma Instruments. Then, to my astonishment, he took a sledge hammer and swung it full force against a gleaming hull. It went right through the fiberglass into the foam core. Then, to the horror of my conservative soul, he proceeded to do the same thing to another boat. This time the sledge hammer bounced off harmlessly. The dramatic demonstration made an indelible impression on my curious mind. It confirmed my own findings about the pitfalls of foam sandwich construction. It showed the advantages of prestressing the fiberglass, a most difficult and precise process if the pressure of the expanding foam is to be sufficient to be effective, without becoming excessive enough to blow the boat, deck, and molds apart. Obviously, Dick worked many hours, destroying many expensive prototypes, developing the techniques which were to prove so successful in the countless production Whalers which followed. I consider myself privileged to have been a spectator at the development of these exceptional boats.

I did make one small contribution to the Boston Whaler success story. As sales soared, production became the primary consideration. Despite winter shipments to warmer climes, demand for Whalers, as for all small boats, was definitely seasonal. Unless production continued at a brisk rate all winter, there would never be enough boats in the summer. The problem was where to store the huge inventory required. Dick decided to build a simple pole building and store boats on end in it. I designed a crane to replace the forks on a Yale fork truck, with a cable fastened at the base, running over sheaves at the top of the crane and down to a hook. Thus, without the complication of a winch, the hook traveled twice as far as the fork carriage, and could be easily engaged in the bow fitting of a boat, lifting it up on end, and carrying it to its storage spot. We use the same system today with the Aldens, but, needless to say, no cranes or fork trucks are required for such light boats.

While Dick Fisher's experiments were leading so directly to the Whaler legend, my own experiments were apparently leading nowhere. The one and only kayak traveled many miles off Cohasset, year round. Some of the risks I took with it I would not repeat today. In controlled experiments, in the warmer water of summer, I capsized it and tried to get back in. With its small cockpit, and solid foam construction, it floated very high in the water, even if I flooded the cockpit. It was easy to right it while swimming, but very difficult to raise my entire weight over the side without capsizing it again. Furthermore, it soon became clear that in the course of struggling to get back aboard, I could lose control of the boat, and in any kind of a wind I could never swim fast enough to catch it. Therefore, in the winter, in a hard westerly, I always tied the painter around my waist. This did not solve the problem of hypothermia. Even in the summer, one can quickly use up a lot of energy trying to get back into an unsinkable boat, and this, combined with our cold northern water, and possible panic, can lead to disaster. I once witnessed a race in New Jersey where a man capsized an inner-liner boat. Though full of water, it floated high above the surface, and, try as he did repeatedly, he was unable to raise his entire body that far above the cold water. He refused help, although we could all see that his strength was diminishing rapidly. Fortunately, he was not far from shore, and was able to swim to shallow water with his boat. Knowledge and caution are all-important ingredients for safety in small boats. One element of danger, often forgotten, is hypothermia. In a struggle for survival, the body cuts down circulation to the extremities to preserve blood heat for the vital organs. This reduces power in the arms and legs, and destroys the reasoning power of the blood-starved brain. Today, I automatically try to keep a friendly shore close by to leeward (looard) when it is blowing hard, particularly in the winter, when there are few, if any, boats around, and both air and water are much colder.

I am always appalled to see novices set out in small boats, however unsinkable, oblivious of the fact that they are going with the wind away from shore, with no assurance that they will be able to make it back against the wind. Capsize, equipment failure, or hypothermia (far more threatening if the victim is wet) can militate against a safe return to shore. I have towed in more than one grateful sailboard aspirant unable to return against the wind.

I made a second kayak by the same design and construction methods as the first, longer and wider. It was fifteen feet long, and twenty-one inches wide, making it more stable and faster at full power. It had greater carrying capacity for fishing gear, picnics, and small children. It was quite effective in catching striped bass off Cohasset. I made a rudder for it, so that it could be steered with the feet, a great help while playing a big bass and trying to get the boat to head in his direction.

White water kayakers, led by the inimitable Bart Hauthaway, used to congregate at the two-way rapids under the Mill Bridge at Cohasset, for slalom competitions. Naturally, I had to try their kayaks, and they tried ours. They did not like ours because they tended to go in a straight line, and I did not like theirs because they would not go in a straight line, unless held skillfully on course with the paddle. Furthermore, because of the round, rocker bottoms, they were not as fast. The sea kayaks were far in the future.

Our good friend, Francis Hagerty, had been in the business of making racing shells. He found the competition from Pocock, who at that time built his shells in rent-free space at the University of Washington, too severe, and sold his shell business to Joe Garafulo, still building fine shells in Worcester, Massachusetts, under the name of Worcester Oar and Paddle Company. I bought all of our kayak paddles from Joe, enjoying watching his deft strokes with a plane as he shaped the Sitka spruce into beautiful spoon blades. Francis had an old unrigged eight rotting under his shop, and he let his son, Peter, and several friends paddle it around to complete destruction, amid much laughter and merriment.

He also had a single, in which he used to row off Cohasset on calm days. The single was badly in need of repair, but he was too busy to fix it. Douglas was becoming quite a skilled craftsman, having built some very fine violins, one of which was used by the first violin player of the Hingham Symphony Orchestra. Douglas and Francis made a deal whereby the former would fix up the scull, keep it in our garage, and use it whenever he wanted, and the latter could also use it as well as retain ownership. At last I had a chance to row a real racing shell, a privilege which had so far eluded me. On calm days we would bring it down to the yacht club, take turns rowing it, wash it off with fresh water, dry it, and return it to the overhead slings in the garage. Despite our best efforts, the fin was constantly being damaged, requiring continual repairs. But it provided a lot of fun and a great experience, and despite our lack of skill and training, it went much faster than our kayaks. Francis Hagerty went on to found the very successful Cohasset Colonial Furniture Company, and his passing was quite a blow to all of us. His widow, Mary, donated a trophy in his name, for the winner of the Alden race around Minot's Light. For me, it was quite nostalgic to stand on the white sand of Sandy Beach, where I had spent so much time with my children and kept my second kayak, and see almost the entire beach filled up with Aldens, lined up on the sand in front of the Hagerty house.

Unfortunately, my marriage to the former Sylvia Van Ness ended in divorce. Such an event is always a most traumatic experience for the children, at almost any age. I will always regret the pain and suffering this caused my five children, but life must go on, and unhappy memories, while not forgotten, are softened by the passage of time.

Later I married Marjorie (Dean) Burbridge, also divorced, and with four children. Life is full of coincidences, and events which seem, in retrospect, somewhat amusing. One blustery southwest day, my wife, Sylvia, and I, with Jane Cox as an additional crew, were racing home to Cohasset from the annual club cruise. Jane, being the lightest, did a great job of pumping out the constantly filling bilge, on the leeward side, while we sat on the windward rail. Ed Hills (father of Liz O'Leary, head rowing coach at Radcliffe) was leading, in a very close race, just ahead of Gregg Bemis. For a crew he had Marjorie and her husband, Herbert Burbridge, both sitting on the windward rail. We were third. The strain of the gusty wind on the sails proved to be too much for Ed Hills' mast and it collapsed. The sudden loss of the heeling force caused the boat to right itself abruptly, throwing Marjorie into the cold water. There is no way that even such a good swimmer could catch a 210 in that wind, despite the lack of mast or sail. Gregg Bemis saw the accident and immediately forfeited his now winning position in the race to go to the rescue. Inexplicably, or perhaps as a result of developing hypothermia in the icy water, Marjorie refused assistance and continued to swim, getting farther and farther from the retreating dismasted boat. When a lobsterman came along later, she was more than glad to accept a ride ashore. Meanwhile, the accident having eliminated my principal competition, I won the race and one of the few trophies I ever received. Thanks to the lobsterman, I also won, years later, a new wife.

The second kayak seemed so good that we decided to make a mold from it. Douglas undertook to perform this exacting and laborious task. The boat became a plug from which to make the mold. Making a prototype, or "one-off," out of fiberglass requires considerable sanding and filling to make it look presentable. But to make a plug this is only the beginning. The surface must be absolutely fair, with no irregularities to be repeated on all production boats. Furthermore, unless it is as shiny and smooth as a mirror, the mold cannot be released from the plug easily, and the production boats cannot be released easily from the mold. The whole process of designing a boat, making a plug, and then a mold, is an expensive and time-consuming one. Unfortunately, there are some despicable people in the boat business who take the easy way out, and use someone else's boat as a plug. This is called "splashing" and it is pure and simple robbery. A book or an article, which are only specific arrangements of common words, are easily protected by a simple copyright.

Fortunately, several states now have strict laws against "splashing" and there is a movement afoot to make it a crime nationally, protecting the creators against the robbers.

When the plug finally passed the inspection of Doug's critical eye, he made a mold from it. Our first boat from this mold was quite an adventure and a far cry from the near-perfection we achieve today. We gradually eliminated some of the bugs, one by one, and second son Charlie made several more kayaks one summer. But neither production nor sales showed promise of any kind of a viable business. Any one who wanted a kayak at that time seemed to prefer a white water or down river one.

Marjorie's mother loved to ride in any kind of a boat, but, unlike her daughter, she had no interest in taking part in its propulsion. I had taken her as a passenger in the peapod, which she enjoyed tremendously. After Marjorie and I were married, I decided to make a wider kayak in which I could take her mother as a passenger. At the same time, I decided to make a miniature kayak for Marjorie's youngest son, Dickie, five. We made the two boats at the same time, by the same process as the previous ones, doing the fiberglassing in the living room, as it was winter.

The little one, which Dickie named *Yot* was only eight feet long and nineteen inches wide. It was just right for a little boy, but quite a challenge for an adult. We found that by tying a rope around the boat over one's knees, it was possible to do an Eskimo roll, as we did in our other kayaks and Marjorie's white water kayaks made by Bart Hauthaway. We used to teach people this roll in our heated swimming pool. I never had any trouble rolling over. It was only in coming back that I was not always successful, despite considerable practice. I once capsized in the rapids and extricated myself from the boat without getting my hair wet, having such a compelling desire to avoid being carried rapidly downstream, upside down, among all the rocks, that reflex action took over, and released me, with bloody thighs, before my conscious mind had a chance to figure out a solution. We took many kayak trips, Marjorie always in a white water one, which she preferred; Dickie in his little kayak; and I and any others in our boats.

The other new boat, which we named *Dot*, for Marjorie's mother, Dorothy Dean, took shape as I carefully sanded away excess Styrofoam, constantly sighting along the emerging hull in an effort to create a shape which would harmonize with its element. It was thirteen and one-half feet long, and twenty-four inches wide, to provide just enough displacement for two small people, with little to spare. I made the bow very sharp below the waterline, which had a lot of reverse curve, or hollow, like a good ship. With a wide foredeck, this allowed plenty of flare. I made the mistake of shaping the stern in a somewhat similar way, ignoring the fact that the function of entering the water is different from that of leaving it.

Sad to say, Marjorie's mother died before the *Dot* was launched. The boat came to life as its namesake was leaving it and soon began to undergo all kinds of tests. The bow turned out to be even better than I had expected. It knifed into waves and threw solid water and spray out to the sides, lifting the bow up over a wave and landing with a satisfying muffled whoosh on the next one. It did not pound as much as the other kayaks, even though it was wider. The bow wave in still water folded over far aft of the stem, indicating little resistance for a boat of such dimensions.

The stern, however, was another matter. It dragged down far below the indicated hull speed, so that its performance was little better than a white water kayak. Speed is always a relative matter. We are used to wide variations such as between walking at three miles per hour and running at fifteen, or driving a car which will far exceed the usual speed limit of sixty-five. Then we fly in a jet at over five hundred and watch others go twice that, and talk casually about rockets going twenty-five thousand. Coming down to the ancient world of hand-propelled boats, differences in speed seem almost insignificant between a wide, heavy skiff at three miles per hour and an eight-oared shell at thirteen. But these slight differences are very noticeable, and a kayak which performs poorly for its length is hard to accept.

As I paddled and observed the *Dot* for many months, I became more and more disgusted with the design of the stern, realizing just how it was detracting from the exceptional performance of the bow. One day, on the spur of the moment, I took a saw and cut the stern off, being careful not to have a straight cut which would make it difficult to attach a new stern without an undesirable concentration of stress. I then took a stern made out of our mold and joined it to the bow, not without some difficulty in fairing together the unmatched parts.

The completed hull was sixteen feet long, longer than any of our previous kayaks. As I stood contemplating the result of the crude graft, it suddenly occurred to me that this boat could be rowed with a sliding seat, like a shell, a concept I had dreamed of but never followed through. Old Town Canoe Company made a nice portable sliding seat rig out of mahogany for use in their canoes. The seat had wheels attached to fixed axles under it, and the track was about the same length as that of a racing shell. They had failed to take into account the fact that racing shells have rolling axles to reduce friction, allowing the seat to travel further than the length of the track. Nevertheless, with reckless abandon of my conservative financial tendencies, I hastily purchased one of these units, along with a pair of their seven-foot-six-inch spoon oars, with leather sleeves and buttons on their round looms.

When I first tried rowing the unusual combination, I felt like shouting "Eureka." The sensation was nothing short of breathtaking. The power of my legs, always lying idly in the bottom of a kayak, was free at last to more than double the available horsepower. The boat, with its new, more efficient stern, was able to utilize the additional power without having the squatting or dragging effect of a displacement boat when driven too hard. Despite the limitations of the rig, the combination seemed sensational to me. Marjorie, who had always viewed our kayaks with a jaundiced eye, was immediately taken with the new creation and wanted one too. I generously offered to buy the materials for a duplicate for her, providing she helped with the construction. She immediately jumped at the opportunity, with her usual enthusiasm.

First I faired up the joint of the two dissimilar parts of my boat, using clay for the largest gaps at the deck and topsides, the bottom being already reasonably fair and smooth. Next we used the hull as a male mold and built the second boat around it. I then designed built-in tracks, longer than those of the Old Town Rig, made out of round stainless steel tubing, right in the bottom of the boat. I was concerned about keeping the center of gravity as low as possible. I made riggers out of fiberglass, secured through reinforced holes in the deck, so that they were easily removable. The seat was made of plywood, covered with the foam rubber which came from the Braintree dump. The stretchers (footrests) were made of wood, attached to the bottom and the deck with fiberglass, so they were not adjustable. The seat was very low and not attached to the track in any way, so that it could take off at the slightest provocation. I made some oars with spruce looms and leather buttons, and fiberglass spoon blades. The new boat had a molded fiberglass backrest in the bow, pivoted so that the rower could lean against it to rest, or fish, or have a beer, or it could be rotated around for a passenger in the bow to lean against. It could also be

Marjorie rowing a more recent Alden. She won a good many Alden races, including the women-over-forty division in two national championships and all the Alden races on the Charles which she entered. Photo: Ann Grinnell.

used for kayaking, stern first. But kayaking gradually diminished, especially in the winter, when the better exercise of rowing served to keep one warmer, and the extra power was a welcome safety factor in sudden high winds.

With the two boats, Marjorie and I could row happily along the coast of Cohasset and gunkhole in all the creeks and inlets. It was a little disappointing to find that when we stopped to talk to friends in sailboats at their moorings, none even noticed that we were no longer in kayaks. We did not care, for we had no intention of making any more rowing shells. We were satisfied to have just the two unique boats for ourselves.

With most of our children grown up and self-supporting, Marjorie persuaded me that it was no longer necessary to endure the frustrations of trying to sell fork trucks for a dying company. Consequently, in 1970, I accepted a job with the John Alden Company in Boston, and left the world of big business forever. My job was not connected with design at all, but brokerage and marine insurance. It was great to be back in the boat business and apply myself to the task of becoming familiar with all that had taken place in the twenty-three years I had been away from it. I had to hit the books once more to pass the insurance exam. We had listings of many fine boats for sale, mostly wood sailboats. There were several Concordias which I considered exceptional bargains at sixteen to twenty thousand dollars, but I never succeeded in selling any. Mr. Joe Plumb, of the tool company, had commissioned a beautiful eighty-two foot schooner, designed by Walter McGinnis and built by Quincy Adams Yacht Yard. I had first seen her at Fairhaven Marine when I was selling Marine Travelifts . It was love at first sight, and I went on a tour of the entire boat, escorted by Captain Miller, who sailed year round with Mr. Plumb. She had been launched as *Cecelia J.*, but changed to *Dorothy G* in accord with a change in wives, the second, whether by plan or happenstance, having the same number of letters in her name as the first. When Mr. Plumb died, his estate put the boat up for sale, listing her with John Alden. I was thrilled at the chance to sell this magnificent vessel and described her in glowing terms to anyone who might be interested, as well as many who were not. But my efforts were all in vain. She was sold to a man named Shippers from the Netherlands, and sailed across the ocean by Captain Miller with the new owner and other crew. Captain and boat were in their glory as they ran easily through the heavy weather for which she was so ably designed. The new owner, however, was more than frightened, and as soon as he reached terra firma, put her up for sale. She was purchased by Prince Ranier and his Princess, the former Grace Kelly, daughter and sister of two of America's most famous scullers. They used her mostly for receptions at the mooring, and I concluded that I would hear little more of the *Dorothy G.* How wrong I was!

One of the nuisances yacht brokers have to endure is the typical ne'er-do-well who has saved up four or five thousand dollars and wants to purchase a large schooner to sail around the world. One must always be polite, but it does waste time. One day I was alone in the office, trying to finish up some work in time for a late lunch. I became aware of someone entering the outer door, and talking to the receptionist. Presently she came into my office and said that the man was interested in a boat to sail around the world. I groaned inwardly, but I had no choice but to have her send him in. He extended a huge muscular hand in greeting, and announced, "My name is Johnson, Irving Johnson." I was overwhelmed at being face to face with one of the greatest of all sailors, about whose many adventures all over the world in square riggers and his own famous *Yankees* I had read so much. It turned out that he was looking for a boat for a friend, and at lunch, after showing him what we had that might be suitable, I listened to a yarn about one of his trips which still seems unreal to me. He was in a canal in Venice, in the second *Yankee*, tied up to a dock, about as safe and snug a position as could be imagined. It was evening, and he and his wife and another couple were down below enjoying a quiet evening. Suddenly, for no reason, he got up, went up on deck, and doubled all the dock lines. Shortly thereafter, a tornado struck without warning, breaking loose and damaging many boats, but not *Yankee.*. He must have felt the drop in pressure, familiar only to one long experienced in the inscrutable vagaries of the weather.

I had not been at the Alden Company long before I began to find out about the far-flung enterprises of the owner, Neil Tillotson. He had purchased Commercial Wharf and Lewis Wharf for a very low price, and later sold both at a tremendous profit, retaining space on the former for the Alden offices and his penthouse above. He traveled all over the world and spent most of the rest of his time at his home at The Balsams, in Dixville Notch, New Hampshire. We always knew when he was in Boston, for the first thing in the morning there would be executives of big companies and others waiting to see him. For all his financial acumen, he was, and still is, very modest, kind, and considerate, the very opposite of the stereotype rapacious business tycoon. He once spent a good fifteen minutes explaining to me his admiration for, and appreciation of, janitors. He liked to form partnerships with promising entrepreneurs, each having exactly half the stock, so that there was no controlling interest.

One such partner was Everett Pearson. He and his cousin Clint had founded the Pearson Company, probably the first really successful manufacturer of fiberglass auxiliary sailboats. After selling the company to Grumman Aircraft, Clint started the Bristol company, and Everett went into various fiberglass fabrications, eventually becoming a partner of Neil Tillotson in the now very successful boat-building firm of Tillotson-Pearson, Incorporated. I soon met Everett Pearson and immediately developed a great admiration and respect for him. He is a brilliant executive, charismatic, dynamic, full of enthusiasm, bubbling over with new and creative ideas, but never pompous or unkind to lesser individuals, or inclined to become involved in petty personality conflicts. Everett is the antithesis of many of the essentially insincere and conniving company politicians I had encountered in business.

When he expressed an interest in manufacturing our little rowing shells, my thinking began to change abruptly. I was sure that Everett, with his vast experience in fiberglass construction, his inquisitive mind ever seeking new materials and methods, and his efficient factory organization, could build all the boats we might require, to the highest standards of quality. The problem was, would anyone want to buy them? The fact that they seemed ideal to Marjorie and me was no guarantee that anyone else would feel the same way.

One possible obstacle was removed when Neil Tillotson gave his blessing to the project. With advancing years, he seems to get younger all the time, as far as undertaking new ventures. He wisely made the stipulation that if we went ahead, I would have to pay for the molds and tooling and guarantee the sale of twenty boats. This confronted me with a difficult decision. My carefully hoarded savings would be gone forever, in exchange for some worthless tooling if the project failed. I figured that I could sell one boat to my generous mother and a couple more to devil-may-care friends, but then I would be stuck with seventeen white elephants.

I tried to analyze the situation objectively, calling on my meager knowledge of the entire rowing scene at the time. As I saw it, there were two distinct worlds of rowing. One included the various optimum boats for unlimited competition. The big boats, in which each rower handles one twelve-foot oar (called a sweep), were the pair, with and without a coxswain; the four, with and without a coxswain; and the eight with a coxswain. The sculling boats, in which each rower handles two oars, or sculls, approximately nine-feet-nine-inches long, were the single, the double, the quad, and the almost extinct octopede. The dimensions, shapes, and construction of all of these boats had evolved over the years in an effort to get the maximum speed from their human propulsion systems over a short course on perfectly smooth water. Use of all of these boats was limited almost entirely to a few Ivy League schools and colleges, and exclusive clubs, some of which to this day do not welcome the fair sex. Americans seemed to retain a certain snobbishness about rowing, possibly derived from their former rulers in England. Although exercise was beginning to be recognized as a significant factor in health, the one form now widely acclaimed as the best of all, rowing with a sliding seat, seemed to be a secret jealously guarded by its elitist practitioners.

There is a story, for which I cannot guarantee the veracity, of a young man from the Midwest who went to Harvard. Upon his graduation and return home, his friends had a party to celebrate. They asked him if he thought the Easterners were snobby. "No," he answered, "I rowed on the varsity crew for three years, and by my senior year everyone in the boat had spoken to me, except number 7."

There had been widespread belief that in order to learn to scull, one had to begin in a wide, heavy wherry, such as I had enjoyed rowing at Kent. Having attained a certain degree of proficiency in it, one advanced to the wide comp, which looked like a racing scull to the uninitiated, but was considerably wider and slightly shorter. From that, one graduated to the narrow comp, a similar but more challenging practice boat. Only after mastering the narrow comp could one venture forth in a true racing scull. But the British and Germans had already proved that all these steps were unnecessary, and sculling schools in America were soon to prove that almost anyone could learn to scull within a week without having to buy so many boats. Thus the demand for a series of practice boats approaching a racing shell design was already falling off before I designed the Alden. The question was, would any of the sliding seat rowing fraternity have any use for a boat which was not like a racing shell at all, except that it was rowed with a sliding seat?

The other world of rowing included all of the people who, like myself, had grown up with a love of rowing in peapods, dories, White-halls, Adirondack guide boats, Saint Lawrence skiffs, and other sea-worthy, stable, and versatile boats with fixed seats. These people were inclined to view with scorn the snobby landlubbers who required per-fectly flat, protected water to pursue their narrow, single-purpose sport. On the other hand, hardly anyone from the racing world had any use for the slow, heavy, fixed-seat boats of the other world, or their plodding, fishing, picnicking, bird-watching adherents.

Would the people of both worlds look with scorn on our little boats, which really were not a part of either one? Certainly we could not compete with the racing shells for speed. Even if we redesigned for greater length and narrower beam we would not have a boat which would be eligible or qualified to race against racing sculls. And how could we expect someone used to carrying three or more people in choppy water to settle for something that could carry only one in addition to the rower, and that only in comparatively calm water? Was there a possible compromise between the two worlds of rowing? Could we find enthusiasts from both worlds willing to give up their precon-ceived ideas and prejudices, and give up some of their customary boat qualifications in exchange for others? If we could not, a lot of time, money, and effort would be wasted. If we could, we would be starting an entirely new sport.

I reasoned that while the racing people might scoff at our compar-atively slower boats, there were many things that some of them might want to do which would be difficult or impossible to perform in a racing shell. Although a young competitive sculler, aspiring for national or international honors, would be repulsed by the thought of carrying a child with him, a few years later, matrimony, paternity, and the physical deterioration of stressful mental work without exercise might alter his thinking. Others might relish the opportunity of rowing wherever water, rough or smooth, was within driving distance. Still others might be enticed by durability, stowability, or the safety of stability in cold water. As for the people in the other world of rowing, I was to learn eventually that most people buy boats primarily because they like the way they look and go through the water. There are exceptions, such as the owners of large power boats which seem to offer more and more shoreside amenities, speed at frightful cost in fuel, space for more and more guests, and last, but not, I suspect, least, the opportunity for the ostentatious display of wealth to the envy of all who behold them.

In addition to all of the other advantages of a canoe, there is the fact that it glides silently through the water like no other boat. Dedicated canoeists even disdain the use of the more efficient double-bladed paddle of a kayak. Few kayakers are lured by the advantages of other self-propelled boats. Proponents of Whitehalls love their wine-glass sterns, regardless of the fact that double-enders are faster (mother nature is too smart to mistake a narrow skeg in the water for the gradually decreasing displacement, at any loading, of a double-ender). To each his own, and woe betide anyone who projects sales figures on the premise that everyone will switch to a boat which offers specific advantages, such as speed. Variety is the spice of life, and it is a great thing that so many types of self-propelled boats thrive today. The only sad part is that so many people, particularly children, are lured away from all self-propelled boats by the easier but less rewarding amusement provided by power boats and their shoreside accomplices, such as television and motor bikes. While adopting a live-and-let-live attitude toward all other self-propelled boats, the question remained, would any of their adherents be interested in a new type of boat incorporating some, but not all, of the characteristics they seek, and offering others which might, or might not, prove more valuable? It was a gamble and also a challenge.

I have always liked challenges and have never hesitated to be out of step with the regiment. In fact, I rather enjoy being on the unpopular side of an issue if I think I am right. I decided to risk everything on my ideas and went ahead. Mr. Tillotson very kindly agreed to let us use Mr. Alden's prestigious name for the new boats. I had met John Alden, whom I admired greatly, but he had died long before I designed the Alden Ocean Shell. As Neil Tillotson pointed out, he owned the Alden name and it was due to the generosity of this fine gentleman that we were able to introduce our unique boats under such a famous name.

With the Alden name, coupled with the fact that it was a truly revolutionary boat and not just another look-alike, almost all of the major boating magazines gave us editorial recognition. In addition, we used paid advertising, the cost of which was quite a shock. We emphasized the exercise value of rowing, as we have continued to do to this day, using eye-catching phrases such as "Do you jiggle when you jog?" "Tennis not your racket?" and "Golf not your bag?"

We introduced the boat officially at the Boston Boat Show in 1971. Everett Pearson had taken Marjorie's boat, *Marj's Barge*, and used it as a plug for the mold. His people did an amazing job of smoothing up the rough hull, and when I saw the first production boat as I picked it up to take to the boat show, I was astonished to see how shiny and perfect it was compared to our crude efforts with its predecessors. The new boat attracted a great deal of attention at the show, and it seemed that everyone wanted to try it out. I scheduled any number of demonstrations for the following Monday, in front of our offices on Commercial Wharf. I feared pandemonium when all those people showed up, interrupting my work in brokerage and insurance, so I enlisted my nephew, Richard Martin, to come in and help out. He sat there all day long reading boating magazines. Not one person showed up.

Later on, many people came to try out the new toy. They had to climb down a slimy ladder to a big camel where I kept my boat. Then, after a brief demonstration and instruction, they set out into Boston Harbor. Tugs went by close to the end of the wharf, where their approach could not be seen, leaving huge wakes. No one swamped or capsized, however, for which I was grateful. One of Boston's biggest sewers spewed tons of raw sewage right in front of the pier, however, detracting somewhat from the ambience of a first row in a strange boat. The miracle of Massachusetts is that now, eighteen years later, the same sewage issues forth from the same place.

One man flew up from New Jersey in a private plane, cheerfully putting up with the polluted water to try out the new shell, which he ordered immediately after washing his hands. Another man saw me rowing while he was looking out of the window of his office, high above the streets of Boston. He watched to see where I landed and then promptly walked down and bought one. Once when I was enjoying a row at noon, a man working at the top of one of the new highrise buildings began throwing heavy objects down at me. I probably broke several records getting out of range, noting one more reason why Boston Harbor was not the ideal place to teach rowing to novices.

With the increasing interest in the shells, I became more and more excited and optimistic about the venture. I found myself becoming disappointed when a telephone call turned out to be about brokerage or insurance.

One day a notice in a post office caught my eye. It was for one of the ten most wanted criminals still at large. Nothing unusual about that, except that this particular felon, who was said to be armed and dangerous, had a consuming interest in sliding seat rowing and might be expected to seek opportunities for participating in his favorite sport. I took a copy of the notice and hung it over my desk, adding the notation that here was a prospect for an Alden Ocean Shell. This little joke suddenly turned quite serious when a man who appeared to resemble the picture entered the outer office when I was alone. Realizing that if he came in and saw the notice he would know that I knew all about him, and that there is an efficient way to take care of people who know too much, I hastened to tear down the notice as surreptitiously as possible. Fortunately, it was a false alarm, but I never replaced the notice.

Brokerage was not working out to my satisfaction, for various reasons. Leaving the Alden Company solved several problems. The boats were still made by Tillotson-Pearson. Mr. Tillotson said we could continue to use the Alden name. Cohasset was far better for demonstrating the still novel boats, and commuting was eliminated forever. The problem was, how could the spasmodic sales of these little boats support our dwindling but still extensive family? We were encouraged one day when Pen Higginson, a leading supporter of the Friends of Harvard Rowing, called up. Marjorie was in the office in our Cohasset house, which doubled as a laundry, and answered the phone. After a brief introduction, the conversation went something like this:

PH: "I want to buy two of your shells."
MDM: "Would you like to try one out?"
PH: "No, I want to buy two of them."
MDM: "Wouldn't you like to see one first?"
PH: "No, I just want to buy two of them."
MDM: "Why do you want to buy two of them sight unseen?"
PH: "Harry Parker said I should buy them."

The great rowing coach at Harvard had not only prevailed upon me to equip the boats with full-size racing oars, which in retrospect was a most fortuitous development, and been instrumental in the first purchase of Aldens at the Union Boat Club, he also highly recommended them to others. Other coaches, many of whom I had never met, were also beginning to recommend our boats for older people, recreational rowers, and even competing oarsmen for practice in the off-season, when water is cold or the usual rowing situation is not available.

As expected, Cohasset proved to be a far better place to teach rowing and demonstrate than Boston, and more and more people found their way there to try out the new sport. I clearly remember a doctor from Rhode Island who arrived with his somewhat domineering wife. She immediately started to admonish him not to buy that boat, before he had even seen it. He was able to go out in it only after assuring her that he was only going to try it out. As he returned to the float, I detected the faint glimmer of a smile of satisfaction creeping across his face. In between further commands not to buy the boat, he asked me a few questions about it, standing on the porch of the yacht club. Leaning against a flagpole, he idly put one hand in his pocket. "Take your hand out of your pocket. You're not going to buy that boat," came a final command from his loving spouse. I often wondered how she might react to a medical report attributing his possible sudden death to stress and lack of exercise. Fortunately, in later years, I found many thoughtful and caring wives surprising their spouses at Christmas or birthday with the Alden they wanted but refrained from buying. And recently it is increasingly the other way around.

In talking to prospects, one question kept recurring: Why was it called an ocean shell? I explained that we rowed them regularly in the open ocean, as that is what they were designed for. Often this explanation would be greeted with, "That may be all right where you are, but where I live the wind blows pretty hard." There did not seem to be any answer to this objection, until one day I was out rowing in tropical storm Doria. The wind was clocked at a nearby weather station at over 80 knots, making it a hurricane, but in Cohasset Harbor, an anemometer on a Grand Banks 42 registered only 61 knots. Nevertheless, it was a good opportunity to compare performance of the Alden with the peapod, and, besides, it was fun to test the power of the wind in the comparative safety of the harbor. I suddenly thought that if I could get a picture of this, it would answer a lot of questions. I rowed ashore quickly and ran

AEM in 62 m.p.h. winds of tropical storm Doria. After an hour this early version of the Alden had two cupfuls of water in the cockpit. Note fiberglass riggers connected to the deck and pivoted backrest for a passenger in the bow. Photo: Ann Grinnell.

around frantically looking for Ann Grinnell, a talented professional photographer and good friend, while constantly checking the wind, which had already started to diminish and threatened to die out altogether before I could have it captured on film. Ann lost no time in getting down to the yacht club with her equipment; I reembarked in the Alden; and we got the shot which was used in our brochure for many years. Bailing out the couple of cupfuls of water which had entered the cockpit, I reflected that, while the photo would serve as a dramatic proof of the boat's capabilities, we should never recommend that a novice venture out in such extreme conditions. Caution is always the watchword, and Davy Jones always has room for more people who insist on defying the elements while neglecting to consider all of the facets of the situation.

It was most gratifying to see people "turn on " to rowing in our boats, and each sale was an exciting event. But, realistically, from an

Two children in the spacious cockpit of an Alden Single. Photo: Marjorie Martin.

economic standpoint, sales were far from reassuring. I had never regarded the boats as a road to riches and never set as a goal the accumulation of wealth. At the same time, I was not unaware that just a nominal standard of living would require some regular and dependable income. There would be long, hard winters, with little boating activity. Some other job appeared to be a necessity. Marjorie, however, was more optimistic. She reasoned that whenever I went cruising, I always went to the Isles of Shoals, like a salmon returning to its birthplace. Why not move to Kittery Point, where we would never be more than a few miles from the beloved islands? Living expenses would be less, and, although far removed from the major job opportunities, I could always go back to lobstering (on the more commercial basis which would meet with Admiral Rock's approval). Half convinced, I dropped a few hints about possibly renting a house in Kittery Point. Within a week, we were sipping sherry in the huge living room of Storer Decatur, a former 210 owner, descendent of Stephen Decatur's family, and also a direct descendent, on his mother's side, of George Washington's secretary, Tobias Lear. Storer was a delightful man, with a great sense of humor and a most engaging manner, especially when describing events of the past in a voice containing all the echoes of history. He had a house with ten bedrooms, which he was anxious to rent to us for a nominal fee. When he later led us through the house, I paid little attention to the antiquated kitchen and the numerous other rooms, but then we walked with him down to the old stone dock which went with the house. George Washington had landed there to attend services in the nearby Congregational church, and Admiral Farragut had broken his nose in the process of landing there to visit the Decaturs, possibly following a tot of rum on board his ship. Many of the big stones had been surreptitiously removed to build a house, but I could see that enough remained to serve our purposes. My mind was made up then and there, and, Marjorie being similarly inclined, the deal was concluded by a handshake.

It happened, whether by coincidence or design (my design, as accusers claim), that the move from Cohasset to Maine was scheduled for the same time as our first venture to the In-The-Water Boat Show at Annapolis. Marjorie handled the entire moving operation with her usual good natured efficiency, while I set out for Annapolis with her sons Rusty and Dick. The former built a small platform out of scrap wood, which he nailed to a bulkhead. This served admirably as a dock from which interested people could set out in the Alden, after brief instructions. The interest we generated was quite gratifying, as numerous people stood in line to try out the strange new boat. Only a few actually purchased a boat, but the exposure was initiating the long process of educating the boating public about the pleasures and health benefits of sliding seat rowing in a boat which neither swamped nor capsized in the sometimes turbulent waters of Annapolis.

Nature's needs were met by portable facilities marked "Men" and "Women," brought in on pallets by an outside contractor. After we had loaded our car with the boats, signs, literature, and other paraphernalia for the long trip to Kittery Point, I decided to take advantage of the opportunity to make a final trip to one of the units marked "Men." While there, I could hear fork trucks, not Yale, scurrying about, picking up crates and boxes from various exhibits. I did not pay much attention to the proceedings, being otherwise occupied, until I heard Dick shout frantically, "Don't take that one, my father's in there." Attending to the needs of nature ended abruptly. Thus the first of nineteen Annapolis Boat Shows ended for us.

*A young lady easily carrying an Alden Single with the Oarmaster removed.
Photo: unknown.*

Kittery Point seemed refreshingly quiet and peaceful after Cohasset. We spent many hours down at the old stone dock, where I soon built some wood steps and an outhaul, the better to access an Alden, at a modest investment of $36. The water was clearer and colder than at Cohasset, and there was no shortage of interesting creeks, coves, and islands, in addition to the wide Piscataqua River and the open ocean beyond. We led lazy, relaxed lives, readily fitting in with the fishermen and other residents who had already discovered the pleasures of a small town. Unfortunately, this ambience was not to last. More and more people from the cities gradually but relentlessly moved in, bringing money to push up real estate values and property taxes, and the frantic pursuit of entertainment, which many of them were trying to escape. We were guilty of the same thing, in a way, as our initially silent phone began to ring, and the boat business, almost imperceptibly, began to expand. It takes a sound philosophy and determination to save time out of each day for calm reflection, watching the tide come in and enjoying all that nature has to offer, far from the madding crowd. Hopefully, I will never be carried away by the prospect of financial success and will continue to be grateful for the many other blessings life has to offer, ever mindful of my own horse theory, which follows:

I am the last one to qualify to pontificate about horses, having never spent more than thirty or forty-five seconds seated on one of the most docile of the species. However, I understand that a horse must have something to eat to avoid death by starvation. But if you put a horse in a room full of oats, he will eat continuously until he dies, or so I am told. In the modern world, man's food and other necessities are easily acquired in exchange for money. The problem is in acquiring the money. But here in the United States, today, the opportunities for making money are virtually limitless, particularly if morality and ethics are not allowed to interfere. All too many pursue the almighty dollar relentlessly to the exclusion of everything else. The more they have, the more they want, and the less time they spend understanding and appreciating the deeper values in life. As it must to all of us, death comes to take them away, and there is no opportunity to turn their money into traveler's checks, and take it with them. It is as though they had been to a party and spent the whole time stashing food and drink behind a curtain, only to find the party ending before they have eaten or drunk anything, or enjoyed the company of the other guests.

One of the many people who came to Kittery Point to try our boats was Bill Trafton. He arrived while two of my granddaughters, Cheryl and Jill Perry, aged 5 and 3, respectively, were visiting us. After introductions we all walked down to the dock. Bill walked with a slight limp, barely perceptible. I pulled the Alden on the outhaul in to the steps, whereupon Bill calmly removed a prosthesis, including shoe and sock, and set it down at the top of the steps. I thought the girls' eyes were going to pop right out of their heads, but Bill explained the situation most objectively and to their complete satisfaction. He had no trouble handling the boat and rowed in many a race, including the grueling Isles of Shoals one year when a sudden blow made it quite choppy.

The first year ended with total sales of not the twenty for which I was obligated, but one hundred and sixty-five. The Alden Ocean Shell was on its way.

AEM and Marjorie in the prototype of the Alden Double. After extensive testing it became the plug from which the mold for production boats was made. Photo: Edwin Hills.

21 • *The Double*

as we began to talk to more and more people about rowing, it became evident that there was considerable interest in a double shell. We had to consider the pros and cons of making such a boat, and, if so, what characteristics it should have. As a starting point, we turned to the racing double scull. A fragile craft, about thirty-two feet long and sixteen inches wide, its dimensions had to be close to the optimum for its assigned duty. Years of racing, all over the world, gradually determined what variations increased speed, and what did not. A longer boat would operate at a lower speed-length ratio, reducing residual resistance, but it was already long enough to minimize this type of resistance at the maximum power output of two humans. More length would increase wetted surface, and hence frictional resistance. Less length and more beam would decrease wetted area and frictional resistance, but residual resistance would increase at a greater rate. For speed in flat water, the king on the hill was already there, and the only way for us to compete for this qualification would be to build a similar racing shell.

Whatever we did, other than making a true racing double, we would be sacrificing speed. If we were to sacrifice speed, we would have to offer as many other desirable characteristics as possible if we wanted to have an acceptable boat. We decided to cut the length almost in half in order to gain two advantages which we considered of primary importance. The first is seaworthiness. While most people can readily grasp the elementary fact that length increases speed potential, it is not always so easy to understand how adversely it affects seaworthiness. For an easy demonstration, get a two-by-four about five feet long, and cut a foot off one end. Put the short piece in some water that has little waves in it. You will see that the wood bobs up and down on the waves without getting wet on the top. If you push it slowly through the waves, it still rides up over them, despite the fact that it has the worst possible bow design. Now take the longer piece, and repeat the process. You will see that the increased length alone inhibits the lifting of the bow, and the smallest waves readily wash over it. Our proposed double could not be considered at all seaworthy if the slightest waves washed up over the bow. Furthermore, with two people rowing in a double, there is a lot more inertia to inhibit pitching. If they were sitting side by side, pitching would be facilitated, and there would be less tendency to bury the bow, but there is no way that a double shell could be designed that way, for obvious reasons. So a shorter length and greater beam was indicated for seaworthiness.

A second consideration was portability and stowability. A 32-foot boat would not fit in any garage, and would be awkward to carry on a car, particularly a compact one. The more overhang, the more chance of damage. Our conception of a recreational boat had to include easy stowing and carrying, for few owners would have the boathouse and float of the average club or other rowing organization. And a recreational shell taking up as much space as a racing shell in an already overcrowded boathouse would not be likely to be popular.

Another problem illustrates the difference between a racing shell and a recreational shell. With the former, two rowers get together, either on the spur of the moment, or as a racing team, and take out a double from a boathouse. If one is not there for any reason, the other merely goes out in a single. With individual ownership of only one boat, this is not possible. Rowing a racing double as a single from either the bow or stroke position is not practical, to say the least. Furthermore, while idle passengers are not welcome in racing shells, there is no reason why recreational rowers should not be accompanied by non-rowing companions. Our built-in rowing rigging as used in the Alden single was no more adaptable for such variations as the rigging of a racing shell. The question inevitably arose: if it can't do things which are impossible in a racing boat, why not get the higher speed racing scull? We agonized over this problem for a long time before deciding that we would have to design an easily removable, self-contained, portable rowing apparatus in order to have a viable double. Designing such a unit presented not one but many problems which at first seemed to defy any solution. Solving one only introduced others. But, still firmly believing that there is no such thing as a problem impossible to solve, we went doggedly on, trying first one approach and then another, convinced that without what became known as the Oarmaster, the double would never be as versatile as we thought it had to be.

In retrospect, the problem with the double was a blessing in disguise. The self-contained Oarmaster, incorporating all the rowing rigging in one easily portable unit, not only made it possible to convert the double from single to double or single with passenger in seconds, it made the hull much lighter and easier to carry or stow in limited space. Furthermore, since all of the rowing stresses were confined to the rugged metal structure, the problems we had been having with the riggers and stretchers eventually pulling out of the fragile fiberglass of the deck on the single were eliminated once and for all before they arose on the double. Using the same Oarmaster in the single was so logical it is surprising it took us so long to make the decision to convert that now popular boat to its use. We initiated a unique program whereby we bought back the original seats and fiberglass (later aluminum) riggers from any owner wishing to upgrade an older boat to employ the Oarmaster. We used the returned parts to supply other owners of the older boats with free replacements of parts lost or broken. We tried to design all of the many high-tech improvements we made on the Oarmasters over the years to be compatible with the older models, so that owners could upgrade their rowing equipment at modest cost, and race on even terms with the owners of the very latest.

Having settled on the dimensions of the double and designed the Oarmasters for it, it was time to design the boat itself and build a prototype. By using the tried and true Styrofoam method, design and construction could take place concurrently. This was just as well, for suddenly time was becoming critical. It was fall, and winter was just around the corner, and many of the forthcoming operations would be difficult if not impossible in cold weather. The Decatur house had a large barn, but it was completely uninsulated and unheated, militating against the use of epoxy resin. To make matters worse, I was scheduled to go into the hospital to part company with a gall bladder. (The operation was not a success; people still said I had a lot of gall.)

Marjorie helped me glue the blocks of Styrofoam together and cut out the shear and deck at side lines. Then the final shaping began. I lamented the fact that the bow had to be so full, but it had to have the displacement to carry the expected weight up over waves. I pondered sanding off a little more here or there, knowing all the factors to be considered in the final compromise of conflicting desirable characteristics. The process took longer than I would have wished, and it was getting too cold to use epoxy in the barn. Thanks to Marjorie's good nature, we brought the boat in to the dining room table without any disturbance of the domestic tranquility and completed the fiberglassing in that unlikely location.

The schedule of events following construction was as closely timed as a shuttle launching. First, we had to test it with two rowers, one rower, and one rower with a passenger, hoping to be able to find some rough water as well as smooth. If the tests proved satisfactory, we would take pictures of it for literature and advertising. Then we would take it to Harvard for Harry Parker and Lloyd Dahman to try it. Finally, we would take it down to Everett Pearson to use as a plug for the production mold, after which I would check in for my appointment at the hospital.

The tests went well, and I was generally satisfied with the design. The day we took it to Harvard a northeast storm was raging, with high winds and heavy rain. It was a Saturday, and a football game was scheduled for that afternoon. When we arrived at the Newell Boathouse, there were crowds of football enthusiasts seeking shelter on the porch. They had set up their picnics, many including tablecloths, candles, and wine, their spirits undaunted by the conditions beyond the roof. I couldn't help thinking "There will always be a Harvard." We had the boat rigged for two pairs of nine-foot-nine-inch oars, which we were using more and more by this time.

Harry and Lloyd never hesitated about taking the boat out, despite the conditions. They had both performed the remarkable, to me, feat of rowing out to the Shoals and back in racing singles. Harry sometimes rowed across the Piscataqua River to Kittery, defying the fierce current and attendant whirlpools, which are so threatening to narrow boats. I remember talking to him one day during a pause in our respective rowing trips, when, a few minutes after he headed back across the river to New Castle, I landed a forty-pound striped bass. If anyone could duplicate that in a racing scull, it would be Harry Parker.

As I watched the two husky oarsmen giving a power ten to the new double, wave making was readily apparent, dramatically illustrating the limited speed potential as compared to a double scull. I noticed the same thing later when Tiff Wood and Charlie Altekruse put on an exhibition quarter-mile sprint race in two Alden singles. I had some doubts about the acceptance of our boats by the rowing fraternity and soon found several members of that august group judging our boats on the basis of how closely they resembled racing shells. By this criterion alone they fell short. I thought that Harry Parker recognized their other attributes from the start and understood what we were trying to do. Proof came after they landed and ordered a double for the Union Boat Club then and there, even though we could give them no idea of price or delivery.

For pictures we called upon Ed Hills, a marine photographer of note and an old friend. I had not only raced with and against him in the 210s, but we had also shared space in his father's barn for winter storage and spring painting. He brought his daughter, Liz, with him. I had known her since childhood, when she called herself "Yo-yo." Ed took numerous photos of the new boat prototype, in all configurations including paddling as a canoe and a kayak.

After the filming was completed, Liz tried out the boat. Having been brought up around the water in all kinds of boats, she had no trouble handling it, but no one can master the sliding seat the very first time. Little did any of us suspect that she was soon to become a member of the first U.N.H. women's eight (along with Marjorie's daughter, Dianne Burbridge), an Olympic silver medal winner, head coach at Radcliffe, and coach of the American Olympic women scullers, under her married name of Liz O'Leary.

After its brief but successful forays on the waters of the Piscataqua and Charles, the prototype was turned over to the capable hands of the Tillotson-Pearson craftsmen, completing the tight schedule on time.

The double proved its versatility at an ocean race in Lynn, Massachusetts. As a number of Alden singles maneuvered around by the starting line, Bud Halsey appeared in a double, rowing with an Oarmaster in the bow position, accompanied by a young lady sitting comfortably in the stern. I thought to myself "This guy is crazy if he

AEM rowing the double with a passenger, and Marjorie rowing a single. Photo: Ann Grinnell

thinks he can have a chance with that extra weight in the stern. But when the five-minute warning gun was fired, Bud rowed in to the beach, the young lady stepped out, and he moved the Oarmaster to the middle position, arriving at the start before the final gun and winning the race.

As time went on, new uses for the double came to light. Every boat and ship is adversely affected by weight in excess of that for which it was designed. This is reflected in the Plimsoll marks on the sides of ships. These give the maximum allowable draft in various conditions, such as Winter North Atlantic, Fresh Water, etc., as specified by the American Bureau of Shipping or Lloyd's, etc. In racing singles, there are boats designed for heavyweights and lightweights, and sometimes a boat is designed for the exact weight of the rower. A heavier

Douglas and AEM in the production double.

person sinks an Alden deeper in the water than a lightweight. At the lower waterline the boat loses both speed and seaworthiness. As weight approaches or exceeds 250 pounds, the double, rowed as a single, becomes more viable. The double can take a couple and one or two small children. It can carry a lot of supplies, as Jill Fredston found out in rowing 2,500 miles through the open water between Seattle and Nome, Alaska. A young man from Yale and a young man from Harvard rowed the entire length of the Erie Canal in one. The larger displacement of the new boat fulfilled many needs.

Although we always recommended the double for anyone weighing over 250 pounds, we heard of a man who, despite weighing 270 pounds, purchased a single. Reports, which we never checked, indicated that he liked the single so much that he carried it inside his station wagon and made his wife ride on the roof.

Despite the remarkable versatility of the double, we often caution couples who plan to row together. All too often it turns out that only one is really interested in rowing regularly, and the rowing enthusiast is stuck with a boat which is not as easy to carry alone and is bigger than necessary for ideal responsiveness. Better to get one single and see what other interest develops. Another single, or a double, can always be purchased if the need arises later. Many couples ride bicycles together, but seldom on a bicycle built for two. We try to recommend the boat which will be most satisfactory in the long run, rather than the one on which we make the most money.

The Union Boat Club had one serious criticism of their new double. Several members enjoyed going out in the ocean as a refreshing change from the confines of the Charles River. The racing shells did not take kindly to this treatment, and on one occasion suffered considerable damage. The Alden was much better, but the oarlock height presented a problem. The riggers had a fixed elevation, which could not be altered. Oarlock height could be adjusted a fraction of an inch by adding washers on its pin, between its shoulder and the rigger. This compensated for the overlap of the oars, which placed one hand above the other, and would force the corresponding blade deeper in the water if the oarlocks were the same height. Although many people in this country row left over right, others do not. The washers could be moved from one side to the other by removing the cotter pins from the oarlocks, a time-consuming process but quite possible to accomplish. It did not solve the problem faced when considerably more clearance is required in rough water or when heavier oarsmen weigh the boat down so that it is lower in the water. The Union Boat Club people convinced me that we should try to devise some quick and easy way to raise and lower the riggers, preferably from inside the boat, out on the water, without any tools. This was quite an order, and it resulted in much agonizing, head-scratching, and sketching of Rube Goldberg devices which were far from practical. Finally we came up with the simple solution which had eluded us for so long. The rigger was made to pivot around the main frame, secured in any position by two adjusting screws which served to hold the base of the rigger out from the main frame, forcing the end of the rigger down. Although we have made improvements over the years, the basic system continues to impress beginners and veterans alike. Since it is patented, no one else can use it. Naturally, this results in more emphasis on other adjustments, such as pitch. An oar blade should have its top edge a little ahead of its bottom edge while it is moving through the water toward the stern. This is called positive pitch. If the blade has no pitch, or negative pitch, it tends to dig down into the water, with disastrous results. Pitch is therefore important and has been provided in various ways. Wood oars are sometimes made with positive pitch, or the same effect is produced by putting a wedge under the plastic sleeve at the oarlock. The simplest way to assure positive pitch is to design it into the forward face and the bottom of the oarlock, and this is what we do in the Douglas oarlocks. A cam action at the pin of some oarlocks makes them truly adjustable. Tilting the member to which the oarlock is attached makes a corresponding adjustment to the pitch, but only when the oar is perpendicular to the boat. The pitch diminishes as the oar is moved forward or aft of this position, a most undesirable but little understood, phenomenon. With a modern high-tech oar, about which more later, pitch adjustments are unnecessary. On a recreational shell, the distance between oarlocks, or spread, does not seem to require adjustment, although our experience indicates it should be greater than on a racing shell. This has to do with what our British friends aptly refer to as the gearing. The more of the oar shaft, or loom, that extends inboard of the oarlock, the more leverage, or mechanical advantage, there is. Each stroke requires less force, and therefore a higher cadence, or stroke rate, can be maintained. Since a recreational shell offers more resistance than a racing shell, more force is required on the oar handles, and a lower stroke rate is necessary. A slower, harder stroke is not such good aerobic exercise as a faster, easier stroke. Increasing the spread compensates in part for this, and that is why we increased the spread from sixty inches to sixty-four inches. To sum up, minor adjustments in pitch and spread appear to be relatively unimportant in a recreational shell, while oarlock height adjustment has proved to be most important.

With increasing activity in the Aldens, our beautiful *Barnacle II* had less use. Sailing is always more time-consuming than rowing, and we were becoming busier. We transported the Aldens around for demonstrations by land and sea. Depending on either the wind or a small outboard motor for propulsion made scheduling uncertain, and weather had to be considered when towing two Aldens. It was time to consider a bigger, faster boat which could carry the Aldens safely instead of towing them. Our friend and neighbor, Russ Smith, knew of a lobster boat for sale in New Harbor. We drove down there one winter day and met the owner, Russ Brackett. He was soft-spoken and calm, with a good-humored twinkle in his eye, and the independence and self-sufficiency I so admired. He was getting on in years and had decided to give up lobstering and sell his beloved boat. It would have been easy to sell his boat locally, as it was certainly the fastest, most sea kindly, and best looking boat in the harbor, but Russ was reluctant to have to see someone else running, and possibly abusing, his boat.

We shoveled some of the new fallen snow out of his skiff and rowed out to the *Marion B.*, riding gracefully at her mooring but also covered with snow. The cabin contained nothing but two narrow benches, making a V in the bow, and then the biggest V-8 engine that Buick made. The sharp bow at the waterline, flaring out in a beautiful concave curve to the wide forward deck, did not escape my admiring notice. She was planked with white cedar and fastened with Monel. From the brief inspection I could guess the performance in rough water, an estimate which was more than adequately confirmed later. My mind was made up, but I took great pains to conceal my enthusiasm. I said nothing to Mr. Brackett, except "Goodbye," but a few days later I called him up. The conversation was as follows:

AM: "Liked your boat."

RB: "Thought you would."

AM: "What's the lowest price you would take for it?"

RB: "Price I'm asking."

AM: "I'll take it."

When Russ Smith and Marjorie and I came down later to take my prized new purchase to Kittery, it was not quite the boat I had agreed to buy. The twin mufflers, which I had observed were quite rusted, had been replaced with new ones. Quite a different experience compared to buying a car. As we fired up the engine and left the dock, I looked back and waved goodbye to Russ Brackett, who stood there with the unmistakable glint of a tear in each eye. He was as fine a man as I ever hope to meet, and I was fortunate in being able to see him many times later, before he joined the other friends who are no longer with us.

Barnacle III, *the lobster boat which served admirably as a tender for the Aldens.*
Photo: Marjorie Martin.

In due course, I made some alterations to *Barnacle III*, as I renamed my first power boat. With a single piece of plywood, I made the two benches into one large double bunk. With some more plywood I made a simple box over the engine and made some canvas curtains to enclose the deckhouse in bad weather. A small alcohol stove and a portable head completed the transition from lobster boat to cruising yacht. A few discerning people tire of pouring endless supplies of fuel into a great box, slightly pointed at one end, which, according to current wisdom, constitutes a motor yacht. Too high and wide to be safe in rough water, creating the gigantic waves that spell wasteful inefficiency and threaten the eroding shoreline, as well as small boats and people, they are at their luxurious best tied up to the various electrical and other umbilical cords of a marina. The more enlightened observe lobster boats, knifing over waves safely and easily, with little disturbance of the environment, and adding their own grace to the surrounding natural beauty. They opt to own one, but some, unfortunately, try to bring aboard all the shoreside amenities of the "yachts." Archimedes' law cannot be circumvented, and all that weight takes the poor lobster boat down to a most inefficient waterline, where its performance leaves a lot to be desired. Such was not the case with *Barnacle III*, for her new displacement was hardly more than the old.

We were out at the Shoals one day when Russ Brackett was there on his son Norman's seiner. I rowed over in an Alden to talk to him. He was most interested to hear about the changes we had made and happy to learn that his favorite boat was receiving such good care. He wanted to come over and see her forthwith. He had a little skiff, but to my astonishment he said he would like to row over in the Alden. For an older man, somewhat overweight, who had never rowed with a sliding seat, this seemed to present quite a challenge. I like to teach beginners at our low float, in the protected waters of Chauncey Creek, after a session on the X-oarcizor in the boathouse. Embarking from the high deck of a big fishing boat to the choppy waters of Gosport Harbor is quite another matter. But Russ never hesitated and soon was landing at the side of his old boat. To my relief, he seemed to approve all of the changes we had made. As we were leaving, he asked, with a twinkle in his eye, "Have you opened her up?" I am not obsessed with speed in a power boat and had been cruising at a modest 10 knots. But I hadn't been able to resist the temptation to "put her in the corner" once or twice to see what she would do wide open (22 knots).

With increasing numbers of Alden owners, it was inevitable that some of them would want to see how fast they could go in relation to others. A race between an Alden and a dory or peapod wouldn't make much sense, except possibly for someone on an ego trip or suffering from some insecurity who would like to play with a stacked deck. On the other hand, it would be equally foolish to have a race between an Alden and a racing shell. But a race where all of the rowers were in identical boats would be just as fair and exciting as a race between the obviously faster racing sculls.

I began to think about how a race could be organized and where it could be held. It suddenly dawned on me that it could not be anywhere else but the Isles of Shoals. It was certainly appropriate that the first race of Alden Ocean Shells should be on the open ocean. Then there was the continuity of the strongest thread of my early life, which had great appeal for me. I like the idea of roots and connections between the past and the present and the future. The thought of a group of our little boats rowing out to the magic islands which played such a big part in my life gave me a great feeling of nostalgia. Surely my father, Mr. Brewster, Uncle Oscar, and all the other people who were a part of my life at the Shoals would be pleased could they look down and see what was taking place.

I decided to start the race just off the Decatur's dock, which we thought of as ours at the time. One end of the starting line was to be our lobster boat, *Barnacle III*, from which I could start the race, using my built-in and very loud whistle. The other end was to be my little original *Barnacle*, perched high on a ledge, with square sail set and a little pennant flying. I had purchased a silver cup as a perpetual trophy, named the Barnacle Cup. As the scheduled day approached, I became increasingly nervous and excited. Supposing no one showed up? Supposing more people than we could take care of appeared on the scene? Supposing our fickle weather treated us to a horrible storm?

When the great day finally dawned, the sea was calm, but there was a thick fog which insisted on hanging around despite numerous entreaties to burn off. A dozen contestants drove their cars down over the field to the dock and started unloading their Aldens. Among them was John Pickering, who went to St. Mark's School in the winter and rowed his Alden back and forth to work in the Friendship area in the summer. He was one of the few in the first race to have the benefit of formal coaching, and he not only won that one but also the ones in the next two years. He went on to become captain of the Harvard lightweight crew, and, on the spur of the moment, took the place of one of the heavyweight oarsman who was injured by a rock, thrown from a bridge over the Harlem River by a friendly New Yorker who evidently did not approve of the elitist sport of rowing. John also became a sculler of note in Philadelphia. It was no disgrace to be beaten by John Pickering. Other participants in that first Alden race were Hargy Heap and Dr. Michael McGill, both winners of the race in later years. The youngest was Jim Loutrel, son of my good friends Fran and Ellie, rowing a fast and furious stroke with seven and one-half foot oars. Because of the thick fog, I decided, reluctantly, not to send all the little boats, most without compasses, out to the Shoals, and shortened the course to round the whistling buoy at Kitt's Rock and return. In subsequent years in unfavorable weather we have used an alternate course through Little Harbor and out through the river. This has seldom been necessary, but I have always believed that it is better to err on the side of caution. A compass is a navigational aid, but no guarantee that an inexperienced person can locate a small island in the middle of a fog-covered ocean.

After the race, everyone returned to the Decatur house for lunch and a drink I concocted called a Cransauvod, made of one quarter vodka, one quarter sauterne, and one half cranberry juice. This seemed to dispel whatever disappointment was caused by the weather, and there was general agreement that the race was a lot of fun. Rocky Keith suggested that the Alden owners form an association to encourage further races. This idea met with general approval, but, as usual, working out the details presented a problem which appeared to be beyond the capability or willingness of the assembled company. Except for Ernestine Bayer.

When she married Ernest Bayer, winner of a silver medal at the 1928 Olympics in a straight four, treasurer and also president of the National Association of Amateur Oarsmen (now U.S.R.A.), referee and judge, and dedicated supporter of rowing, Ernestine faced the prospect of becoming a rowing widow. Instead of fighting rowing, she joined it. Founding the Philadelphia Girls' Rowing Club, she rowed in all the racing boats with distinction and encouraged others of her sex to fight the prevailing male chauvinism which, unfortunately, was a part of the elitist mystique of rowing at the time. When no money to send women abroad for international competition was forthcoming from any organization, she borrowed the necessary funds, being careful to pay back every cent. The first American women's crews did not fare well in international competition and faced scorn from some quarters in their own country. But Ernestine never gave up, and gradually the ladies made progress in the uphill battle.

The Bayers lived in Kittery Point when we arrived on the scene, and they were among the first to buy Aldens. Ernestine and her

Ernestine Bayer in her Alden single. She, more than anyone else, was responsible for the growth and success of women's rowing and the Alden Ocean Shell Association. A most deserving member of the Rowing Hall of Fame. Photo: Marilyn Chapiro.

daughter, Tina, coached the first women's crew at U.N.H., using their Alden double in a swimming pool to teach the fundamentals to the novices, including our daughter Dianne and Liz Hills. Their first big race was at the Head-of-the-Charles. Unfortunately, only seven rowers showed up for the start. Undaunted, Mrs. Bayer, at age 65, jumped in the boat and rowed the three miles without batting an eye. The culmination of all of her efforts came in 1984 when the American women's eight won the gold medal at the Olympics. At the annual meeting and banquet of the United States Rowing Association that year, all nine members of the women's triumphant eight were inducted into the Rowing Hall of Fame. In a fitting tribute to the many contributions to women's rowing which led up to the great victory, Ernestine was also inducted. In answer to many requests, the great crew put on an exhibition row on the Schuylkill the next morning. By a strange coincidence, once more only seven rowers showed up, and Ernestine, now 75, pulled a sweep in that famous boat.

The fledgling Alden Ocean Shell Association was just one more challenge for Ernestine Bayer. She volunteered to be secretary and treasurer and soon had everything well organized. She wrote long personal letters to anyone who enquired about the association and transferred some of her enthusiasm for rowing to all with whom she came in contact. She participated in many Alden races and, with her daughter, continues to run the Alden race on the Charles, immediately preceding the Head-of-the-Charles Regatta.

At first, it was relatively easy to keep track of the few members who joined the Alden Ocean Shell Association. But over the years, numbers increased dramatically, until today there are about seven hundred, and there are more and more races each year. Ernestine relinquished the job of treasurer to Beverly Garber to ease the burden of paperwork and resigned as secretary in 1988, as her eightieth birthday approached. Both worlds of rowing owe her a tremendous debt of gratitude, and her name will never be forgotten where oars churn the water, whether from an eight or an Alden.

Paul Coolidge was another to participate in that first Alden race. I first met him at Kent School, where a group of us used to listen to classical music on a state-of-the-art (of more than fifty years ago) phonograph in the music room. Paul lived in the Wentworth-Coolidge house in Portsmouth during the summer and would often appear on the *Sightseer,* wearing a sword fishing (guinea) hat, for a visit with us. After graduating from Harvard, he acquired a Friendship sloop, in which he managed to install a grand piano. The unlikely combination made the pages of the *National Geographic.* Paul founded the Allied Resin Company in Weymouth and provided me with all the fiberglass and resin for the kayaks and first Alden Ocean Shells, as well as the valuable technical advice without which I might still be muddling about, covered with rapidly curing resin. It seemed quite fitting that Paul Coolidge was unanimously elected the first president of the Alden Ocean Shell Association.

Over the years, the Association has sponsored many races all over the country. As more and more members attended rowing schools, such as Craftsbury in Vermont and Florida Rowing Center, and trained oarsmen such as Olympic medalists Charlie Clapp and Brad Smith, and champion scullers Gregg Stone and Tiff Wood began participating in Alden races, the quality of rowing improved considerably, and it became more and more difficult to reach the top in the bigger races. With handicaps for age and sex becoming more accurate with years of experience, races were won by people of all ages, from teens to over sixty. A spirit of good sportsmanship seemed to be established as a precedent, and race results were generally accepted gracefully, despite the fact that it is human nature to want to win. Participants worked long and hard to improve their rowing techniques and physical condition, but there was a remarkable lack of the win-at-any-price syndrome which seems to invade,like a cancer, so many sports. The boats are essentially the same, and one of the few rules prevents them from being altered in any way to increase speed, although other alterations such as fishing rod holders, compasses, rear-view mirrors, etc., are allowed. Improvements which have been made over the years are always designed to be easily and inexpensively retrofitted on the older boats, and none are designed to increase speed. There has been remarkably little sign of efforts to win by equipment alterations, and virtually no accusations that races were won by unfair means. Just a group of people of good will competing for the fun of it.

At one Isles of Shoals Race, I was starting the contestants in groups, at timed intervals, as is the custom in this ocean race. First to start, women over 60, then men over 60, and so forth until the last to start, men under 40. As I started the countdown for this last group, I noticed that two boats were far behind the starting line and would have to start rowing full speed immediately to get to the line on time. I warned them over the bull horn to do this, but they ignored my advice and didn't take a stroke until after the others had crossed the line. It was Charlie Clapp and Brad Smith, veterans of the eight which won a silver medal at the 1984 Olympics, rowing for the Union Boat Club, generously giving all of their competitors an added head start. I thought to myself that it didn't take them long to pick up the spirit of Alden racing. Despite his self-imposed handicap, Charlie Clapp was first on elapsed time, and he told me afterwards that he really enjoyed the challenge of racing in rough water (which it certainly was that day), the lack of pressure and tension, and the friendly spirit of the competitors. It is my hope that legal bickering and hard feelings never mar the races in the boats which mean so much to me.

John Pickering rowing the first production Martin at the Head-of-the-Charles in 1975. He actually went faster than 92 of the racing shells. Note the absence of a coaming (or wash box), which was added later for greater seaworthiness. Photo: Edwin Hills.

22 • *The Martin*

*W*ith the Alden Single and Double, we were able to satisfy the needs of most potential recreational rowers. Our clientele covered a broad spectrum of ages, sex, physical condition, previous rowing experience, and future aspirations. We were not distressed to find some, particularly the younger ones, going into the racing shells. Instead, we were proud to have introduced to the sport of rowing some who went all the way to the top ranks of competition. We were content to leave the manufacture of racing shells to the various good builders who specialized in that field. But a question remained: was there a need for something between an Alden and a racing scull?

Having by this time (1975) rowed with many Alden owners, I observed that the vast majority rowed the boat well below its potential hull speed. No boat is faster than the speed corresponding to the power applied, and the fact is that most recreational rowers apply much less power than a young competing athlete. I once rowed an Alden beside a very nice, elderly lady in a racing scull. She rowed well but with very little power, and the Alden kept right up, going at the same stroke rate. Nevertheless, the fact remained that some big, strong, and accomplished rowers could get the Alden up to its natural hull speed, beyond which additional power is largely wasted in wave making. A single scull would do the same thing but at a higher speed, and no ordinary mortal could apply sufficient power to reach it. A boat with the same shape as a single racing scull but reduced in length and increased in beam would reach its hull speed with far less power. I have tested such a boat against an Alden and found it to be slower at full power, even though it was more than four feet longer.

As we considered designing another boat, we came to the conclusion that while we did not want to go to the extremes of a racing shell, we should come up with a boat which would not reach its limiting hull speed with the power that any human could apply. This would make it satisfying for the biggest, strongest, most skillful young athlete in an all-out short sprint, even though for maximum speed the racing boat would still be superior. If this requirement were to be met, we would have to sacrifice some of the recreational benefits of the Alden. The challenge was to preserve as many as possible, lest we come up with a boat having the same limitations as a racing shell without its ultimate speed.

I decided to stay with the flat bottom, giving more stability than a wider round-bottom boat. I also decided to retain a straight keel, thereby eliminating a troublesome fin or skeg. I gave the bow even more flare than the Alden, necessitating a very full deck line, to help it lift over waves, although I was fully aware that regardless of the flare, such a long, narrow boat would never be as seaworthy as the Alden in really big waves. Having decided on the design parameters, I deserted the primitive design and construction methods which had proved so successful with the Aldens and reverted to the more orthodox methods I had devoted so many years to learning. I drew up the lines to scale, sighting each curve from various angles and making changes as I saw fit. From the resulting offsets, I drew full-size sections, from which Douglas made wood forms, and set them up on a rigid frame. Always fascinated with new materials, I bought some C-Flex fiberglass to try. This ingenious product consists of fiberglass cloth with fiberglass rods running through it. The rods are like thin, untapered fishing rods, easily bent to any shape, but stiff enough to maintain fair curves. I couldn't believe how easy it was to work with. Marjorie and I "planked" the prototype in no time at all. The hard and time-consuming part came later, when we had to add fiberglass mat and resin, and sand and fill, sand and fill, first with more fiberglass, and then with automobile body putty. This added a great deal to the weight, but in subsequent trials we allowed for this disadvantage. We had many people row it, tall and short, light and heavy, sprinting, challenging waves, and testing the flotation of the two foam bulkheads. Performance was about as expected: no one could make the stern drag down. We decided to call it the Martin Trainer, which proved to be a poor choice for a name. Some people mistakenly thought we intended it to be used for training them to row Aldens, whereas our intention was that they would use it to train for rowing a racing shell. That idea, too,

Hargy Heap rowing a Martin in rough water. Despite its greater length, its bow lifts over waves instead of the waves washing over the bow. Photographer unknown.

was erroneous because the new boat, while a little less stable than the Alden, was hardly necessary as a step toward a racing scull. It had already been proved that beginners could be taught to row directly in a racing shell, let alone making the easier transition from an Alden to one. The idea of advancing through a series of narrower and narrower boats had already been discarded. Owners and dealers soon began to refer to the new boat as the Martin, so we followed suit, like the tail wagging the dog.

To save weight, the first boats were made without coamings, with a deck made out of sailcloth. This proved to be a mistake, for despite our warnings that this boat was for protected water only, and forbidding its use in the Isles of Shoals Race, many owners insisted on taking it in waves for which it was not intended. Consequently, Douglas designed a fiberglass deck with a high coaming surrounding the small cockpit and made a wood plug from which a mold was made. Tillotson-Pearson had a hard time making the coaming, because it was flared out in a reverse curve to keep water out of the cockpit. It was

Douglas rowing a production Martin. Many improvements had been made and an admirable record of racing victories was established. Despite its potential for speed, the cockpit of the Martin remains remarkably dry in considerable chop. Photo: Ann Grinnell.

worth the extra expense and trouble because the boat proved to be very dry in choppy water. Although we never recommended it, the decked model survived some really rough water, particularly in winning more than once the Catalina to Marina Del Ray Race in California, a distance of more than 30 miles in the open Pacific. We still did not allow these boats in the Isles of Shoals Race.

Another use which we neither envisioned nor approved was racing against true racing shells, a basically unfair contest. But our friend John Pickering, three-time winner of the Isles of Shoals Race, wanted to enter the Head-of- the-Charles Regatta in the novice singles division and did not have a racing scull. He asked if he could borrow one of the first Martins. We could hardly turn down this request, and besides, I was curious to see just how much slower our new boat was. John, to my surprise, finished in about the middle of his division, posting a time faster than 92 of the racing shells. The race officials, wisely, I think, ruled out any boats other than true racing shells in all future races.

Our life in Kittery was almost too good to be true. Our little business consisted entirely of educating people about the joys and health benefits of recreational rowing with a sliding seat. This was creative selling at its best, a far cry from the dog-eat-dog competition of the fork truck business, where numerous hungry competitors sought to discredit Yale by making statements and innuendos which simply were not true. Our only competitors were the makers of running shoes, bicycles, and other sports equipment. Our elegant lobster boat, *Barnacle III* swung from her mooring, ready to take us, along with two Aldens on top of the deckhouse, out to the Shoals, or down east to the many islands and coves that were often deserted. We could never have guessed what kind of a dark cloud loomed over the horizon.

A little newspaper, called *Public Occurrences* appeared suddenly from nowhere. The editors haunted real estate offices to pinpoint land on which options were being purchased. They printed a map on the front page, showing all of this land in ominous black. The dark shadow, like a cancer on an X-ray, started in the peaceful college town of Durham, New Hampshire, with a thin line running right down to the ocean at Rye. Furthermore, one of the islands at the Shoals, Londoner's (Lunging), was also black. Was this all a coincidence? Was someone trying to put together land for a big commercial venture? If so, what? Some of the more astute suggested an oil refinery, but that seemed too horrible to contemplate, and certainly not very practical.

We had not long to agonize over doubts. Aristotle Onassis announced that he did indeed intend to build a mammoth oil refinery in Durham, with pipelines going down to the ocean at Rye, and thence under the sea to a supertanker terminal at the Isles of Shoals. I immediately wrote a vitriolic letter to the editor of the *Portsmouth Herald*, fully expecting it to be consigned to the circular file. But, to my astonishment, it was published the next day, and several people called up to express their agreement and congratulations. They also begged me to go to a reception Mr. Onassis and Governor

Meldrim Thomson of New Hampshire were planning to hold shortly. I explained that the reception was only for the press, politicians, influential business people, and friends of the project, in none of which categories I could qualify. But on further reflection, I decided I could not let my good neighbors and the beloved islands down without at least making some attempt, so I called up Peter Booras, the top Onassis representative in the area. He was not there, but I boldly left a message for him to call me back, convinced that the matter would end there. As it turned out, it was only the beginning.

They did call back and put me and Marjorie on the list of invited guests, for what reason I could not guess. We headed out toward the reception in Manchester, fearful of running out of gas, due to the shortage which Onassis undoubtedly expected to lend support to his project. It was quite a reception, with two open bars and unlimited *hors d'oeuvres* featuring shrimp and similar delicacies. Best of all, there was a very good orchestra playing not rotten roll and other children's music, but real jazz.

An announcement came over the loud speaker to the effect that the governor would soon escort Mr. Onassis into the ballroom, where he would deliver a short speech and then circulate among the merrymakers. Several drinks and shrimp later he appeared, and it was immediately apparent that his photographs had more than done him justice. He was surprisingly short for such a powerful personage, reminiscent of Joseph Stalin, and Marjorie had to stand on a chair to see him, though we were not ten feet away. He said he was going to build a refinery which would be "cleaner than a clinic." Then he introduced a Mr. Greene as the world's foremost authority on oil refineries and a Mr. Eugene Harlow as the world's foremost authority on tankers and tanker terminals. He said they had come to answer any questions and, without further comments, bid us all adieu and circulated hastily out the back door.

Perhaps because of my background in designing and building tankers, and years of experiences at the Isles of Shoals, I was intrigued by the thought of trying to find out just how much this Mr. Harlow knew that would qualify him to design a supertanker terminal at the storm battered islands. I approached him without delay and began to ask questions. He made a most transparent effort to avoid me, desperately trying to become involved in conversations with others. I pursued him with the persistence of a heat-seeking rocket, until finally he ran across the room to avoid me. This attracted the attention of some of the ever-present reporters, and they asked who I was and why Mr. Harlow seemed so anxious to get away from me. This was the beginning of a battle that was to become quite intense over the next several months.

Nancy Sandberg of Durham Point immediately organized a group of housewives, professors from U.N.H., and other concerned citizens of the area called "Save Our Shores" (S.O.S.). Led by her indomitable spirit and boundless energy, they raised money, put advertisements in various publications, made posters and stickers, and held endless public meetings to rally support for opposition to the schemes which were seen as a brutal rape of the seacoast area to further enrich one of the world's wealthiest money-grabbers. I fully supported this effort, but it seemed that they were so well organized that I could add little to defend Durham from a refinery. The Isles of Shoals were another matter.

The barren islands were of little concern to many people in the area. But if my life could be considered a wheel, with the spokes the many interests and activities extending out to the rim to support life and happiness, the Isles of Shoals were certainly the hub. The thought of carelessly handled oil contaminating those pristine waters forever made my blood boil. If there were anything I could do to prevent such a tragedy, I wanted to join the effort in whatever capacity my qualifications would be most effective. I talked it over with my friend and neighbor, John Hallett, and he pointed out that while S.O.S. was a noble effort and had many sympathizers, the fact remained that the region had to have oil to survive, and S.O.S. was concerned only with derailing the Onassis effort, without offering any alternative solutions for the oil shortage. He persuaded me to join him in forming The Committee for Regional Oil Planning, and with his connections in the oil industry, he knew a great deal about the options.

John, as co-chairman of our little committee, researched alternative sources of oil for the region, to reassure people intimidated by the dire predictions of New England oil shortages if Onassis were to be stopped. Meanwhile, I conducted a hasty review of everything I had learned about tankers and diligently studied the copious literature on tanker accidents and oil spills. It was fascinating, and at the same time sickening, to dig out the facts about the supertankers that Onassis was proposing to land at the Shoals. Time dims the memory, but the gist of the most awesome facts remains these many years after the refinery battle.

The tanker barons, of which Onassis was but one of many, seemed devoid of any consideration for the environment, mankind, or the standards of morality which we like to associate with enlightened civilization. Fortunes could be made in one voyage of a colossal tanker. The cost of ship construction was modest compared to the profit potential. Yet there seemed to be a competition between tanker owners to see who could build and operate the cheapest fleet. A small tanker carrying thirty thousand tons of crude oil was usually divided into about ten big tanks, each holding about three thousand tons. These are awesome numbers, especially when one climbs down a long ladder into the huge, dark cavern of one of the tanks or imagines the release of such a volume of lethal oil should a single puncture occur. The super tankers carry ten to twenty times as much. In ten or twenty times as many tanks? That would require more bulkheads, the cost of which would reduce the estimated twenty million dollars a year Onassis spent on entertainment, and that would never do. Each tank thus held more oil than the weight of the battleship *Massachusetts.* Mysterious explosions occurred with dismal frequency in an empty thirty to sixty thousand ton capacity tank. No one could see how the remaining vapor could be ignited without any visible source of flame or spark. Finally it was discovered that the enclosed area was so colossal it created its own weather patterns, including lightning storms.

In 1970 the *Arrow,* one of about 60 tankers owned by Onassis, hit a ledge off Nova Scotia, spilling oil which cost the Canadian Government $8 million to clean up. What did the owner pay? Not a penny, because he had created a separate company to own each of his ships, and after a spill, he simply dissolved that company. Although even small fishing trawlers carry two radars for safety, the *Arrow* carried but one, and that was sectoring and therefore ineffective. The single depth sounder had been broken for some time. The captain was incompetent but willing to work for substandard wages. The facts about the tankers and the oil transportation industry were appalling, and I set out to study them as thoroughly as I had studied for the Webb exams and to make them known to as many people as possible.

We raised money to support our little committee and spent it as fast as it came in on a series of pamphlets, most of which I wrote. We gave these out to S.O.S. and any other groups or individuals who were concerned. The first was entitled *It Could Happen At The Isles Of Shoals* and featured a photograph of the tanker *Torrey Canyon* breaking in half in moderate seas southwest of England. Inside were shocking facts about this and other tanker disasters, as well as hazards and wave conditions at the Isles of Shoals.

It was an inspired group that the threat to the seacoast brought together so spontaneously, and they worked in unusual harmony. Social and economic backgrounds were put on the back burner or forgotten, as were political persuasions. But we faced a formidable foe. One of the first contributions to our committee was five dollars from an Isles of Shoals lobsterman named Norman Foye. He was about my own age and had grown up on Cedar Island, only half a mile from our house on Appledore. Norman had a great sense of humor, along with his typical Shoals independence and absolute integrity. Once he was approached by a visiting "yachtsman" from an imposing luxury "yacht." The owner, an apparent success in the world of greed, was accompanied by two superficially good-looking young ladies, whom he was evidently trying to impress. Having taken into custody the lobsters he had so imperiously ordered, he handed Norman a one hundred dollar bill, winking at the young ladies as though to say "watch this poor hick try to deal with more money than he has ever seen at one time." Norman never batted an eye as he calmly pulled out a roll of bills and peeled off more than ninety dollars in change. We received many other contributions, none very large.

The sum total of all of our contributions, plus those received by S.O.S. and other groups, were as a drop in the bucket compared to the almost unlimited resources of Onassis. Furthermore, it was demonstrated once again that money attracts political forces. The battle was developing into a classic David and Goliath struggle, and we were not Goliath. Furthermore, Onassis had an enviable track record, never having lost a battle in his insatiable quest for money and power.

A series of meetings were held in schools and other public buildings, in various towns adjacent to the affected area. Speakers were chosen to explain different aspects of the proposal. For instance, a pipeline specialist from U.N.H. would explain the immensity of the 12 huge pipes between Durham and the Shoals, some of which were to carry refined products to be loaded on tankers destined for Europe or wherever the best price was forthcoming. The long-suffering local citizenry were not to receive the additional heating oil and gasoline so glibly promised. Some one else would explain that the refinery would be built by out-of-state labor experienced in such work, destroying the myth that jobs would be created for local people. I was often called upon to share my rapidly increasing knowledge of the technical failings of super tankers. John Kingsbury, of the Shoals Marine Laboratory on Appledore, run jointly by Cornell and U.N.H., was by far the most inspiring speaker. He had put his life and soul into building the laboratory, and had quickly fallen in love with the islands. He at once sensed the importance of the Laightons and all the others who had loved the islands before his coming there. He had been largely responsible for restoring Celia Thaxter's garden, and had taken care of the Laighton graves, where I had said my last good-bye to Uncle Oscar so many years before. He had great love and respect for Norman Foye, whom he always invited over to Appledore each year to lecture the students on the noble profession of lobstering. The lectures were always full of the irrepressible Foye humor, as he stood up in front of one of his lobster traps, facing the young and enthusiastic audience, saying, with a twinkle in his eye, that he was going to try lobstering for a few more years, and if he then didn't like it, get a job in the Navy Yard. John disdained the use of notes or the ever present microphone. He spoke from the heart, and reached the hearts of those who were privileged to hear him. He explained that he had picked the Shoals for the laboratory because of the unusually clear water, the clearest on the East Coast, I believe. Even without a major spill, the inevitable small daily doses of oil would render the laboratory untenable.

The endless meetings, speeches, and preparations absorbed a lot of time and energy. One night it seemed that all was quiet on the oil front, and I made myself a drink and sat down to relax as I read the evening paper before dinner. I was reading about a meeting in Rye that very night when I was shocked to see my own name as one of the speakers. Marjorie quickly made me a sandwich, which I consumed on the way to Rye, and I arrived just in time to contribute my latest information on oil tankers. The Olympic (as the proposed refinery was called) representatives made their own presentations, with costly charts, graphs, and movies. One of the latter showed the construction of a small pipeline in the Middle East. There was a huge explosion, like a mini nuclear bomb. Some one asked what it was. The explanation that they had run into some ledge brought gales of laughter from the audience, most of whom lived above or near the solid granite which formed almost the entire route of the proposed pipeline. All of Olympic's presentations were followed by question and answer periods. I invariably used these opportunities to address hostile questions to Mr. Harlow, who seemed to cringe every time I stood up. His wife later told me, in a pathetic appeal for mercy, that it was affecting his health. I replied that he did not have to participate in the attempted rape of our seacoast. He seemed to be a decent man as I got to know him, but the truth was on our side, as I am sure he was aware, and only Onassis money kept him in the battle.

One politician who was on our side had the unlikely name of Dudley Dudley. She was a state representative, and when Governor Thomson threatened to override the upcoming town votes against the refinery, she introduced a home-rule bill to prevent him from forcing it down their throats. The Olympic people knew that the home-rule issue would make or break them. They purchased a special inset in the local papers, urging people to call their representatives and urge them to vote against home rule. They included the names, addresses, and telephone numbers of that massive deliberative body. We used this convenient list to make our own telephone calls. I soon found that those who did not depend on Seacoast votes were not enthusiastic about stopping the refinery. However, I found a way to make them wake up. I asked if they knew that the oil complex would require more than eight million gallons of water every day. When a lack of concern was shown, I advised that there was no way they would be able to get that much water from the seacoast area, and where did they think the water would come from? I answered my own question: "Lake Winnipesaukee." This brought the desired response: "Over my dead body." The tide was finally beginning to turn.

The last big confrontation was in a packed hall, with the entire Olympic team up on the stage, with all of the long-awaited details of their proposal. Local and national television cameras ground away as tension mounted in anticipation of the promised question and answer period to follow the formal presentation. When my turn came, I asked Mr. Harlow what they intended to do about the Canadian oil spill they had caused, for which they had not paid a cent. Eugene Harlow had evidently had enough of my hostile questions and turned to Vice President Nicholas Papanicolaou for a reply. The young executive had been educated at Harvard and spoke faultless English with a cultured accent, which could hide neither his arrogance nor his ignorance. He said that Onassis had paid in full for cleaning up the mess. One of the Canadian officials saw the exchange on television and called me for details, for Onassis still had not paid anything. Our friend from across the border wanted to revive the case, in which he had played an active part.

The most dramatic part of the whole performance came later when Bob McDonough, a young lobsterman, stood up. He asked, with almost uncontrollable emotion, what would happen to him and the other fisherman if the blasting and oil spills decimated the lobster population and took away their sole source of making a living. The same young vice president who had replied to my question gave an answer in a cold, self-assured, and supercilious tone: secondary effects of accidents were not the concern of Olympic. After the meeting, Bob came up to me and apologized for losing his cool. "On the contrary," I replied, "I think it will have a great effect on public opinion." And indeed it did. The contrast of the young fisherman, bravely trying to protect his honest livelihood, facing the personification of the abuse of power and money, deeply moved those who witnessed it, in person or on television.

Onassis was thoroughly defeated on all counts, an entirely new and upsetting experience for him. Not long after, he left the planet he did so much to destroy. The Isles of Shoals survived the threat, as they had survived so many vicious storms over the centuries. The next summer, at the conclusion of the race, I pointed out to the assembled rowers how lucky we all were to still have such an unspoiled destination.

Following the dramatic Onassis episode, *The New Yorker* published a long article on super tankers, which later became a book. They talked to me for nearly five hours by phone, checking on technical details. Later there was a small oil spill off our own Kittery shores, and the State of Maine brought suit against the owners. I was asked to be an expert witness, and the assistant attorney general and I went down to Boston to inspect the ship. We climbed the gangway and went up to the officers' wardroom, where we were given a cup of coffee. The owners were drinking Scotch and gin, though it was only ten o'clock in the morning, a little early for the sun to be over the yardarm. I talked at great length with the captain, who impressed me as being an extraordinarily fine seaman, though very modest. The log for the last voyage showed five days in force eleven winds. This proved to be too much for the thin plating at the bow, rusted dangerously by many trips carrying molasses, which is very corrosive. The current owners had paid very little for the now unseaworthy vessel, hoping to clear a big profit on a few more trips with oil. Their luck ran out. The captain had saved the ship by heaving to with the bow held into the wind, the great seas sweeping the decks all the way to the bridge. He had turned it around to go before the wind to allow men to get up to the bow to make temporary repairs. Without his courage and skill, all lives and the remains of the ship would have been lost. I climbed down to the bottom of the tank which had spilled oil. One of the top plates was ripped open. Little evidence of oil remained, but I was still apprehensive about the foul air which could deprive one of oxygen. I was glad to get up on deck, where my more prudent legal companion had observed the scene in comparative safety. The case was settled out of court.

One day we took our little granddaughters, Cheryl and Jill Perry, out to the Shoals on *Barnacle III*. It was one of those foggy summer days which I love, providing there are not too many in a row. There is an air of mystery, turning familiar landmarks into vague shapes which loom up suddenly where they are not expected to be. The air seems much saltier and the water deeper. If there is no wind, it seems blissfully quiet, like a gentle snowstorm. After anchoring, we launched our two Alden singles and rowed the girls to the west side of Appledore, one little passenger with each of us. We visited our friends at the Shoals Marine Laboratory and returned to our lobster boat, anticipating the marine supper which would be quite an adventure for the girls. Marjorie set up the little alcohol stove under the steering wheel, and I lowered the canvas curtains to preserve some of the heat from the resting engine below.

Just then the sound of two big diesel engines shattered the silence, and a big Hatteras gradually took shape in the gloom. It approached slowly and stopped nearby, dropping a ridiculous little anchor from the bluff bow. On board were three friends, who promptly hailed us and invited us aboard for a visit. We reembarked in the Aldens and landed at the stern, which seemed like the side of a barn. Climbing up to the lofty altitude of the deck, we entered a spacious area entirely enclosed by curtains and thence into the luxurious cabin. It was all brightly lighted, and the air conditioning shut out the delicious aroma of the salt air. The diesel generator which made all this possible, though well insulated for sound, throbbed continuously, creating exhaust fumes which were more successful than the salt air in seeping in. A most sophisticated hi-fi system flooded the area with the unmistakable music of Benny Goodman. I had first heard these great sounds issuing forth between the scratches of a 78 record on a wind-up portable Victrola in our living room at Appledore. Later, I had squandered months of my meager funds to squire a young lady to the Madhatten Room of the Hotel Pennsylvania, or the Empire Room of the Waldorf Astoria, where the Benny Goodman Orchestra was holding forth. Marjorie had gone to the Spence School in New York, and one of her classmates and best friends was Gilly Duckworth, Benny Goodman's stepdaughter. She had spent many weekends with the Goodmans, swimming in their swimming pool and being serenaded by Benny, playing *Margie* on his clarinet whenever she walked by. She had also gone to choice night spots with the Goodmans, meeting other famous people. The only stipulation in what would pass for a marital contract with Marjorie was that she would introduce me to Benny Goodman, which she did when he came to Cohasset. While I was very happy listening to the King of Swing, the girls were having a great time running up and down the carpeted stairs and investigating all of the palatial amenities. Reflecting on the grandeur of the surroundings, I could only conclude that the simple life on *Barnacle III* was more in keeping with my concepts and instincts about enjoying the Isles of Shoals.

23 • *The Appledore 16*

*b*oats or ships may be more or less seaworthy than others, but from a racing shell to an ocean liner, they all have their limits of endurance in wind and wave. A single Pacific typhoon rivaled the Japanese for damaging the mighty ships of the U.S. Navy. Sea kindliness describes a vessel's performance in rough water better than seaworthiness. A boat may survive adverse conditions at the expense of exposure, desperate effort, well justified worry and fear, and a portion of good luck on the part of the crew. The Aldens had often demonstrated that they could be rowed with comfort, security, and even pleasure in situations quite threatening to a racing shell or its look-alike. But as waves become bigger, steeper, and breaking at the crest, there is no substitute for additional freeboard at the bow, along with plenty of flare. The dory and peapod, with which I was so familiar, were the ultimate in small boat seaworthiness.

Good dories were being made of wood by Lowell's Boat Shop in Amesbury and the Strawbery Banke Boat Shop in Portsmouth, where Douglas translated his violin-making skills into the more rough and ready methods of dory construction, designed new models, and eventually ran the shop until he joined Martin Marine. The best peapods, in my opinion, were made by Jim Steele in Brooklin, Maine. Several of them were rowed by Russ Smith and other members of a most informal club of Sunday morning rowing enthusiasts, who meet in Russ's boathouse to sit around the wood stove to have coffee and spin yarns before embarking. My Alden looked a little incongruous among all the traditional boats. I began to think of designing a boat more like them and perhaps fulfilling a lifetime dream of having my own peapod for which no excuses would be necessary.

In view of my errors in designing the peapod when I worked for Ray Hunt, did I have the courage to try again? Should our next design

Building the prototype Appledore 16 with C-flex. It was quick and easy to plank, but long and difficult to fair up. Photo: Marjorie Martin.

be in the direction of the seagoing peapod or in the direction of a racing shell? Would a peapod designed for sliding seat rowing be ultimately safer because of the extra power for emergencies? Could a peapod without the wide beam required for hauling lobster traps be made stable enough to give confidence against capsizing to the most cautious and traditional of rowing buffs? Could we design a sailing rig more satisfying than my father's of years ago without interfering with the rowing capabilities? It was quite a challenge, involving a number of fateful decisions.

I started drawing up the lines to a one-and-one-half-inch scale. It was not easy to fair them up. I wanted a hard bilge for stability, with a flat bottom amidships, but with extremely fine ends below the waterline for speed and seakindliness, and plenty of flair at the bow. I had as much trouble fairing in the diagonals as builders had experienced with the hard bilges of the Concordias. When the waterlines, buttocks, sections, and diagonals finally all agreed with each other, I drew full size sections.

Douglas transferred the lines to wood and cut out forms as he had done with the Martin. When these had been lined up on a rigid frame, Marjorie, Douglas, and I applied the C-flex, taking more time and much more care in fairing up each rod to reduce the fiberglass work later, tying some rods in place with thread in addition to the usual stapling. When it came to fairing the fiberglass later, I wanted the minimum exposure to the dust, which is so irritating to the skin and seems to find its way through any known variety of clothing. I started working at five o'clock one morning and didn't stop until eight that night. But the heavy power sanding was all done with only one day of itching.

The completed boat was no beauty, but I never claimed to be a patient craftsman, and, besides, it did not seem productive spending a lot of time smoothing and polishing if tests indicated that we should go "back to the drawing board." The first trials, however, were most gratifying, and I decided to take our latest effort to Mystic Seaport to participate in the annual Small Boat Clinic, where the prototype of the Alden had made its first public appearance.

A strong northwest wind ruffled the water around the launching dock, there being considerable fetch for a wind in that direction. As I always did at those events, I availed myself of the opportunity of trying out numbers of traditional boats: dories, peapods, Whitehalls, and others. I noticed that my back was getting soaked with spray. In the meantime the peapod, like an ugly duckling, was attracting little attention. It was a surprise to me that such a knowledgeable group would be so influenced by such superficial considerations. Sad to say, useless glitter often determines sales of automobiles, household appliances, and boats. The designer, like the father of a wayward son, never lost faith in the crudely constructed Appledore and headed it, full speed, into the waves. Despite my long experience and knowledge of the factors involved, I was taken by surprise when it became obvious that it was not only easier to row but also drier than any of the other boats I had rowed.

A year later I returned with another Appledore 16, this one built of cedar and mahogany by Ted Perry, using the WEST® System and finished

AEM rowing a production Appledore 16. This boat has all of the advantages of greater displacement, including stability, sea-kindliness, and carrying capacity, without sacrificing too much of the speed and easy rowing characteristics of the Alden. Photo: Ann Grinnell.

bright. It attracted a great deal of attention. Phil Bolger, whom I had never met, was sitting on a wharf when I rowed by. "If you change anything an eighth of an inch, you'll spoil her," he called out. This was quite an accolade, coming from one of the best of small boat designers. Phil was at Mystic with his friend and client, Peter Duff, of Edey and Duff, builders of the classic Stonehorse designed by S.S. Crocker. We had known Peter and Maggie for some time, thanks to their son Ian and daughter Jane. The children attended many boat shows at which their parents were exhibiting the Stonehorse. They often appeared at our floating exhibit, helping us out whenever they could, in exchange for which we let them row an Alden when things were not too hectic.

Peter formally introduced us to Phil, and we joined them for dinner. They had brought one of the latest Bolger innovations, the Dovekie, made by Edey and Duff. This is an incredibly practical cruising boat, too little understood or appreciated by all but the most discriminating. It can be trailed behind an ordinary car to wherever the most scenic waters beckon. It can be propelled by sail, oars, or a small motor, and wherever it goes, it carries cruising accommodations far superior to camping, though not up to the Ramada Inn standards that so many demand. It can always find a secure and safe berth in the shallowest water, even grounding out at low tide without damage or discomfort, a great advantage when the deep-water anchorages are threatened by high winds or overcrowding.

Marjorie joined Peter and Phil in the Dovekie for the breakfast cruise down the Mystic River the following morning, while I rowed and sailed the shiny wood Appledore. Among other things, Mystic Seaport and the venerable John Gardner have taught many people the joys of small boats. I recall rowing there one year when John was rowing the late Howard Chapelle on the annual cruise.

The Appledore 16 began to enjoy a reputation as a remarkably seaworthy boat. It gave me a great sense of security rowing in the often severe weather of the winter. Rowing in a gale one day, parallel to a banks dory, I observed that the latter seemed to be taking in more spray than I was. But I think the greatest safety factor is the fact that the Appledore goes through the water so easily, and the sliding seat makes so much more power available that one feels confident of prevailing against the strongest winds and currents. There have been times when I have felt panic in a traditional boat upon discovering an apparent lack of forward progress in extreme conditions. Some point out, rightly enough, that one does not get a traditional boat for racing, but they fail to realize the blessing of extra power in an emergency.

With a revived interest in rowing, it was inevitable that at least a few owners of traditional boats would want to compete with others. A get-together of various kinds of boats is always fun, and an impromptu race among people who have never raced before is a novel experience. But a race is a race and not a cruise. There are always those who want to win, which is only human, and no one wants to enter race after race with the distinct disadvantage of a significantly slower boat. The only fair race is in one-design boats, and several different classes can race in the same regatta, just as fours and eights and singles do. But open races do offer an opportunity for manufacturers to demonstrate a speed advantage, thereby hopefully increasing sales. With the Appledore 16, we were to some extent guilty of this questionable practice.

In the first annual race around Gerrish Island here in Kittery, all of our boats were ruled out on the grounds that they had sliding seats. Although I avoid racing in any of our boats, Marjorie and I entered in Russ Smith's peapod, built by Jim Steele. It happened that we won. The following year we rigged an Appledore 16 with a fixed seat, and Marjorie won in that. The same boat won again, with either Marjorie or Hargy Heap at the oars. Instead of resulting in sales to owners of slower boats, cries of foul were heard, some contestants working as a team, with certain ones blocking the Appledore while others rowed by in the narrow waters of the creek. One year Marjorie was informed, seconds before the start that she was disqualified because of light weight. Another contestant gallantly pointed out that his boat was actually lighter, and she was allowed to compete.

One year race day brought very strong southeast winds. The Coast Guard, which had agreed to provide a rescue boat, decided that discretion was the better part of valor and withdrew its offer. No other power boat owner would volunteer for the job. Nevertheless, the race began on schedule, although some contestants had already dropped out. The fleet made a serpentine dash through the narrow winding channel of the marsh which constituted the first leg of the course. As they reached the open ocean, they dropped out, one by one, some swamping. When they started rounding the rocky coast of Gerrish Island, only four boats remained, three big boats, each with two husky young oarsmen, and Marjorie in the Appledore. To add to the contrast, one of our grandchildren was shouting encouragement with repeated urging to "Come on, Grammy." This was a good example of how not to run a race. There is no excuse for taking needless risks with the unforgiving sea. I was gratified that both Marjorie and the Appledore survived, and being last was no disgrace.

A young man from Damariscotta, Maine, was an early Alden owner, and a participant in Alden ocean races. One day he asked us to build him an Appledore 16, of heavier than standard construction, to row around Cape Horn. This would seem to be a foolhardy notion for anyone but Charlie Porter. He was well experienced in all kinds of boats, and he planned everything very carefully. After several discussions, I became convinced that if anyone could accomplish the challenging task, Charlie could. He seemed to temper courage with caution and planned ahead against the crises he knew would arise. Consequently, we built the boat, and he came down to Kittery to test it out. It happened that a couple of newspaper writers were assigned to collect material for writing about our company that day. It was obvious that they were less than enthusiastic about the assignment and disdained taking any notes. I was showing them our boathouse and dock, while they tried in vain to stifle a yawn, when Charlie came in sight. "Who's that?" they asked. When I calmly replied that he was getting ready to row around Cape Horn, they suddenly came to life, and out came the notebooks. But Charlie was not a seeker of publicity and was not inclined to embellish his replies with elaborate descriptions of life-threatening dangers to be encountered. The writers, deprived of the sensationalism on which the media thrive, soon lost interest.

Charlie went ahead with his plans but ran into a logistical problem. He planned to start at Punta Arenas, and he found that the only way to get there was in a small plane, which could not carry an Appledore. He had to revise his plans to substitute a Klepper Arius kayak for the Appledore. This could be folded up into two bags, and he set about making some ingenious alterations so that it could be propelled by his Oarmaster and 9'-9" wood oars which we imported from F. Collar in Oxford, England.

He spent the best part of a year rowing through the maze of natural canals at the southern extremity of South America. Some of his journey followed Darwin's course through the Beagle, while at other times he traveled alone where no human had been since the ancient native settlements were abandoned. Large expeditions had been sent to the general area, manned by many curious and daring explorers, armed with fleets of power boats, food and water, and other supplies and equipment. From the standpoint of archeology, these efforts met with little success, for it was next to impossible to find the right places to dig for telltale artifacts in that vast wilderness. Charlie, obviously unable to carry much food or water in his diminutive craft, had to learn to spot the topography for natural water supplies. In so doing, he merely repeated the efforts of the ancient inhabitants, so many years before. His digging in such sites uncovered evidence more than three thousand years old.

Charlie Porter's voyage was the supreme test of human courage, ingenuity, and endurance. It was also a most severe test of equipment.

Sudden winds of one hundred miles per hour and more, rocky shores, and great distances between refuges have spelled disaster for more than one adventurer. We were concerned about the Oarmaster enduring this environment for a year without any hope of metal repairs. Charlie carried a few spare parts, which proved to be unnecessary. Another young man, in a similar folding kayak, but using a double-bladed paddle instead of Oarmaster and oars, was not so fortunate. He was caught in a fierce williwaw, as the winds are called, and was unable to prevail against it with his double paddle. He was blown ashore on the rocks, where his boat, gear, and supplies were destroyed, and he had to walk over a hundred miles to safety. A dramatic proof of the advantage of the extra power of a sliding seat in an emergency.

One day, when the Cape Horn trip was furthest from my mind, Charlie's mother called to say that he had actually rounded the dreaded Cape. In due course, he returned and showed us the startling color slides he had made. I was most impressed by the sheer beauty of the area, and the thought of seeing it firsthand crossed my mind. But the coward in me has so far prevailed over the adventuresome spirit.

Charlie Porter had provided a real service to the government of Chile in supplying charting information for unknown waters, and he also recorded plant and animal life missed by Darwin, as well as the amateur archeology success following failure by others.

One afternoon Charlie showed up in Kittery with Ned Gillette, an adventurer well known for mountain climbing and skiing around Mount Everest, and Jan Reynolds, an outstanding athlete and holder of the women's record for high altitude skiing. The trio had decided to embark on what might very well be the greatest rowing adventure of all time: a voyage from Cape Horn to Antarctica propelled by oars alone. Douglas joined us in a lengthy discussion of a boat designed for such a venture. I was at first partial to a design similar to the Appledore for stability, seaworthiness, and the maximum speed for a vessel which would of necessity have to be big and heavy. Speed would help them to cross the treacherous waters of the Drake Passage in a "window" between the worst of the westerly gales, which could blow them to the east of the southernmost continent to oblivion. Charlie favored a Swampscott dory concept, but double-ended. On further reflection, I was inclined to agree with him. While I had certainly had a wealth of experience with many kinds of boats in various sea conditions, I had to rely on imagination to guess at the actions and reactions that were likely to occur. A boat too big to be heeled at will by the weight of the occupant(s) would travel sideways at great speed when broadside to a forty-foot breaking wave. A hard bilge, so beneficial in other circumstances, would be more likely to catch and trip the boat over than the slack bilge of the Swampscott. I concluded that Charlie's final design was the best compromise. Ned promptly purchased an Alden, to learn to row with a sliding seat and get in condition for the grueling task ahead.

The aluminum boat, christened *Sea Tomato*, was launched in Camden, Maine, on a sparkling day, and Marjorie and I were there with three of our grandchildren to participate in the first tests. There were two Oarmasters with which to experiment with rowing positions, and various oars. After Charlie and Ned had tried it out, they generously turned it over to us for a very pleasant, but painfully slow, family row around Camden Harbor. Then, with water ballast to simulate the weight of supplies, they turned it upside down with a crane. It immediately righted itself, as planned.

After more than a year's delay, due to continual unfavorable weather forecasts, *Sea Tomato* arrived safely in Antarctica. Thirty-six hours of sailing at the start tended to detract from the significance of the feat in the eyes of purists, for many had already sailed across the treacherous waters. Charlie was not on board, having made other plans.

He built a small cruising sailboat out of steel, in which he proposed to explore further the waters of South America around fifty-five degrees south latitude. He asked us to design and make an Appledore 16 in two sections, which could be nested on the small deck of his boat and quickly assembled and launched to carry out an extra anchor or a line to a tree or boulder on shore in the event of sudden violent winds. When we had completed this project, Charlie and I tested it out in the roughest water we could find off Kittery Point. After passing this test, along with trials of the little boats making up the bow and stern sections, Charlie drove off with the the new creation, and we liked it so much that we added it to our line of boats for those cruising people who like to row in a high performance tender too long for their boats. When Charlie got to Chile in his sailboat, he married a local girl, and we haven't heard from him since.

AEM sailing a wood Appledore 16. This unusual rig makes it possible to sail in what has proved to be one of the finest of rowing boats. The combination of wood and epoxy resin makes for light weight and easy maintenance while at the same time giving the traditional beauty and elegance of the finest boats of yesteryear.

Appledore 16s have since embarked on many lesser adventures, cruising down the Mississippi, along the Maine Coast, and in many other waters, always giving a good account of themselves, according to owners.

The Appledore 16 was becoming pretty well established as a rowing boat, nicely filling in the performance gaps left by the Aldens and the Martin. As a yacht tender, it had carried four adults on one occasion, although this would certainly be an overload under most conditions. It had carried a tremendous load of gear and supplies. Although a race between an Alden single and an Appledore 16, with equal oarsmen, Oarmasters, and oars, would obviously be unfair to the wider, heavier boat, under the usual relaxed effort of recreational rowing, it proved to be not that much slower. With one person, its seaworthiness was being documented over and over again. One traveled down the Mississippi, through the wakes of high-speed tugs and barges, as well as the currents, eddies, and snags encountered by Huck Finn. One is rowed in the worst of winter weather on Long Island Sound. For an extended rowing cruise, sleeping on shore, it would be hard to beat.

It was inevitable that further versatility, via a sail, would sooner or later be requested. Dick Fisher's son had rigged a sail on an Alden single, and a man in Spain had rigged one on a double, neither of which I have ever seen. I cannot imagine that an Alden would be at all satisfactory under sail. The late Marshall Dodge, of "Bert and I" fame, used to paddle an Alden single with a double-bladed kayak paddle, using a backrest and foot-controlled rudder which we made for him. He carried an umbrella for restful down-wind runs, which he said met the life style he preferred. The characteristics of the Appledore 16 suggested much greater adaptability to sail than the Aldens, but left many unanswered questions.

Could a rig be devised which would have minimum conflict with what we considered the all-important functions of rowing, using one or two Oarmasters in three different positions? This immediately eliminated the possibility of a centerboard or the usual daggerboard. The speed would be too great for leeboards, as we soon found out. The final solution was a daggerboard on one side, the added complication of two wells proving to be unnecessary. The mast consisted of two aluminum lower masts, pivoted at the gunwales, and bolted together at the top. Between them was a pivoted topmast, which could be locked in place with a sliding spectacle member, or folded back out of the way, so that the entire mast assembly, weighing only seven pounds, could be folded down inside the boat, resting on the bow seat.

The sail was a roller reefing genoa jib, set flying but furled, the only standing rigging being a backstay clipped to the rudder.

The whole rig left something to be desired from the point of view of the average user. It would not come about from any point of sailing by merely putting the tiller down. It had to be sailed up to a close-hauled mode first, and then the sail had to be helped around both lower masts, before losing all headway and getting in irons. The luff could not be tightened much, because the mast bent in compression. The thirty-three-inch beam, more than adequate for rowing, left little room or extra stability for the hasty position changing of sailing. We spent a lot of time pointing out these disadvantages to would-be buyers, usually persuading them not to buy the sailing rig.

Despite the obvious limitations of the sailing rig, it nevertheless did what it was supposed to do. It was almost completely out of the way when rowing, but in less than two minutes the boat could be under full sail. When wind increased too much, sail area could be reduced in seconds. When a sudden gust puts water in the cockpit, the sail can be furled completely, and, instead of the sail flogging like a flock of angry seagulls, so annoying to sailors of "high performance" boats, a peaceful calm prevails for bailing out and regrouping. And in extreme conditions, the entire rig can be stowed inside the boat, followed by a safe row home. The trusty oars proved to be a boon under adverse conditions. All too often, the wind goes down with the sun, the mosquitoes come out, it begins to get cold, and hunger gnaws. The boat sails painfully slowly, if at all, and the current carries it away from its destination. Few sailboats can be rowed or paddled efficiently.

I once sailed an Appledore 16 in a full gale in the winter. Returning up Chauncey Creek to our dock, I heard a loud report like a gun shot. Upon landing, I discovered that one of our biggest trees had been blown down, narrowly missing compressing a car into scrap. Needless to say, I had been using little more sail area than a handkerchief.

For all its limitations, I still think that the sailing rig in the hands of an agile and capable skipper offers great possibilities. Oth-

The Cape Horn Model. The two halves were designed to nest and fit on the deck of a sailboat bound for the treacherous waters of the Cape. For the less adventuresome this model provides the fun of rowing in a long, capable boat which can come apart to stow in a small space, or become two little boats for young crew members to explore distant harbors. Photo: Marjorie Martin.

ers have equipped the boat with the tried and true spritsail rig, which has its advantages, including easier tacking, but it is not as easy to stow in an emergency. While almost all Appledore 16s, wood and fiberglass, go out as strictly rowing boats, the sailing rig is available for the few special situations where it alone fills the bill. I cannot leave the subject without recalling one day when my grandson, Nathan, then about seven or eight, and I were sailing in the ocean in the Appledore. The wind was moderate, but a high-performance, self-rescuing sailboat had capsized half a mile ahead of us. As we approached, the skipper righted it by applying leverage to the centerboard. It came up quickly, but went right on and capsized the other way. This was repeated several times, as the aging skipper gradually lost strength and body heat in our frigid Maine water. Fortunately a power boat came to the rescue before we reached him. "Unsinkable" and "self-rescuing" do not necessarily mean armchair safety. I have successfully "self-rescued" in a capsized sailboat, but later been only too glad to accept assistance in the same boat under slightly different circumstances.

With the passing years, our little "mom and pop" business of recreational rowing gradually gained acceptance. We never did have any dreams or expectations of making a lot of money, but we were able to pay our bills on time, and, outside of some production problems, the business was not only enjoyable but quite gratifying. A stranger approached me at the Annapolis Boat Show one year and said that I had saved his life. He related that his job in Washington involved a great deal of high pressure and stress. At the end of the day he would drive home through heavy traffic, still "up tight," and grinding his teeth. He would have a couple of stiff drinks to relax before dinner, all to no avail. His dinner would land in a lump in his stomach, and he was becoming so disagreeable to his wife that he feared a divorce might result. Then he got an Alden from a local dealer and rowed instead of drinking. He came off the water refreshed in body and spirit, and, as he said, became a functioning human being again. This one incident gave me a great deal of satisfaction and made up for hours of frustration struggling with late deliveries, quality control, taxes and foolish government regulations.

Both Marjorie and I enjoyed teaching rowing to the people who were interested enough to come to Kittery Point. Some became lifelong friends, and many returned later to have their rowing checked or just to say hello and thank us for introducing them to the sport. We were reluctant to establish dealers, because we feared that some would not take the pains that we did to keep our customers happy. We thought there was no place in recreational boating for the stereotype automobile dealer, schooled in adversary selling rather than creative selling. So we watched the growth of the sport we started with mixed emotions. On the one hand, we sought success as measured in increasing sales. On the other, we deplored the tendency for recreational rowing to become more and more impersonal, with customers becoming distant numbers rather than new friends. Whatever our feelings, we could not control the growth of the sport and had no choice but to roll with the punches, to some extent at least. We began to have a few dealers, hoping that they would share our philosophy.

About this time, another recreational shell surfaced in California. It was called the Torpedo Dory, and the word was out that there would be dealers all over the country, each dealer a "fleet captain" who would organize local races. When I saw the colored brochure, it made our simple black and white specifications seem very crude by comparison. I was worried that we would soon be left in the dust in the very industry we had started. But as I studied the brochure, I saw that it depicted the shape of a racing shell, shortened and widened, with the fin required by a rocker bottom. Also, to my astonishment, I saw that it was made with an inner liner, a manufacturing shortcut sure to introduce many problems. But how were the general public to find out about this except by painful experience?

I was somewhat reassured when I received the following telephone call from California:

Prospect: Is this Martin Marine?

AM: Yes.

Prospect: Do you make the Alden Ocean Shell?

AM: Yes.

Prospect: Is it anything like the Torpedo Dory?

AM: No.

Prospect: Good. I will mail you a check today.

Shortly thereafter the Torpedo Dory faded into oblivion, to be followed by many another inner liner shell.

Like most people, I have always admired those who become successful in any field of endeavor. Outstanding people share certain characteristics regardless of how they choose to apply them. We were honored to find some well known names among the growing list of Alden owners. One of the first was John Hayden, Governor of American Samoa. Although I never met him, I felt that I knew him from his many letters. He used his Alden to carry his skin-diving equipment out to reefs, there to pursue what is a fascinating sport in those waters. He remarked on the seaworthiness and carrying capacity of the boat. He also used to row at night, a delight missed by so many, and he could sneak up to anchored ships to see if they were discharging oil on the pristine waters. No careless captain expected to be caught in the act by the governor in a rowing shell.

Shortly after Governor Hayden ordered his Alden, I received a letter from the I.R.S. I know of no one who becomes elated upon receiving such a missive, and I was no exception. I was relieved to discover that it came from the head of the I.R.S. in Samoa; he wanted to get an Alden so he could race against the governor.

We numbered Rockefellers, DuPonts, and Roosevelts (Oyster Bay; not Hyde Park) among our clientele. The Aga Kahn tried one out at Harvard and ordered five, which we shipped to Switzerland, receiving a check from Paris. A senator, a presidential candidate, two members of the cabinet, Frank Perdue, Ted Koppel, Alistair Cook's wife, and a vice president of General Motors all became owners. Bill Koch, the American cross-country skier who thrilled television audiences by his startling performance in world and Olympic competition in a sport previously dominated by Europeans, came to Kittery one day to find out about rowing. He said that the team was trying to devise effective methods for training in the off-season. As he explained it, running alone did not do it, and the skiing simulators, such as Nordic Trac, were far in the future. Bill was tested on a treadmill, wired for all the vital signs of stress, as the sports physicians gradually increased the slope to the maximum angle and the speed to the highest level. He still had stamina and endurance to spare, meaning that the treadmill could not make him "max out." He returned later with an arm-actuated weight device, which he used at the same time, and was able to reach his limits. This suggested rowing as an exercise that could be even more taxing than cross-country skiing. I showed him the basics, and we set off together, I noting wryly that for the first few strokes I was able to keep ahead of a famous athlete. My success was short lived, however, for he soon caught on to the technique. Several members of both the men's and women's Olympic team followed his example and purchased our boats.

In the world of competitive rowing, skepticism was gradually giving way, as Alden rowers advanced to the most prominent positions in national and international racing in eights, fours, doubles, and singles. There were still those who judged a recreational shell by how closely it resembled a racing boat, like condemning a van because it does not look like an Indy machine, but more and more of the racing fraternity were beginning to understand the theory behind the

Aldens. Some, no longer able to get to the flat water and ideal conditions demanded by the racing boats, were settling for the versatile
Aldens, which could be rowed anywhere within driving distance of
some kind of H$_2$O. Some had both a racing single and an Alden, and
more than one volunteered that if only one boat were possible, it
would be the Alden.

Among the top racing oarsmen to row in Aldens were Tiff Wood
and Charlie Altekruse, featured in the best-selling book, *The Amateurs*,
by David Halbestrom (an Alden owner). It is a great tribute to the
author that a book about the obscure sport of rowing should make the
best-selling list. My favorite part of the book mentions some advice an
older oarsman gave to one of the young Olympic hopefuls: "Just
remember, there is more to life than rowing...but not much." Charlie
was particularly good at teaching rowing to beginners. He understood,
better than most, that neither our dealers nor most of our customers
would ever aspire to row in the Olympics and did not chastise them
for the minor flaws in technique which would be detrimental to a
world-class competitor. Instead he made sure they were comfortable
and happy in the boat. Charlie was a great addition to the rowing clin-
ics we hold for dealers and novice rowers alike. Fred Borshelt, an
Olympic sweep oarsman, served well in the same capacity, and Tiff
Wood was planning to, but the occasion did not arrive until he was
otherwise occupied. One day Tiff and Charlie came to Kittery to row,
and it happened to be almost dead low tide. To get from our dock to
the ocean, one must go down through Chauncy Creek, a distance of
about a mile. At low tide there are a series of rapids, just above the
Chauncy Creek Lobster Pier. One must follow a somewhat serpentine
course to avoid the many rocks just below the surface. I instructed Tiff
and Charlie to follow directly behind me on the course so familiar to
me but unknown to them. This they did, and as we passed the lobster
pier, the lobster eaters on the deck applauded in the mistaken belief
that the old man was beating the two young athletes in a race. King for
a day, or at least a small part of one, until we reached the ocean.

When a Mr. Dalton, vice president of General Motors, ordered a
boat, we soon received an urgent call from the G.M. expediting
department. The gentleman assured me that he was prepared to fly to
Boston to expedite the shipment of the Alden for Mr. Big. We were

behind on shipments at the time, and there was a waiting period of two or three weeks. I said that he could fly to Boston if he wanted, and expedite to his heart's content, but we would ship the boat only after delivering all of the ones ordered previously. He couldn't seem to believe that some ornery, independent, insubordinate cuss from Maine would fail to accord the special treatment expected and usually received by the big brass at G.M. When I finally convinced him that his expediting efforts would be in vain, the shipping department took over. They informed me that they were going to have the boat flown to Detroit. I told them that we had not been able to make satisfactory arrangements for shipping by plane, except overseas, where the long, light package could fit in the tail of a 747. He merely repeated the magic words "We're General Motors," and several days and many phone calls later, instructed us to deliver the boat to Flying Tigers at Logan Airport. At that time, Flying Tigers were not prepared to handle any such load, as their planes were all equipped to handle containers only. It turned out that G.M. purchased the space of several containers to carry our little boat. Quite an honor, but also a possible explanation for the profusion of Japanese and European cars here.

When John Lehman was Secretary of the Navy, he had someone call us up about an Alden. He said that all of the other people had offered to supply a boat at cost, and wanted to know what discount we would offer. The answer was that we would not give any discount at all, but we did offer to bring a boat to Annapolis, since we were going to the boat show there anyway. He decided on the Alden, despite the somewhat un-American approach. He was evidently not one of the many who go for the discount, without checking into what makes up the possibly inflated list price. I remember standing in an Alden, looking over a bulkhead at the Naval Academy, watching a full-dress parade in honor of the visiting secretary.

One day we received a telephone call from Kennebunkport. It was Nick Brady, who was at the Bush house with the presidential candidate and Bob Teeter, who was in charge of polling. They wanted to come down (up) to Kittery to try rowing if they could find a time when Mr. Bush did not require their services. In due course they appeared with their wives, and both rowed, and both bought Aldens. I offered gratuitous advice to pass on to the candidate that if he rowed an Alden instead of driving that Cigarette-type boat he would receive more votes in certain quarters. Despite the fact that he failed to receive, or chose to ignore, such good advice, he won the election, for which I was not sorry.

Along with increasing numbers of orders from the great and not-so-great, we began to get considerable attention from the media. It was quite a thrill to see ourselves on national TV, and read articles in periodicals such as *Sports Illustrated, Fortune,* and the *New York Times Magazine,* as well as various other boating, sports, and exercise publications. The best article was written by a senior writer from *Time,* who was asked to write for the *New York Times Magazine.* His name was Peter Stoler and, like any good writer, he made a thorough study of the sport before setting down any words. He came to Kittery, where we gave him one of our rowing lessons, and he spent a lot of time out in a boat. His article, entitled "The Solitary Joys of Sculling," was so good we have sent reprints out ever since, and we were swamped with orders when it first came out. Peter was later promoted to head the *Time* bureau in Canada, and he bought an Alden. Sadly, cancer claimed him far before his time.

It often seemed difficult to believe that our little boats, which so far have never sold in any really large numbers, and may never do so, were receiving so much attention. It was an unexpected honor that so many prominent people were beginning to see merit in the boats which began just as a personal hobby to be enjoyed only by Marjorie and myself. The same thought haunted me as I sat around a table at the Harvard Club of Boston, surrounded by the officers and directors of the Alden Ocean Shell Association. I, as an honorary director, asked myself how it could come about that these prominent people from the worlds of business, law, medicine, and sports, would take the time, money, and effort to travel from various distant areas to preside over an organization of owners of our boats.

But to me the greatest honor of all ocurred when Ray Hunt called from Tilton, New Hampshire, and expressed an interest in coming to Kittery to see an Alden. I had not seen him for several years, and looked forward to seeing him again. He walked down with me to the old stone dock of the Decaturs, where we kept an Alden in the water. He asked me to row it past the dock at various speeds, a series

A fleet of Martin Marine boats, each designed to meet specific rowing criteria. Clockwise, from top: the Martin, the fiberglass Appledore 16, the double Alden rigged as a single, the Kittery Skiff without its Oarmaster, and the most versatile and popular of all, the Alden single. Photo: Ann Grinnell.

of "row-bys" I was only too happy to perform. When I came ashore he said, "I guess you have got it about right." Coming from Ray Hunt, this was quite a compliment to the design.

Later, Ray, Douglas, and I had lunch together at Padenarum, where he had moved. Douglas was only four years old when I worked for Ray, but now he could discuss design concepts, particularly aeronautical theory, on equal terms. Ray, as usual, was thinking of ways to improve the performance of boats under both sail and power. He showed us a 110, his first design, equipped with a radical and very tall mast, far aft. It carried a huge quadrilateral jib and forestaysail only, there being no mainsail. It had made remarkable speed to windward in light air, and Ray was looking for a way to get rid of the high top of the mast, as well as the jib, in heavy weather. We were unable to come up with any ideas which did not require excessive weight, or Rube Goldberg complication, or both, although we were dealing with a somewhat similar concept in the Appledore 16, and were later to devise a sliding gunter rig which might have worked out. He was also experimenting with a deep-V hull with a centerboard in the bow. This would drop down to facilitate steering at slow speed, but would lift up by dynamic action when planing. Also, this boat had water ballast tanks which could be empty until planing speed was achieved and then filled through the centerboard trunk to hold the boat down in a seaway. Ray was once again ahead of his time, and ballast tanks, so common on ships, are just beginning to find their place on power and sail boats.

When we were exhibiting at the Newport Boat Show, I planned to sneak out for a while and drive over to Padenarum to visit Ray. I called him up, but there was no answer. Later, his younger son, Josh, came over to our booth, and, with tears in his eyes, told me that his father had only recently passed away. Thus ended one of the greatest careers of the century in boat designing. For me, it was a great loss, coupled with regret that I would never have a chance to thank or repay him for all he taught me. It was hard to accept that the great enthusiasm for new ideas and the infectious laugh were gone forever. But whenever I see a beautiful Concordia under full sail in a good breeze, or lying at anchor in a quiet harbor, or drive by the 210 which lives in Kittery, I am reminded that something of Ray Hunt lives on and probably will forever.

One hundred Aldens and Martins gather for the annual Alden race on the Charles, which precedes the Head-of-the-Charles Regatta. Photographer unknown.

24 • The United States Rowing Association

$\mathcal{W}$ hen we first started selling Alden Ocean Shells, it became apparent that among our best customers were the people, mostly men, who had rowed at Ivy League schools and colleges and never forgot the feeling of exhilaration and well being that followed the vigorous exercise. I think many of them, deprived of the opportunity for continued rowing at one of the few exclusive rowing clubs, had already visualized such a boat when they first heard of the Alden. They knew what they wanted and how to use it, regardless of their distance from ideal racing shell conditions. Not only did they require little sales or instruction effort, they were used to careful handling and frequent repairs of fragile racing shells and, perhaps due to gentle upbringing and education, were not as demanding as the general public. Their good-natured tolerance of our early mistakes astonished me.

The seats provided a good example. The very first boats had plywood seats, to which was glued a one-inch strip of closed-cell foam (now purchased rather than acquired from the Braintree dump). We decided to up-grade to a shaped seat and borrowed what was reputedly the most popular one at the Union Boat Club, from which to make a fiberglass mold. When the mold was completed, Everett Pearson asked me to come down and work out a fiberglass lay-up. One of his best fiberglass workers, a very capable lady from Portugal, was assigned to help me out. We made a fairly substantial seat, and when it cured I put it on the floor and stood on it. It promptly cracked and broke in half. We then made another, putting uni-directional fiberglass around the edges to reenforce it. This time it passed the test with flying colors, and I felt that the problem was solved. Sometime later, however, a new (and short-lived) foreman told the lady to disregard my instructions and eliminate the costly uni-directional fiberglass. When I found out about this from irate customers with broken seats, the correct lay-up was immediately reinstated, and all the broken seats were replaced without charge. I had no way of knowing how many of the defective ones were still out there. Talking to an ex-oarsman one day, I asked him the usual questions about how he liked his Alden. When he answered enthusiastically, I asked if he had encountered any problems, to which his reply was negative. When I pressed him further, he said, "Well, the seat broke, but I didn't want to bother you, so I repaired it myself."

On another occasion, Greg Stone, former national champion sculler, approached me after a race and said he had a bone to pick. He had ordered a part but never received an invoice. I asked what the part was, and, from his description, I could tell that it was a stainless steel angle supporting the teak clogs, or footrests, on an early model Oarmaster. I told him that these parts could fail in fatigue, and therefore we had replaced them for nothing. "But this was ten years old," he protested. I replied that the part was defective, and the delay in showing its weakness was irrelevant.

With more oarsmen showing interest in the new boats, I thought it would be wise to investigate their association, then called the National Association of Amateur Oarsmen. I contacted them them at the New York Boat Show, where I met Bill Stowe, a somewhat later graduate of Kent School, and crew coach first at Columbia and then at the Coast Guard Academy. Crew was a new sport at the latter, but after Bill Stowe got going, some of the other college crews must have felt like the slower rumrunners of the past being overtaken by the Coast Guard. The N.A.A.O. was given a booth at the show by management, so that they could promote the sport, hand out membership applications, and sell their rowing gift items. They also had on exhibition a single scull incorporating a new product, carbon fiber, made in England by Tony Baker. I became convinced that, despite our limited advertising budget, we should advertise in their national publication, then called *The Oarsman*. Ernie Bayer was the treasurer at the time, and our first check for advertising helped him to balance their small budget. Although the name and the personnel have changed, we have continued to this day to support the national organization, not only

*Aldens at Sandy Beach in Cohasset for the annual race around Minot's Light.
Photo: Marjorie Martin.*

with our advertising, but also indirectly through the seven hundred
members of the Alden Ocean Shell Association, most of whose dues
go to the present U.S.R.A., and many of whom also contribute to the
National Rowing Foundation to help finance American rowers (male
and female, I am happy to add) in international competition. We are
proud of the fact that so many rowers who started in Aldens have gone
on to achieve such distinction in racing shells, including Andy Sud-
duth and Liz O'Leary. I hope that our boats can continue to support
the U.S.R.A. with money and promising young rowers.

In 1972 the N.A.A.O. again was offered free space at the National
Boat Show in New York. There was a problem in persuading people to
take care of the booth during the ten grueling days and nights of the
show. The few manufacturers of racing shells were booked as much
eighteen months ahead and were not enthusiastic about having the
curious public, particularly the younger members, pound fists on their
exquisite craftsmanship. Neither rowers nor manufacturers had time

to spend explaining why the seats had wheels. Consequently, we were invited to take over the booth, providing we sold memberships and artifacts on behalf of the N.A.A.O.

This arrangement worked out very well for all concerned for several years. Rowing received some good exposure and seemed to be coming out of the woodwork at last; and our boats, the only recreational shells available, were becoming known. Working with the N,A.A.O., I thought I should learn more about the goings on in the world of competitive rowing and began to read race results in *The Oarsman.* The name of Jim Dietz appeared frequently as a constant winner of important sculling races. One day a tall young man appeared at New York Boat Show booth and appeared to be curious about the Alden. I struck up a conversation by asking him if he had ever rowed. When he replied in the affirmative, I asked further questions: With a sliding seat? In an eight? In a single? In a race? Having received positive answers to all these questions, I decided to show off my knowledge of competitive rowing and do a little name-dropping, so I said, "You may have raced against Jim Dietz." "No," he replied quietly, "I am Jim Dietz."

In later years, we shared the booth with a competitor, Art Javes, with his Row Cat. Art had worked in the design office of the Luders Marine Construction Company, a concern not unknown to me. Later he had designed the first really successful sailing catamaran, the Aqua-Cat, still going strong today under the new owner. While the racing scull is king on the hill for speed, the catamaran certainly occupies that exalted position for stability. Although we had done everything possible to increase the stability of a monohull of a given beam, capsize was still possible under some conditions. A sailing catamaran can always turn over, but it is difficult to imagine any circumstances that would capsize a rowing catamaran. For many years some people, being particularly concerned about capsizing in a narrow boat, had toyed with the idea of a rowing catamaran.

Buckminster Fuller, the great inventor of the geodesic dome, among many other ingenious innovations, designed and built a rowing catamaran which he called *The Needles.* When he was over eighty he bought an Alden and drove up to Kittery Point to pick it up. He stayed for some time, and had tea with Marjorie, Douglas, and me. To

Marjorie with first prize in the first Alden National Championships at Toledo. Photo: unknown.

my everlasting regret, I became somewhat tongue-tied and failed to ask him the questions that would have started him on some of his most interesting and pertinent theories, which he seemed so anxious to explain. I was nervous about the subject of catamarans coming up, since I did not want to appear to be lecturing such a great engineer, but at the same time I could not deny my belief that natural laws did not favor the two hulls for speed with limited power. He never pursued the rowing catamaran idea, to my knowledge, and Art Javes was the first to put one in real production.

Art is a thorough gentleman, and we had no hesitation in sharing the booth with him. He never indulged in bad-mouthing our products, though they certainly had failings at that time, and we reciprocated. It turned out that he lived near the city and did not mind staying until closing time at night. On the other hand, he was anxious to get work done at his factory during the day. Living at my mother's house in New Jersey, our preferred schedule was just the opposite, so we took care of his exhibit during the day, and he took care of ours at night. Later, Art Javes' catamarans made a real breakthrough in providing a safe means for paraplegics, quadriplegics, and other physically or mentally handicapped people to row, a great addition to the sport, about which more later.

In recent years, the U.S.R.A. has made a real effort to broaden the base of rowing, and remove the elitist stigma. The change in name signifies a change in attitude toward women in rowing and the growing number of rowing programs in colleges; and private, public, and parochial schools have swelled the ranks of competing rowers. New rowing clubs are springing up, and old, long inactive ones have been revived. The total number of participants has increased tremendously. National teams for the Olympics and other international events can benefit from the increasing numbers of young rowers coming along. Masters rowing is gaining in popularity. But the real potential for growth, most agree, is in the sport of recreational rowing.

More and more health experts are conceding that rowing is the best of all forms of aerobic exercise. It employs more muscles than running or bicycling and does not damage joints like the former, or threaten accidents like the latter(bicycling ranks number one as a source of emergency room patients in many hospitals). Cross-country skiing ranks a close second to sliding seat rowing, but other sports, such as tennis or golf, while far better for health than no exercise at all, are far down the list. Based on the known facts about aerobic exercise, rowing should count its participants in the millions instead of the present thousands.

Can or will the U.S.R.A.do enough to put recreational rowing in its rightful place? That remains to be seen. I am somewhat ambivalent on the subject. On the one hand, it would be most gratifying to see the little activity which we started suddenly blossoming out into a massive sport to rival tennis, running, or bicycle riding. On the other hand, I would be sorry to find our business becoming large and impersonal. I enjoy introducing new people to rowing, teaching novices to row, and keeping in contact with happy owners. Most of our dealers have come here to learn how to teach rowing and learn, firsthand, about our somewhat unusual business policies. As business increases, pressure builds to place more organizational tiers between the owner and management, and rules replace face-to-face decisions. We cannot stop or delay what may become inevitable, but we can at least try to maintain the old-fashioned policies which have so far proved beneficial to all concerned.

AEM sailing the Appledore 19. A little too big and heavy for good aerobic exercise for one rower, this boat proved to be remarkable under sail. Photo: Ann Grinnell.

25 • *The Appledore 19*

*a*ny design may be considered in two parts: concept and execution. The concept of a ship might be to carry passengers or airplanes. The design of an airplane carrier, no matter how well executed, would hardly be suitable for an ocean liner. A motor yacht designed with the concept of providing the ultimate luxury while tied up at a marina might not fare well in the open ocean, however well the concept was carried out in the design. A sailboat conceived for the sole purpose of winning races under the foolish and ever- changing I.O..R. rule might be extremely ugly, unseaworthy, and unpleasant to sail, but if it brings home the silverware, no one can deny that the designer carried out the concept with great skill. The best K-1, or white water kayak, would be unacceptable for a family interested in taking a leisurely trip down a placid river.

The concept of the Alden proved to be acceptable to certain segments of the boating and exercising public, and the execution, constantly updated and improved, found favor with these groups. The Appledore 16 incorporated the slightly different concepts of greater stability, seaworthiness, and carrying capacity at the expense of less speed and portability. The world must decide how well these concepts were executed, but experience indicates a smaller but no less enthusiastic owner response. The sailing rig, in my opinion, made it a most capable rowing boat that would sail, a concept destined to have a far narrower appeal than the straight rowing model. We have considered many alternate sailing rigs, from spritsails to rigid airfoils, but none seemed to meet the requirements of the total concept as well. For the few who are willing to put up with the challenges of sailing it, the sailing model Appledore 16 provides faster and safer sailing than many small boats, in a very capable sliding seat or fixed seat rowing boat. We shall continue to advise those seeking a boat more easily handled under sail to look elsewhere.

The original concept for the Appledore 19 was for a seaworthy open boat capable of utilizing the power of two big, strong rowers. While the Appledore 16 can accept two rowers, and is very satisfactory for husband and wife combinations, it reaches its maximum hull speed with two strong men sprinting, and drags a larger wake rather than going appreciably faster. The 19 concept, with three feet more length, and much more displacement at its designed waterline, was intended to meet this requirement in a much more satisfactory manner. This was the basic idea. I completed the design, and East-West built a prototype, which we tested extensively. As expected, it was pretty heavy for one person to row, but once it got up to speed, it rowed fairly well, although not as fast or as easy a pull as the 16. In my opinion the 19 calls for too slow and hard a stroke to qualify it as a good aerobic exercise machine. In general, good aerobic exercise requires the muscles to change length as much as possible with minimum change in tension. Weight lifting does just the opposite, and, while good for building up muscles on young athletes, it is contraindicated for older people trying to avoid heart attacks. The Alden, with the 64-inch spread (distance between oarlocks) which we introduced after a few years, proved very satisfactory for aerobic exercise. The lower gearing made for an easier pull and a higher stroke. The Appledore 16, offering more resistance, required a somewhat harder pull and consequently a lower stroke rate, but still acceptable. The 19 seemed to me to go too far in this direction to be really satisfactory for aerobic exercise for one person.

With two rowers, the 19 was far better, going at a good speed with an easier pull. In rough water, with two strong rowers, the 19 gave the ultimate feeling of security. Plenty of power, plenty of stability, and plenty of flare and freeboard. With air chambers under the bow and stern decks, it was virtually unsinkable. Although I could not fault the execution of the original concept, the concept itself would fit the requirements of very few people. I used it for its designed purpose only once. We were cruising, anchored in Cuttyhunk, when a severe storm came up during the night. Hargy Heap was aboard, ever anxious to try the most severe conditions. We rigged the 19 with two Oarmasters, a challenging operation with the boat bouncing around in the heavy chop. Rowing gave exactly the feeling of security that was

AEM and Hargy Heap rowing the prototype Appledore 19. Photo: Ann Grinnell.

expected, but in a couple of hours the wind diminished suddenly, and the dinghies that had not braved the storm began to ply the waters of the harbor again. It was obvious that few people would ever require the capabilities of the 19 as a double rowing boat, but for those few, it would be hard to equal.

Another concept for the Appledore 19 was the ability to sail. I did not want any rig which would interfere with rowing, with either one or two Oarmasters or one or two fixed seat stations. The entire rig would have to be capable of stowing inside the boat, and being set up out on the water, like the sails in a whaleboat. I wanted to make tacking much easier and more positive than in the 16. Also, I wanted the center of effort to be as low as possible, for maximum stability. The thirty-nine-inch beam was far less than that of almost any other sailboat of similar length. With these requirements in mind, I designed a ketch rig, with unstayed masts just over eight-feet high. Sliding gunter topmasts gave sufficient leading edge or aspect ratio to improve efficiency. With the small, round topmasts fitting in pockets in the sails, the efficiency of the tops of the sails was much improved. Full battens, tapered toward the luff, gave the ideal sail shape which many boats now incorporate. The aluminum daggerboard, offset to one side, was the same as used on the 16. It could stall and allow the boat to go sideways, like a 110, until it got up sufficient speed to develop the necessary lift. I made an airfoil section for the bottom of the daggerboard, with wings, similar to those first used on *Australia,* as an experiment. It improved upwind performance somewhat, but it had to be installed from under the boat, not the easiest operation from inside the boat in choppy water. Lines from the yoke on the rudder led forward of the mizzen mast to another yoke with a small tiller, where they were secured in clam cleats. Since the tiller could be easily locked amidships, the lines to the rudder could be adjusted to balance the boat on any point of sailing. With the mizzen sheet in a clam cleat, the boat would sail along by itself, although I always held the main sheet to be safe.

Of all the boats I have ever sailed, from the original Barnacle to the 82-foot schooner *Deliverance,* the one I enjoy most is the Appledore 19. It comes down to concepts. Many people judge a sailboat by how many people it can carry if it is a day sailor or how many it can sleep if it is a cruising boat. Space for shoreside amenities is a high priority, and the closer the cabin resembles a Ramada Inn the better the boat. Others want a boat which will win silverware under the latest revisions of the I.O.R. (International Offshore Rule). Many prefer one-design racing, which I enjoyed for so many years in the 210s. Others like to work on classic wood boats, which are a joy to behold and far more graceful under sail than some of the modern offerings. Sheer size has great appeal, leading some owners to an investment of money and time which may not give a satisfactory return. Sad to relate, sailboats of all kinds have declined sharply in popularity, replaced by the instant gratification of simply turning a key in a power boat. If we continue to avoid any unnecessary expenditure of mental or physical energy we will repeat the fate of the ancient Romans, satiated by free grain and circuses.

For myself, I am inclined to judge any boat by how it goes through the water. A high, wide, boxy power boat, forced through the

signal, the four men on each side lifted in unison, to begin the final journey of the deceased in his expensive eternal abode. At this point, the bottom fell out of the coffin, and the corpse landed with a thud on the stone floor. Thus ended the foam casket business.

Both Everett and Neil Tillotson expected recreational rowing to take off like a skyrocket, as the Sunfish had done. They were the first of a long line of people who had the same expectations. My views were more realistic and still are. Despite the great health benefits of rowing, and the now generally accepted doctrine that rowing is the best of all aerobic exercises, without the injuries of running or the hazards of bicycle riding, it seems that the general public has not really embraced the sport during the twenty years that it has been available. I expected a modest but steady growth, and that is the way it happened. Everett, on the other hand, was prepared to set up a very efficient assembly line, using an overhead powered chain conveyor, as soon as conditions warranted it. Although demand for the Aldens did not diminish as did the demand for other boats in the recession of the early seventies, neither did it escalate rapidly as so many expected. When business returned to normal, Tillotson-Pearson began the dramatic ascendancy that has brought them to the prominent position in the sailboat and powerboat business which they enjoy today. The Aldens, representing a relatively small dollar volume, required undue attention to quality control, shipping, and the little details which are important to owners. The little shells no longer seemed to fit in with the direction the growing boat manufacturing company was taking.

Meanwhile, Dick Tatlock, a nephew of Dick Fisher, and an enthusiastic Alden owner, asked us to consider having our boats built by the company he worked for, Hyperform, in Hingham, Massachusetts. It seemed to be a good suggestion, for several reasons. They were making very fine kayaks and were well versed in the lightweight, flexible construction which would bend instead of fracturing when subjected to the stresses of rocky rapids. They were much nearer to Kittery Point, facilitating quality inspection and pickup of boats on our trailer. And they had none of the big boats which seem to distract attention from the smaller ones. We decided to move our molds to Hingham and left Tillotson-Pearson on the best of terms and mutual understanding.

Hyperform built the Aldens to high standards of quality, and the new arrangement was quite satisfactory for some time. Unfortunately, Sam Galpin, the owner, got carried away with the idea of making the kayaks out of plastic, in a rotational mold. He had a dream of turning out finished hulls with hardly any of the hand labor required for fiberglass. Many others, before and since, have had the same dream, usually with disastrous results. Hyperform was no exception. They ceased production of fiberglass kayaks for their dealers, anticipating much greater success with the new process. When this did not pan out, they went into bankruptcy, leaving the Aldens without a builder.

We were fortunate in being able to make arrangements with Lincoln Canoe Company, in Waldoboro, Maine, to take over production. This worked out fairly well for several years, although we did have some delays in shipments during the busy season. Then another concept came on the scene at Lincoln Canoe Company (just reorganized as Maine Marine Company). The idea was to shrink the lines of an I.O.R. boat down to 16 feet and promote it as a canoe, sailboat, and rowing shell. A prototype was steamrollered in to the Small Boat Clinic at Mystic Seaport, without the usual advance registration and permission. There it demonstrated its qualities. As a canoe it failed to meet the basic requirements of being narrow at the bow and stern for easy paddling, and light for portaging, or launching from a car top. This boat, at 140 pounds, was far too heavy, and the I.O.R. beam was excessive. Although any floating object can be paddled, as I had proved in a becalmed 210, nothing paddles like a canoe.

It required a dagger board in order to go in a straight line when rowing, and the sliding seat was entirely too high. It seemed like a joke to the salty people at Mystic who tried rowing it. Then, with a great deal of delay and difficulty, the sailing rig was set up. It distinguished itself by becoming the only boat to capsize under sail that day. I warned the Lincoln people to have nothing to do with it, but, beguiled by the promise of big money behind the project, they went full speed ahead, tooling up to make four boats per day, while the plug for the new Appledore 19 gathered dust in the background. I couldn't see how their new boat could succeed, given what I considered such a flawed concept. For paddling, there is nothing like a canoe, and many fine builders had been improving on the original

Indian design for years. For sliding seat rowing, we had been supplying the Oarmaster to canoe owners and manufacturers for some time,
as we still do. Sailing rigs for canoes are available from many manufacturers. In short, it appeared that all three of the highly touted functions could be performed far better by other boats. Unfortunately, my
dire predictions were not long in being fulfilled. The company soon
went bankrupt, owing large sums of money to many trusting suppliers.
Lincoln (renamed Maine Marine in connection with production and
financing arrangements with Honnor Marine in England, makers of
the famous Drascome boats) went into bankruptcy, from which they
never recovered. Because of the financial connection with the failing
American company, Honnor Marine also went into bankruptcy. Many
others suffered drastic financial losses from the boat reputed to be
able to do so many things. Unbelievable though it might seem, the
same boat returned, with new financing, new location, mostly new cast
of characters, and new plastic construction, only to go bankrupt again.
Once more the beguiling prospect of big money in the rowing business proved elusive.

The episode was a disaster for us, involving great financial loss and
leaving us without production when we needed it most. Every cloud has
a silver lining, however. Ted Perry, who had married my daughter
Lorna, had been heavily involved in the skiing business in Lake Placid.
Like Lorna, and her brother Rod, he was a certified ski instructor and
ran a retail ski business as well as representing manufacturers. But a hidden talent in woodworking gradually surfaced, and he moved his family
to Kittery Point and began building our wooden boats. Like many
purists, he disdained becoming involved with fiberglass.

With the crisis resulting from the downfall of Lincoln, I used my
best sales technique, acquired through years of selling fork trucks, and
then selling the public on the sport of rowing, to persuade Ted to take
on the production of our fiberglass boats. Fortunately it worked, and
his company, East-West Custom Boats, began making all the Martin
Marine boats, fiberglass as well as wood. Although it was difficult to
learn the entirely different techniques of fiberglass construction, the
boats soon began to meet the highest quality standards ever, and from
then on we never had any serious production delays.

Douglas rowing the Kittery Skiff. Built from a kit by do-it-yourselfers, this little plywood boat provides the least expensive way to get into sliding seat rowing. Photo: Ann Grinnell.

26 • Special Equipment

i nevitably, there were gaps in our varied line of recreational rowing boats. Such is the diversity of requirements, limitations, and preferences of individual potential boat owners that no one manufacturer can ever hope to satisfy them all. Following our original and constantly reinforced thinking that a recreational boat, of any kind, should always seek to provide activities impractical or impossible in a racing shell, rather than pursue the hopeless quest for duplicating its speed, we continued to look for new ways to provide characteristics desirable to some of the people out there who might be induced to trying the joys and health benefits of sliding seat rowing.

One neglected area seemed to be the aspiring home builder, who would enjoy working with wood, providing it was not too complicated, and would like to reduce the monetary investment by an investment of time and skill. I thought often, over a period of several years, about a simple plywood boat. I made little sketches of various approaches but threw them all away as various objections arose. A V-bottom would allow a pretty satisfactory shape, but seemed too complicated for the novice builder. A rocker bottom would be easy to build but it would require a vulnerable skeg or fin to maintain any directional stability, and the stern would drag down at less than satisfactory speeds. A flat bottom in the middle would be ideal in many respects, but bending it up into anything but a pretty flat arc at the ends was out of the question. Slitting the ends of the plywood would help but still not allow enough twist. I had not given up, but the project was definitely on the back burner, when I suddenly thought of shaping the ends out of foam, allowing a straight keel, no skeg, and some transitional shape from the arc of the bottom to a reasonably sharp bow and stern below the waterline. This seemed to be a good compromise for a shape but very fragile structurally. Ted thought of the perfect solution: use solid pine ends, shaped by the same multiple cutting heads used by Hargy Heap to make ornamental ducks and decoys for L.L.Bean and mahogany seats for our Oarmasters.

Thus was born the Kittery Skiff. It was not as fast nor as seaworthy as the Alden, for the subtle hollow waterlines and generous flair could never be duplicated in plywood. But it was the same weight, at 40 pounds, making it easy to handle, and responsive to minimal effort at the oars. Being a true double-ender, with bow and stern identical, and being completely open, it lent itself to turning the Oarmaster around and rowing stern first, with a passenger in the bow, the latter moving to a position to give ideal balance under any conditions of weights or heading to the wind.

Hundreds of the kits went out by truck, plane, and ship, each one complete to the last detail, including Gougeon epoxy, hardener, and metering pumps, all pre-cut parts, and even rubber gloves. Our business in Australia started with the easy-to-ship kits, and they kept it going until molds for the Aldens could be set up. The British Maritime Museum bought one so that their key people could have hands-on experience in combining solid wood construction, as in dugout canoes, and plank-on-frame construction. On discussing this with the renowned John Gardner, I was surprised to learn that our "new" method of construction had been used many years previously, in many lands, albeit without the wonders of epoxy resin, in the transition from solid wood to plank-on-frame construction.

Making the Appledore 16 in two parts proved quite a challenge, and after testing out Charlie Porter's, which was the first, we found various other applications. Each half, with the lower bolt holes bunged, could become a little dinghy, allowing the offspring of a cruising family to explore a new harbor in one, while a parent went ashore for supplies in the other. The nested halves could be carried inside a van or station wagon, or in the back of a small pickup truck. One more way to make sliding seat rowing available in sometimes difficult circumstances.

With the boom in exercise equipment, and rowing gradually beginning to come out of the closet, a rowing machine seemed like an inevitable development. The Dreisigackers invented a most ingenious rowing machine called the Concept 2. It employed a bicycle wheel with

Carolyn Hanson working out on one of the first X-Oarcizer units. Unlike the so-called rowing machines of the discount stores, this unit gives a true rowing stroke, and does not tend to injure the back. And most of the apparatus serves double duty in a boat. Photo: Ann Grinnell.

small paddles attached to the spokes to give air resistance. The combination of this air resistance, increasing with speed, and the inertia of the wheel gave a realistic facsimile of rowing on the water. Sophisticated measurements of input effort gave a good comparison of competitors, helping coaches to select the best members for a crew and providing exercise and competition in the winter for all kinds of people.

It is not surprising that the "bottom-liners" saw the rowing machine as a new source of profit. It was a simple matter to conclude that two arms, moving in a vertical plane, would be far cheaper to manufacture than any type of oars moving in a horizontal plane, as in a shell. Consequently, such machines began to appear, accompanied by clever advertising hype and selling at outrageous mark-ups. As more manufacturers got into the act, competition became severe. Prices came down, discount stores provided volume distribution, and ways were found to reduce cost and quality still further.

Unfortunately for the gullible consumers, these were not really rowing machines at all. For each increment of the leg drive, the handles increased in height, traveling in a vertical arc around the pivot points. The powerful leg muscles pushed against the hips, but the resistance was increasingly high on the body, putting a severe strain on the back.

We decided that some Alden owners, landlocked in the winter by fresh-water ice or severe weather, might like to keep up their rowing regimen on land for reasons of health. In the Oarmaster they already had most of the ingredients of a real sculling machine. It remained to design some form of hydraulic resistance which would duplicate a hard catch and an easier finish, as in a boat. This proved to be no easy task, and many problems arose to block the way. The final solution was the current X-oarcizer. More people bought them than we had at first visualized. Some non-rowers bought them for exercise in the winter, planning to use the Oarmaster in an Alden, or other boat, in the following spring. Some bought them because their doctors advised them to discontinue using their discount-store "rowing machines" because of back damage. Wives gave them as Christmas presents to their husbands, or vice versa, leaving the recipients to buy Aldens later on.

I found any kind of exercise for health alone, such as a stationary bicycle or our own X-oarcizer, considerably boring, and participated only when heavy rain or extreme weather prohibited the fun of being out on the water. We did find, however, that the X-oarcizer was ideal for teaching beginners to row, and encouraged all of our dealers to follow our example. Learning to row without the added complications of navigation, wind, current, and stability, added one more dimension to our versatile line of rowing boats.

So we were tempted to think that we had helped make rowing available to everyone. But not quite. We perhaps shared, unconsciously, the old, and fortunately dying, common reaction to handicapped people, defined by the unspoken words, "I'm sorry your active life has ended, but please don't embarrass me by appearing where I am enjoying my favorite sport."

While we did nothing, others perceived a great opportunity to make it possible for severely injured people to participate in the great sport of rowing. Art Javes, a fine gentleman and designer of the Row-Cat, surmised that his catamaran would have enough stability so that a paraplegic, having no control of upper or lower body, helpless to counteract a tipping tendency, could not capsize while rowing. Art decided to make this equipment available to people with spinal injuries and other disabilities. It remained for courageous victims to volunteer to experiment, and people of good will to devote the time to the teaching and difficult logistics.

Doug Herland started life with *osteogenesis imperfecta,* or brittle bone disease. Several bones broke during his entrance into this world, and at least one or two more followed during each year of his childhood. When, at 12, he was swimming, an aspiring diver landed on top of him, shattering the bones in both legs. These finally fused together but in a shape bearing little resemblance to what the Creator intended. Doug's hopes and dreams of a career in baseball, never bright, were utterly shattered forever. He could not even walk without crutches. He was left with only one thing: an indomitable spirit.

Someone suggested that he try rowing. I don't understand how he did it, but somehow sheer willpower overcame the seemingly insurmountable obstacles of mastering a racing single scull. Doug was hooked, and he set out to learn everything he could about his new sport, from equipment, to rigging, to stroke efficiency, to training, to racing strategy. Rowing so improved his muscle tone and coordination that he was able to walk without assistance. He became a coxswain for the sweep-oar boats: pairs, fours, and eights. He coached crews. Rather than indulging in self-pity over his own handicaps, he started to think of how he could help others. He began to teach and promote rowing for the handicapped.

One by one, people with various disabilities were finding out that they could row. With the blind, it was comparatively easy in an Alden double, or even a racing double, because they could feel and hear the proper motion, and a sighted person could take care of navigation and maneuvering. Impairment, or even total loss of one leg proved to be surmountable, and even paraplegics found that they could venture out on the water by themselves in the untippable Row-Cats. But a

Herland collects bronze

From News Tribune sources

LAKE CASITAS, Calif. —Doug Herland, former Pacific Lutheran University coxswain, enjoyed his greatest moment of success yesterday as he accepted an Olympic Games bronze medal in the pairs with coxswain rowing competition.

Herland, a 1973 PLU graduate, was the cox in a shell with Kevin Still of Los Angeles and Robert Espeseth of Champaign which finished third behind Italy and Romania. The Italians won the gold with a time of 7:05.99. The U.S. team finished in 7:12.81.

That was just part of one of America's finest showings in Olympic rowing. The U.S. also collected a gold medal and three silvers yesterday.

Paul Enquist, a Seattle commercial fisherman and a member of the Lake Washington Rowing Club who competed at Washington State University, teamed with Bradley Lewis of Corona Del Mar, Calif., to win the gold medal in double sculls with a clocking of 6:36.87.

Other Seattle rowers involved in medal victories were Alan Forney of Edmonds, who was on the second-place fours without coxswain; former University of Washington athlete Charles Clapp, who was a member of the second-place eights with coxswain; and John Stillings of Edmonds, a member of the silver medal-winning fours with coxswain team.

John Biglow of Bellevue finished fourth in single sculls.

AP Laserphoto

Doug Herland celebrated bronze medal-win

Doug Herland celebrates a great victory. An indomitable spirit, he conquered seemingly impossible obstacles to win a bronze medal in the Olympics, and developed rowing programs which included even the most severely handicapped. Photo: Associated Press.

quadriplegic? This was the unconquerable Mount Everest of rowing. Doug Herland believed it could be done.

He persuaded a quad to allow himself to be strapped into a Row-Cat in a heated swimming pool. Doug tied the immobile hands to the oar handles. Then they cast off, with Doug sitting facing his student and manipulating the oars. The quad's arms, mechanically connected to the oar handles, had no choice but to follow the motion of rowing. Gradually, Doug reduced his effort on the oars, but the boat kept going. Finally, he removed his hands altogether, and still the motion continued. A quadriplegic was actually rowing, for the first time ever, as far as I know.

Since that time many others became involved, either rowing or organizing and assisting, and sometimes both. Dolly Driscoll, a noteworthy Philadelphia competitive sculler, received a debilitating spinal injury but came right back into rowing, learning to participate all over again, however cruel the new rules, and organizing the Philadelphia Rowing Program for the Disabled. Each year the Bayada Regatta, sponsored by the Bayada Nurses, brings disabled rowers from all over the country to the fabled waters of the Schuylkill to compete in well organized races. which rival any regatta for excitement, fun, and good-natured competition.

Out in Toledo, our friends were jolted by a telephone call from a paraplegic named Jim Reisig. He wanted to know why the Toledo Rowing Club, supposedly making rowing possible for everyone, ignored the handicapped. The somewhat lame answer was that the equipment was too expensive. When advised that the price of a Row-Cat single and double would come to four thousand dollars, he arrived the next day in his wheelchair with a check for the full amount. When they admitted that they had inadvertently forgotten oars and freight, he promptly produced further funds to cover them. Since then he has been a spark plug for handicapped rowing, participating, helping and encouraging others, and providing an inspiration to all who are burdened by physical limitations.

Doug Herland continued to be a small bundle of energy. He worked up a program called Freedom on the River, to encourage cities and towns to set up rowing programs for the handicapped. Later he widened his goals, sensing that handicapped people did not want to be herded into separate rowing programs, akin to leper colonies. Why not have programs that included everyone: competitive able-bodied rowers, inner-city kids, recreational rowers, and handicapped rowers. He called it Rowing in the Main Stream, and he wrote a very comprehensive prospectus for the program and sent it to various government agencies in a quest for a grant. Alas, he was advised that there was no money for this kind of program, available funds being earmarked for more important matters, such as studies of the sex life of the butterfly. Ninth inning, two outs, two strikes.

Meanwhile, another of Doug's goals was to get into the Olympics. He obviously did not have the physical qualifications to pull an oar in the world's toughest competition, but he was a good cox. He went to the national selection camp to try out for a position steering and directing one of America's only crews in the pairs, fours or eights events. He was turned down cold, and about to return home, defeated once again.

But in 1984 there was a wise stipulation that any crew could challenge the selected national crew, and, if they won, take their place in representing their country. A couple of husky oarsmen named Bob Espeseth and Kevin Still joined forces with little Doug Herland and challenged the selected pair with coxswain. Miraculously, they won and went on to win a bronze medal in the Olympics. As many times as I have seen him do it, my eyes always moisten when I see Doug, standing on his small, tortured legs in front of a crowd of rowing hopefuls, pulling out his well polished prize possession, the Olympic medal.

After the games, there was a sponsored tour around the country for all the medal winners, who were feted at various receptions. They ended up at the White House, where they each had their pictures taken with President Reagan and Nancy. Doug looked very diminutive standing between them, but completely undaunted, as usual. He suddenly pulled a copy of his prospectus out of his breast pocket, blithely ignoring the possibility of quick aggressive action by the Secret Service, and handed it to Mr. Reagan, saying, "Mr. President, I would like a second opinion on this."

Shortly thereafter, he received the grant and began traveling around the country setting up his Rowing In The Mainstream program in several cities. When he was in Baltimore, he and his dog,

Eddie, came over to Saint Michaels to visit us and spend the night on *Barnacle IV*. The next day, when we were all going ashore in the Appledore 19, Doug asked if he could row. I always feel uncomfortable in any kind of a rowing boat unless I have the oars, but I couldn't resist the opportunity of being rowed by an Olympic medal winner.

Chris Keim, an astonishingly young octogenarian from Oak Ridge, Tennessee, having devoted his considerable talent to the atom bomb, was redirecting it in retirement to helping both mentally and physically disadvantaged people to enjoy the pleasures and benefits of rowing. When Art Javes wanted to retire, Chris was instrumental in arranging for the Row-Cats to be built in Oak Ridge so that equipment for handicapped rowing would continue to be available.

One day Doug Herland called up and began to give me a well organized sales pitch. Production of the catamarans was falling far behind schedule. There were Aldens practically everywhere that any rowing programs had been set up. In other areas they were readily available, and owners should be easily persuaded to loan them to new programs. They were easy to transport, and took up little space to store. Why couldn't we design a device to make an Alden sufficiently stable to allow a spinal injury victim to row one?

We were already supplying Oarmasters to the Row-Cat people at cost, as our small contribution to handicapped rowing. The engineering involved in producing a suitable stabilizing device for an Alden could never be justified by the small volume to be expected. But it was a challenge which I could not, in good conscience, turn down. I began to make sketches of possible pontoon configurations. Long pontoons could travel at rowing speeds in an efficient displacement mode, but they would be cumbersome to handle, in and out of the water, and would interfere with the transfer between wheelchair and boat. Short ones would be traveling above an efficient speed-length ratio, causing undue resistance. Planing hulls seemed to be the answer. But in any waves, spray thrown out by the bows would land on the rower. I finally hit on a Sea-Sled shape, hoping that the late Mr. Albert Hickman would not object to having his ideas plagiarized in a good cause. I carved two of the floats out of Styrofoam, a process with which, by this time, I was not entirely unfamiliar, and covered them with fiberglass. I decided to support them with two sets of riggers, to give directional stability, and to insure against inadvertent failure to secure some fastener, which, if not redundant, could result in capsize.

For a fixed seat to meet all of the various requirements, I called upon Douglas, now doing more and more design work for the company. I suddenly realized that everything we were doing was based on pure hunches and assumptions. We could test for stability, and we could row it, but what about a spinal injury victim? Only he, or she, could determine if the rig was viable. Obviously, we needed a qualified test pilot.

Over in nearby Exeter, Richard Tobin had been devoting endless hours to the cause of rowing for the handicapped. He had set up an organization, acquired Row-Cats and the later Omni-Cats, modified equipment to suit the circumstances, and become the unquestioned leader and spark plug of handicapped rowing in the area. He very kindly arranged to meet us at his facility, and have there some of his troops who volunteered to try out our experimental rig. Douglas and I and grandson Nathan, who showed great empathy for the physically impaired, journeyed to Exeter, bringing an Alden single and double, and an assortment of seats, rigger extensions, pontoons, oars, etc. For the first time we were able to experience reality, where the theoretical and the practical meet. As a result of this, and later trials, we were able to learn a great deal about designing equipment for this special application. While some of our ideas proved to be faulty, it was gratifying to see that the basic concept was sound. Above all, as was confirmed so many times in the months that followed, the courage, optimism, good will, and appreciation for whatever we did, shown by the handicapped rowers, amply rewarded us for our efforts.

Several came down to Kittery Point later, and we made a portable ramp to facilitate making transfers and launching. One enthusiast was Dwight Hamsley. He had been a star football player at Portsmouth High, selected as all-state. A fall from a tree in Hawaii made him a quadriplegic, potentially ending a promising active career just as it was beginning. But Dwight found strength in a strong religious faith, boundless optimism, and determination to make the most of remaining opportunity. He disdained the usual electric wheelchair, preferring to strengthen the few muscles over which he still had control in a manually powered chair. He learned to paint, with immobile fingers, and produced an original movie. He was a natural for rowing and became our chief test pilot.

He held on to an impossible dream of rowing out to the Isles of Shoals: seven and one-half miles of never completely docile open ocean. He insisted on practicing for the big adventure, and I sometimes went with him. He would row down the mirror-smooth waters of our creek, to the Chauncey Creek Lobster Pier, a mere half-mile away, at a painfully slow pace. Showing unmistakable signs of exhaustion, he would turn around reluctantly, and that would be it for the day. I didn't have the heart to tell him that he could never make it to the Shoals.

But he persisted, day after day, going a little further each time. When he got out to the mouth of the harbor finally, he encountered some very small waves, which completely shattered his rowing rhythm and efficiency. The goal seemed further away than ever. But Dwight wanted to set a date and time for the event: four o'clock in the morning, before the wind and the sun came up (having minimal sweat glands, quads are most susceptible to heat). We arranged to have Paul Sadler, who had a big Boston Whaler with a mast and boom, be an escort. In an emergency, we could lift Dwight out of the Alden in a sling. On more than one scheduled day, we all got up at four, and stumbled out in the dark to check the weather. A strong wind from the east, and all bets were off.

Finally, on a day when the crane was not available, conditions seemed ideal. But Dwight and his helper did not show up. We called and got no answer. We waited in suspense, watching the hands of a watch turning inexorably toward a no-go situation, confirmed by the first crimson rays of the sun. Dwight's alarm had failed to go off, but he finally arrived. Douglas rowed over and got the Energy 48 from her mooring, while we launched Dwight in the Alden with pontoons, and Marjorie and I shoved off in an Appledore 16, armed with drinking water and Shaklee energy bars to fuel Dwight along the way. I reflected on how vulnerable Dwight was, despite the well meaning escort. Any number of possible circumstances could spell disaster. If we had to abort the mission, it was by no means certain that we could get his heavy and almost inert body up over the side and into the safety of the cockpit of *Barnacle IV* . But part of the fun, excitement, and stimulation of life involves risk. Not Russian roulette, but calcu-

Dwight Hamsley, a quadriplegic from Rye, New Hampshire, arrives at the Isles of Shoals in an Alden equipped with stabilizing pontoons. Rowing is for everyone. Photo: Marjorie Martin.

lated risk where skill and courage can prevail, as in skiing and other active sports. Are handicapped people to be denied this zestful living because those who would help fear lawsuits? It seems that we have far too many greedy lawyers (50 times as many per capita as the Japanese), advertising contingency fee services, and far too many greedy people seeking something for nothing, as willing to take a chance on a risk-free frivolous lawsuit as a sweepstakes ticket, or a government handout, however unjustified. Dwight wanted, with all his heart and soul, to take this risk. We decided to accept the consequences, whatever they might be.

The Loran on *Barnacle IV* gave constant readings of miles to go, decreasing at an agonizingly slow rate. We relayed this information to Dwight, who could not turn his head to check his destination. As the islands, so familiar, and yet always a new thrill to approach, began to become more clearly defined, we tried to describe them to Dwight, to encourage him to keep up the effort, although it was obvious that he was getting tired. Then, to my horror, the wind began to pick up, and the chop made rowing increasingly difficult. But Dwight struggled on, though I suspect he didn't quite believe our assurances that he was almost there. Finally, we asked him to stop and turn his boat around, so that he could see where he was. Marjorie captured on film the look of pure ecstasy that came over his face as he discovered that he was actually in Gosport Harbor.

The special equipment had proved itself. More important, the increasing numbers of special people who began to use it proved that even severe disabilities cannot foreclose the solitary joys of sculling. The pontoons, adjustable fixed seat, and adaptive Oarmaster are listed on our regular price list, but we make them available to any bona fide adaptive rowing program or anyone wishing to donate them, at a much lower price. This does little for the bottom line. But the bottom line has never been our prime consideration, and as long as we can continue to live as we do, the pleasure of seeing supposedly immobile people rowing and racing is a deeper reward.

The launching of the Energy 48. It was a momentous occasion for us, seemingly full of promise for sisterships to follow. But the criteria did not meet the agendas of those able to afford expensive power boats. Photo: Ann Grinnell.

27 • *The Energy 48*

*t*here was quite an oil shortage during the seventies, the
result of many factors, with some of which I was familiar
through the battle with Onassis. My aging mother was
advised that setting the thermostat above 65 would be considered a
crime, and vital automobile transportation was sharply curtailed. At
the same time, popular versions of the "motor yacht" were burning 40
to 100 gallons of supposedly scarce fuel per hour, just to entertain
their well-heeled owners. It seemed that such a highly visible waste
would have to stop. Even today, automobile manufacturers must pay
huge fines if their cars do not average the legal minimum gas mileage.
It seemed to me that perhaps the world was ready for a more graceful
and fuel-efficient life on the water.

A motor boat with an easily driven shape might have been a welcome little alleviation of the fuel crisis, as well as a means of luring
some people back to a more relaxed way of enjoying life on the water.
While *Barnacle III* was in many ways a most satisfactory boat for cruising with two Aldens on board, demonstrating them in many a harbor
along the coast, it was a little incongruous for us to be seen in a boat
with a transom stern. Slowly the germ of an idea began to take shape.
If the Appledore 16 was so easy to row, a larger version should require
proportionately little power to attain the same speed-length ratio.
With a much longer length, this should translate into a cruising speed
sufficient to satisfy retiring sailors and others having a true appreciation for life on the water.

For a long, light-displacement boat, I did not think I could improve
much on the lines of the Appledore 16. Much as I enjoy drawing lines,
the only plans which always seem totally absorbing, my conservative
nature called attention to the saving in paper if I simply used the lines of
the Appledore 16, changing the scale from one and one-half inches to

the foot to one-half inch to the foot. I added six inches all the way around, a straight, vertical element above a knuckle at the shear line. This was a compromise to allow minimum headroom below decks. I was only too aware of how many boat designs have been ruined aesthetically by the insistence of full headroom everywhere, just like a house. If the amenities of a house are more desirable than the grace and performance of a boat, why not stay ashore? Many well-heeled owners compromise with a floating luxury hotel, seldom unplugging the umbilical cord of a marina, far from the ocean waves which could spell disaster. There are "trawlers" with impressively high, flared bows, but with waterlines so blunt that in perfectly calm water the bow wave comes halfway up the stem. A respectable wave has but a short distance to rise to bring green water over the bow.

The Energy 48 was conceived to forego many of the shoreside amenities dictated by current wisdom in favor of a more kindly motion in the water. To glide along in relative quiet, like an ancient steam yacht of years gone by. To slice partly through and over the usual rounded summer waves without pounding. To hold a nearly straight course in following seas, with minimal steering effort, and no fear of broaching. To traverse the tranquil inland waters at a comfortable 10 miles per hour without making huge waves to threaten small craft and erode the fragile shoreline. To be self-sufficient at anchor in a deserted cove, with the necessities for two people to live in reasonable comfort but without some of the shoreside luxuries.

The above criteria were established as an unalterable set of parameters. I realized that this concept was not destined to find favor with the vast majority of motorboat enthusiasts, regardless of how well the criteria were met. But, approaching the end of a life devoted to being out of step with the regiment, I had no qualms about being, once again, the lone believer in generally unacceptable ideas.

Translating the unusual concept into reality proved to be quite a challenge. My son-in-law, Ted Perry, favored wood construction, as did Douglas and I. We were well aware of the advantages of gluing wood with epoxy, having already had considerable experience with the process in the Appledore 16. We had no hesitation in deciding to go with the West System®. Ted and Douglas went out to Bay City, Michigan, and spent three days absorbing wisdom from Meade Gougeon, my idea

Barnacle IV *on her first trial run. The way she slipped quietly through the water with hardly any wake was a source of never-ending delight. She proved to be the ideal boat for slower, quieter cruising, the opposite of current trends. Photo: Ann Grinnell.*

of the epitome of honesty and objectivity in engineering. His excellent ideas were incorporated into the structure, which we strengthened still further as a tribute to inbred conservatism. When big seas later tossed the unusual new boat around considerably, I had no regrets.

Starting at the stem, *Barnacle IV* has a three-foot void compartment (what a waste of space!), terminated by what is called in a ship a collision bulkhead. If the bow is smashed in a collision, the boat will not flood. If the rest of the boat should flood, the air chamber will add to the considerable buoyancy of the wood. Above the air chamber is a full-width shelf for clothes and linen. Next aft is a huge double berth, extending from side to side, providing comfortable backrests and making it impossible to fall out. Then there are foot lockers on either side, also serving as seats. A partial bulkhead separates the forward quarters from the head on the starboard side and the shelves and hanging locker on the port. A single step leads up to the deckhouse, with steering station to starboard, with the helmsman's seat built over a refrigerator equipped with a Sea Frost holding plate, the first refrigeration installation sold by this estimable company. It makes ice most efficiently from an engine-driven compressor, eliminating many problems, including dead batteries. The galley, featuring a compressed natural gas stove with oven, the only safe stove outside of electric, is on the port side. Thus the galley slave is not sent down to Siberia to prepare meals but instead may enjoy the view and the company of the skipper. A comfortable settee on either side completes the deckhouse, with a wood stove burning only teak, mahogany, and oak, for the cold, rainy days that have been known to occur occasionally in our part of the world. The huge open cockpit is encumbered only with a heavily sound-insulated box, under which a small diesel purrs away unobtrusively. At the stern (pointed, to be sure) there is another big double berth, accessible only through a flush hatch. To the surprise and chagrin of amenity seekers, there is absolutely nothing else in the entire compartment. This was named the after fornicatorium by Gary Hoyt, a great innovator and authority on sensible and practical things nautical if not nice. I have never checked on activities in the after cabin, it being far removed from the forward quarters, unlike some much more luxurious vessels which separate amourous couples by a mere three-eighths of an inch of sounding-board-quality bulkhead.

Altogether, the Energy 48 offers pretty sparse accomodations for its length, and the little engine must seem like a joke to the power-hungry set. In retrospect, it is not surprising that we have yet to sell one, despite advertising, appearances at boat shows, and numerous exposures to the yachting public. We are in the same position we were with the Aldens twenty years ago: trying to sell an idea rather than one more product in current demand. We would hope that most boat owners get as much enjoyment out of their boats as we do. If any are looking for more satisfaction from life on the water, we are here to help them. The following random scenes from *Barnacle IV* trips might suggest possibilities:

Launching day. The radical, and really experimental Energy 48 is poised on the ways of Dion's Yacht Yard in Kittery, awaiting the signal that will start her slow, controlled descent into her element. There is none of the drama and suspense of the wildly speeding Navy ships whose initial contacts with salt water I had so often assisted. Nevertheless, there is an air of excitement among the small group of well-wishers, and, for me, overwhelming suspense. How would the reality of floating, and moving through the water compare with my calculations, expectations, and dreams? The answers are only a few minutes away, as little ripples of water creep up the red bottom toward the white boot-top and the inevitable dark blue (Endeavour Blue) topsides.

As I take the stainless steel destroyer wheel and inch the throttle forward, I cannot help smiling. It is so smooth and quiet, and the bow wave is a mere ripple, folding over gently far aft of the sharp stem. It is all very well to say that I planned it that way, but, as Robert Burns reminds us, "The best laid plans o' mice and men gang aft agley." All too often boats do not live up to expectations. Extensive tests and trials further confirm my hopes and expectations, and I am generally satisfied that the concepts, however controversial and even repugnant to the multitudes, have been implemented with some success. Later experiments with engines, propellers, interior arrangements and details result in various improvements. The sailing rig, designed only for reaching, proves to be more trouble than fun, for us, at least. The folding A-frame mast and roller-reefing sails interfere with the all-important function of quick and easy stowing and launching two Alden Ocean Shells, which always live on top of the deckhouse. No experiments are ever totally in vain, and one always learns something from them. There is a certain satisfaction in acheiving a speed of 10 mph in a 48-foot boat with only 200 square feet of sail, and 19 m.p.h. with the little engine and the sails, surfing down the waves in a hard sou'wester.

We are anchored in placid Perry Creek, on Vinalhaven. Another typical summer day starts with a thick fog, and not a breath of air. On auxiliary sailboats anchored nearby, owners fret and complain about Maine weather, finally moving out into the fog under power, hoping for clearing and a breeze in the afternoon, lest another day of a precious vacation be wasted. We launch the Aldens, and head off around Calderwood Neck, never losing sight of the rocks and spruce trees of the shore. We stop at a deserted island for some wild raspberries, and then at a bleached rock formation in Winter Harbor for a refreshing swim and a picnic lunch, always carried in the spacious cockpit of Marjorie's Alden. One more stop to gather some mussels for dinner, and then back to *Barnacle IV*. By this time the almost inevitable (but not quite) sou'wester is beginning to gather momentum, and we set sail in the Appledore 19. After checking out all of the interesting boats in the Fox Island Thoroughfare, we land next to the ferry slip at North Haven, pick up some groceries at Waterman's Market, and indulge in an ice cream cone.

We are heading south, toward Charleston, South Carolina, on the Intracoastal Waterway, our almost flat wake and quiet engine hardly disturbing the abundant wildlife and the fragile shoreline. Our compact Chart Kit shows a narrow, winding channel through the marsh grass to the east. We slow down and take it, watching the fathometer for shallow water. Instead, it shows as much as 50 feet in spots. A couple of dolphins cavort nearby, oblivious to the almost silent passage of the long, narrow boat that presumes to share their territory. After half a mile, we turn into one of the narrower branches and anchor. Within minutes, both Aldens are in the water, and we are off to satisfy our curiosity about the origin or destination of the main channel. We are not held in suspense long, for in less than half a mile we row through an inlet where the usual opaque water gradually turns crystal clear, and we are in the open ocean, with completely deserted white sandy beach stretching into the distance, as far as the eye can see, on either side of the inlet. Have we died and gone to heaven, or is this the promised land that so many seek in vain? Several days pass without any thought of weighing the anchor. Days of rowing through the endless wetlands, swimming skinny from the deserted beaches, and sailing in the 19, sometimes out in the ocean and sometimes along the inland waterway. Our last day, we are having a leisurely breakfast, drinking in the magnificent scene in the early morning sun. Some dolphins are having their breakfast beside us. To the east there is no sign of human life, save for a little house and dock on the far shore, which we have not seen fit to disturb. To the west, above the marsh grass, we see an endless procession of high superstructures, topped by fully enclosed flying bridges. with occasional "tuna towers," partially enclosed, above. They are traveling at high speed, their mammoth engines turning shameful supplies of fuel into smoke and noise which even acres of high marsh grass cannot completely eradicate. Their huge wakes break on the fragile shores, eroding the edges, whether wild or individually owned. Constant dredging and repairing cost landowners and taxpayers alike great sums of money each year. Like the migratory birds, the ostentatious "yachts" are returning North in the early spring, but there the similarity ends. The boats are leaving crowded marinas in Florida for crowded marinas in the North, there to enjoy their own and their close neighbors' varied hi-fi and TV programs. Why the great hurry to accomplish this minor change of scenery baffles my possibly narrow mind. Surely God must be somewhat offended that His best handiwork is so often ignored and desecrated, in favor of ruthless accumulation of wealth and the most visible evidences of its overabundance.

These depressingly negative thoughts are interupted by a gentle knocking on the hull of our boat. There is Andy Magwood in his little skiff. He says he has noticed that we seem to appreciate his secluded corner of the world, and in his polite and charming way, he wants to say hello. Like so many of the real people who live close to the sea, he immediately exudes the basic honesty and good will that are so lacking in the world of the bottom line. We ask him aboard, and he relates that he, and his father before him, have lived in the lone house in that vast expanse of wilderness virtually all his life. He explains that he has the oyster rights to all the marshland delineated by little weathered signs with his name and number, and promptly urges us to help ourselves. On second thought, he departs, and quickly returns with a tremendous bucketfull, on which we later gorge ourselves. He invites us ashore to his house, where we meet his charming wife, and he proudly shows us some of the handiwork of his father. There is a handsome door, the top of which is gracefully curved and sloping, which his father retrieved from the wreck of a schooner. A large, robust tree, whose first shoots poked through the earth when his father died. The love and respect for his father, so often lacking in some quarters today, is abundantly apparent, especially when he leads us, with obvious pride, to a wood boat designed and built by his talented parent.

Like his forebears, Andy makes a modest living selling oysters, following the time-tested practice of "boarding" them. This consists of placing the newly harvested oysters on planks between high and low tide, where the little ripples on the rising and receding water wash away the mud. Since oysters often live above low tide, they are not harmed by the practice. One day, without any warning, three armed men landed at the Magwood dock, to demand, in the most arrogant tones, that all "boarding" cease forthwith to avoid fines and jail. Such is progress under an ever-burgeoning bureaurocracy.

We are crossing Penobscot Bay in a brisk westerly, the ruffled blue water dotted with towering whitecaps. The Energy 48, as usual, is having an easy time in the following seas, followed closely by the Appledore 19 on a short tether. The latter is bouncing around considerably, being pulled up short from time to time in a jarring action which I deplore. A little more forethought and a little less laziness on my part could have secured it in the safety of the cockpit before we left the sheltered waters of Tennants Harbor. A little spray is accumulating in the bottom of our faithful follower, but not enough to threaten on such a short trip. A few "modern" sailboats are about, some under reefed main, some under jib alone, and most under bare poles, using power. Later we sail in the Appledore 19 at thrilling speed, watching a skilled and hardy windsurfer enjoying planing back and forth in the nearly empty Fox Island Thoroughfare. The Herreshoff 12 fleet is out in force, racing as usual, in the somewhat extreme conditions which old Mr. Nat so ably anticipated when he designed these superb little boats. Not surprisingly, the race is won by Linc Davis, over eighty, but with the same acumen which made him the scourge of the 210s in Marblehead so many years ago.

Over the last ten years, many people have expressed admiration for the Energy 48, circling her in their dinghies or invited aboard for a complete inspection. So far, no one has quite had the right combination of courage, means, and shall we say eccentricity, to acquire a similar vessel. Like Alcoholics Anonymous, we cannot force anyone to change his or her way of living, but, likewise, we are always available should the occasion arise.

28 · Oars

*a*s soon as Douglas was old enough to comprehend words, he began to ask questions, standing up behind the front seat of a car (no longer allowed, I understand), sitting in the 210, playing on a beach, or in a tidal pool. By the time he was seven, he had learned just about everything I could teach him, and I had learned to be careful about expressing hasty opinions in front of one so honest and retentive. One day when we were sailing, a rather unattractive sailboat appeared in the distance. When Douglas, as usual, asked what it was, I replied that it was a tub. An hour or so later, as we were slowly beating up the narrow channel into Cohasset, in the quiet of a dying wind, we overhauled that very boat. In an unusually loud voice, Douglas announced the proximity of "that tub." I hastily assured him that it was a boat and not a tub. "But you said it was a tub," he corrected, pointing at the adjacent vessel for emphasis. I tried to hide behind the tiller, desperately searching for a way to end the discussion quietly and gracefully.

Though never an enthusiastic swimmer, in the following years Douglas spent endless hours in his Rookie, *Silver Moon*, and then his ll0, *Invader II*. He taught himself the theory of rowing, and then sailing, trying out new things, like sailing backwards, always completely self-sufficient in a boat. As time went on, he studied every printed page he could lay hands on, including the encyclopedia, in which he sometimes quietly pointed out errors. After three years at the University of Maine, he studied sculpture at Rhode Island School of Design. These formal studies did not interfere with various other projects, such as making and designing violins, designing lights to accompany classical music, hang gliders, airfoil skate sails, and, always, sooner or later, back to boats.

In the early days of the Aldens, oarlocks presented a problem. We did not want to use the readily available round ones used for fixed seat rowing, but we were not ready to go all the way to the gated square

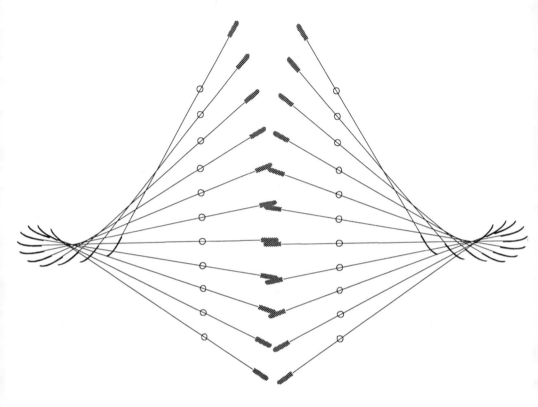

The pattern an oar blade actually makes in the water during the rowing stroke. Understanding this phenomenon led to the concept of a blade as an efficient wing, propeller blade, or tail of a fish, rather than a paddle wheel or parachute offering resistance only. Drawing: Douglas Martin.

oarlocks used in racing shells. My thinking, long since proved faulty, was to use fiberglass oars, with a very narrow flat area near the button, to give a hint of indexing the blade in the squared and feathered positions, with an oarlock slightly squared. Douglas came to our rescue and worked all one night to produce a beautiful wood pattern of just such an oarlock. As we quickly turned to using regular wood racing sculls, a corresponding oarlock was called for. We wanted to stick to solid manganese bronze, designed to eliminate the troublesome gate. It is sad to read of a favorite crew losing a race because a gate has come loose. But it could be a lot worse for a recreational rower, alone on an angry sea. Furthermore, surfing down following waves often requires strong backing on one oar to avoid broaching, and the plastic oarlocks are not designed for such stresses. Douglas designed and built a new pattern, which served us well for many years. We had the oarlocks cast by a foundry in Connecticut, and we had a standing order for an ample quantity to be shipped each month, without constant communication.

One month, the oarlocks were late, but Ted wisely had a reserve supply and assumed that some production delay would be resolved before we ran out completely. As time went on, and our reserves dwindled, he became concerned, and called the foundry, only to find that the phone had been disconnected. After considerable Sherlock Holmes investigative effort, he found that the I.R.S. had resolved some difference of opinion by shutting down the foundry, without warning. Ted explained that we owned the pattern, and had a proprietary right to any oarlocks in process, for which we were more than willing to pay. The arrogant voice on the other end of the line refused to consider any logical solution, and our lawyer could do nothing because they insisted on a Connecticut lawyer. Government servants have the mighty power of the country, including the army, air force, navy, and marines behind their every decision, however cruel and unthinking, but they have no responsibility for the results of their decisions. Power corrupts. The more power, the more corruption, and the greater the attraction for small people who could not make it in the real world of private enterprise.

Once more, Douglas came to the rescue and, within hours, appeared with a new and much improved pattern, which began to sire oarlocks in a small local foundry in record time, allowing us to replace some plastic oarlocks which we had been forced to use, before many of them had failed.

Meanwhile, we were importing all of our oars from F. Collar, in Oxford, England. Essentially a two-family, two-generation business, my initial contact was with the original Mr. Scaldwell, who personified all that one would associate with the best of British disdain for the bottom line. His calm voice over the transatlantic telephone solved many a problem for us, and after meeting him on the occasion of our first visit to England, we were saddened to learn of his passing shortly thereafter. The business continued exactly as before, under the guidance of his son, Richard, the late Mr. Collar's son, John, and Keith, a genius at shaping wood by hand, the head carver, and the only non-family director of the company. We received many compliments on the exceptional beauty of the finely finished wood, and, since Collar sweeps and sculls won numerous competitions all over the world, including the Olympics, we had nothing to be ashamed of, particularly when Collar oars were compared to domestic ones of inferior design and materials. Other oar makers, both here and abroad, solicited our business, but we remained loyal to our friends in England, who had come across the ocean to visit us and had entertained us royally when we went to England, arranging for us to row at Oxford in a racing single and visit the simple country churchyard, so appealing to me, where Winston Churchill now rests from his mighty labors.

But, as our business increased, and good silver spruce became scarcer, we began to run into shortages of oars. Substituting domestic oars in desperation was not acceptable, as we were forced, in good conscience, to replace them as soon as good oars again became available. By this time, Douglas was running the wooden boat shop at Strawbery Banke, the historic preservation project in Portsmouth, New Hampshire. He was designing and building wood dories and skiffs, while explaining the time-tested process to curious tourists. It seemed logical for him to employ some of his free evenings making oars for us, supplementing our increasingly inadequate supply from England.

As usual, Douglas took nothing for granted. As he started cutting into a pile of Sitka spruce with the intention of carving a set of beautiful traditional sculls, he detoured into an offhand experiment. Thinking of an oar blade as a drag device similar to a parachute, he glued eight vertical slats on the end of an old oar shaft and went for a row. Much to his surprise, water did not flow through the slots between the slats as the "picket fence" blade raked the water. Instead, the water flowed nearly parallel to the shaft as the blade moved laterally, away from the boat and back, following a fishhook-shaped path. The implication was startling but irrefutable: the natural motion of a blade in the water caused it to function as a wing, not a parachute. The motion of the blade was similar to the sculling motion of the hands that most people instinctively use when treading water (and which, when incorporated in his freestyle swimming stroke, made Mark Spitz invincible until others caught on).

This sudden insight called into question every design characteristic of traditional sculls. How much was form logically following function and how much was tradition? In the days before good waterproof glue, it was easiest to make blades long and narrow. Also, making the inner edge of the blade pointed gave an easy transition to the shaft, or loom, and reduced the tendency to split when encountering an object in the water. The Germans had already proved that the long, narrow blades, such as I had used at Kent School, were not as efficient as their shorter, wider ones which were eventually adopted for virtually all competitive rowing. If blades are actually wings, why not follow the principles of fluid dynamics to improve efficiency by making the blades still shorter and wider? New construction methods with wood and epoxy would allow freedom from old structural constraints. Laminated blades, not subject to splitting, could be cut off abruptly at the inboard end to form a better trailing edge and they could be attached to the shaft at a more advantageous position and angle.

The traditional sculls were abandoned. The pile of spruce served instead for numerous experiments and prototypes that culminated in a product, the Douglas Feathor. The blades of the Feathor were essentially rectangular in outline and cold-molded to provide both transverse and longitudinal curvature. For hydrodynamic reasons, the blades were glued onto the back of the hollow shaft which was made with a turned-up tip much like a ski. They were met with scorn from traditionalists, but more and more people who tried them with an open mind began to prefer them. When we offered a choice of oars with all of our boats, the Douglas Feathor's slowly pulled ahead in sales.

But Douglas was never satisfied. Nine years later we gave permission for him to conduct some basic oar research on company time. To measure the lift and drag coefficients of blades without the expense of a water tunnel, he took advantage of a nearby tidal sluiceway. A catamaran made from two Alden singles supported a gimbaled force gauge that could suspend a blade at any desired angle in the smooth flow of an outgoing tide. It was significant that in the three-knot current of the sluiceway, a traditional blade produced very large forces far more than necessary to push a shell.

To document the fishhook path of the blade, he attached a wire, extending vertically below one blade tip, and rowed an Alden over a

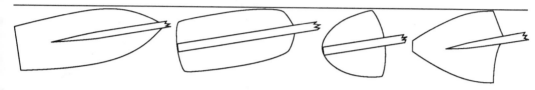

Stages in the development of the Douglas Deltor. Left to right: traditional spoon blade, square-bladed Douglas Feather, half-ellipse-bladed Douglas Feather, and Douglas Deltor. Drawings: Douglas Martin.

mud flat, where, on the last of an outgoing tide, the wire could trace the blade's motion in the mud. When the tide dropped, the tracing could be accurately measured.

Analysis of the stroke geometry showed that on a shell, blades were constrained to move through the water nearly as fast as the boat in the early part of the drive (far faster than the three-knot speed of the tests in the sluiceway) yet at mid-stroke the inboard end of a traditional blade came to rest as a stationary pivot point and contributed nothing to thrust.

The data suggested that blade area could be dramatically reduced if the remaining area was distributed in a more vertical manner and given a good shape. For a quick two-minute test, Douglas sawed off the inner two-thirds of a Feathor blade, leaving the tip looking like a hammerhead shark. When he rowed with the tiny blade on one side and a large standard blade on the other, the boat kept a straight course!

Within a few months, we introduced a blade having an almost round forward edge and a straight trailing edge, with roughly one-third the area of either the traditional blades or the square Douglas oars which were in production. To my astonishment and the many others who began to use the new, smaller blades, they seemed to make the boat go just as fast, if not a little faster, with less effort. We made the new blades optional on all of our oars. We even sent some to F. Collar in England for them to incorporate on their fine sculls. Alden buyers, having a choice of several kinds of oars, began to show a preference for the new blades. While the American world of racing largely ignored what appeared to be a breakthrough, the British, thought to be so chained to tradition, began to buy them for racing shells.

We decided to couple the new blade geometry with an advanced carbon fiber shaft. Over the course of many months of research, experiment, and very costly tooling, Douglas, working with Mark Currier, Ted's right hand man at East-West, came up with a carbon-fiber loom with a square section. This was a real breakthrough, for it offered greater strength and stiffness for the weight, an easier oar to feather and square, a more stable oar because of pulling the blade through the water rather than pushing it, and less wind resistance on the recovery. The blade for the new shaft was still in question.

One day, I had an appointment with a quadriplegic to row with our pontoon rig at 10 a.m. Rather impractically, I set off down Chauncey Creek in an Alden, equipped with a fishing rod and spinning reel, a choice plug, and a gaff and a hammer, on the slim chance that I might get lucky with a bluefish outside, although it was already after 9. But anyone, however undeserving, can have a lucky day, and just before 10, I was walking up to the house with a sizable bluefish as the quad's van pulled into our driveway. Douglas, who had come over to help in the transfer from wheelchair to boat, asked, in his quiet way, if I would save the tail of the bluefish.

I seemed to detect a hint of plagiarism of the work of the Greatest Designer of All in subsequent experiments with oar blades, as they bore some resemblance to the tail of my bluefish. The shape that evolved seemed to be quite superior to anything else. Among the many people who have rowed with what are now called the Douglas Deltors, there is an overwhelming preference for them.

It is my humble opinion that in the years to come, these unique new oars will be modified and adapted to provide slightly more speed for the racing boats, from single sculls to eights. Doubtless many will be involved in the transition from the traditional to the new technology, but Douglas alone should be considered responsible for the dramatic breakthrough. I don't hesitate to say that I am very proud of him.

Most of the family at Dick Burbridge's wedding, 1986. Back row, left to right: Rusty Burbridge, AEM, Marjorie, Alise Burbridge, Dick Burbridge, Maureen Martin, Charlie Martin, Douglas Martin, Kate Martin, Kelley Martin, Rod Martin, Cheryl Perry, Ted Perry, Lorna Perry, Jill Perry, Dianne Burbridge, Bob Devin, Bill Burbridge. Front row, left to right: Erin Martin, Maysa Martin, Caleb Martin, Nathan Martin, Taylor Devin, Faith Martin, Anna Martin. Not in picture: Carl Martin, Maja Martin, and their children, Asa and Odin. Photo: Ann Grinnell.

29 • The Big C

*a*s I passed the mystical three score and ten, all the rewards that life could offer seemed to be falling my way. My early goal of becoming a naval architect, which seemed so remote on the far side of the Webb entrance exams, had been reached nearly half a century ago. I never aspired to the acquisition of power, fame, and fortune, and therefore I was not disappointed by failure to control a vast business empire through acquisitions, leveraged buyouts, big deals (questionable or not), political connections, or workaholic effort to the exclusion of participation in the simple pleasures life offers.

By not seeking the grandiose rewards which sometimes prove so elusive, and, when finally achieved, so devoid of deep satisfaction, I was able to take great pleasure in a relatively simple life. I was ever grateful for the priceless opportunity to live by the edge of the sea, where I always wanted to be. I derived great pleasure from the use of the boats, powered by diesel, sail, and oars, which I loved, and had wanted and dreamed of since childhood. Also, I have to admit that I took pride in the fact that I had designed them all.

I had always loved and enjoyed my children, spending endless hours with them, playing in the sand and tidal pools, teaching and encouraging swimming, rowing, sailing, skating, playing hockey, skiing, and, last but not least, living lives of honesty and integrity. Later I had the chance for an encore of sorts with Marjorie's four children, though their childhood was largely spent before I came on the scene. There was a brief period a few years ago when it was fashionable to say "O.K. Coach" when receiving instructions from someone. A young friend used this expression in talking to me, and somehow the title stuck. All of my children, stepchildren, grandchildren, and their friends began using the appellation. Then adult friends and business acquaintances took it up, so that I am seldom called anything else.

As the formative years passed, it was a great satisfaction to sit back and enjoy the results. Douglas, and Lorna's husband, Ted Perry, were ably playing more of a part in the production, sales, and design functions of the company. Charlie became a very capable and objective nuclear engineer, but he found spare time to design and build a beautiful double-ender (what else?) called the Energy 27. I drew the lines, and East-West made the hull of wood and epoxy. Rod, like Lorna and Ted, became a certified ski instructor, shifting from teaching skiing to a more challenging position on the ski patrol at Telluride, Colorado, controlling avalanches, and rescuing their hapless victims, as well as taking care of the usual skiing accidents. Now far from salt water, Rod had managed to finish a fiberglass Appledore 16 hull in elegant wood, which he and his children used when living in Maine, and he now hones his windsurfing skills in the summer when not building houses. Carl once sailed a 16-foot boat from Nova Scotia to Woods Hole, in November and December, and later worked for our company delivering boats to the West Coast and helping with office work.

Of Marjorie's four offspring, Rusty and Billy both acquired captain's licenses, and have spent many exciting hours on the high seas, in various boats, under sail and power. Dicky, the youngest, was building houses and enjoying an outboard (how could he?), but he has sold and delivered Aldens, and he recently distinguished himself in an Alden race, beating his mother. Dizy, having spent a lot of time on the ocean, sword fishing and sailing, was married to Mike Brown, who is in the towing and salvage business, having built a small steel tug, and recently acquired a full-size one as well. Billy and Dizy were both Alden dealers in North Carolina, and the former was highly regarded by Masonboro Boatyard, particularly for the fine woodwork he did on the boats which they repaired. Billy now runs his own boat repair business in the area.

It was most satisfying to have all of the next generation interested and involved in boats, in one way or another. The third generation, rapidly increasing in numbers, had already provided a secretary for Martin Marine Company, oldest grandchild, Cheryl Perry. Nathan Martin, the oldest grandson, had always shown a keen interest in boats, having rowed an Alden across Penobscot Bay and back at the age of seven. He accepted adversity calmly and quietly, seldom letting it erase his engaging smile. One day he and I were rowing across the

AEM and Marjorie. Photo: Pat Sopic.

mouth of the harbor in a rather hard blow, making steep waves which periodically hid him from sight. I was a little apprehensive about one so young in those conditions, but he was handling his Alden skillfully, and was not complaining. As we neared the shelter at the other side, he announced, in a quiet, matter-of-fact way, "Coach, there is something I want you to know. I don't like these waves."

Fortunately, the continuing production of new grandchildren kept me supplied with companions with whom I could keep up, whether rowing or skiing. I was getting as much fun out of my grandchildren as my children had provided, while the latter continued to be a source of great pleasure and satisfaction.

Testimonials, written, phoned, or delivered in person, from Alden owners, were adding a great deal of pleasure to my life. It was especially gratifying to learn that one of our little boats had changed some stranger's life for the better. Many owners dropped in at Kittery, unannounced, just to say hello. Quite a few became good friends, whom we saw, year after year at Alden races, boat shows, and other events, or no special occasions at all. One such owner made a most indelible impression, though I never had the pleasure of meeting him, or even talking to him on the telephone. His name was George I. Willis, and he lived in Vermont. As I learned later, his Alden was his prized possession. Though in his seventies, he rowed almost every morning, carrying his boat up to a special stand and lovingly cleaning it up after each row. One day, after returning from his usual voyage, he completed the rest of the ritual, and then peacefully fell lifeless over his boat. In his wallet was found a well worn paper with the final words of a little pamphlet called "Recreation and Amusement," which I had written and included with every Oarmaster. This chapter ends with those same words. Henry and Mary Riley, close friends of Mr. Willis, sent me some money to be used to promote the sport he loved so much. With it I purchased the George I. Willis Trophy, awarded each year to the handicapped person who contributes the most to help others enjoy the sport, and we include a year's use of an Alden with our special rigging for the handicapped. The first year it was awarded to Dolly Driscoll of Philadelphia, and the second to Jim Reisig of Toledo.

Life for me was very full and satisfying, and I could wish for nothing more than that it continue, unchanged, forever, ignoring the fact that we are all mortal.

One of the first to take a chance, and buy an Alden, was Dr. Mike McGill, of Exeter. He participated in the first Isles of Shoals Race, and went on to win that event more than once, competing in later years against his wife, Dr. Mary Beth Weathersby, who also won the Barnacle Cup one year. I began going to Mike for a physical check-up every few years, whenever I got around to it. I did not have the usual dread of these procedures. In fact I rather enjoyed hearing that my blood pressure and pulse were those of a far younger man, and my cholesterol was unusually low, all the better for an exceptionally high ratio of high-density lipoproteins(HDLs, the good guys in the white hats) to low-density lipoproteins (LDLs, the bad guys, in the black hats). So, with no reason other than a considerable lapse of time, I scheduled a repeat performance of the now familiar procedure in September 1988.

Mike included a chest X-ray, since one had not been done for several years. I was not alarmed when he called up later to request a repeat of the X-ray, explaining that the first one showed a shadow on the left lung, which might very well be only a faulty picture. But the second one confirmed the first, and a subsequent CT-scan provided a 3-D picture series of a definite tumor, which might have been benign. But a biopsy, taken with long needles in the chest, under the eye of the CT-scan machine, while I was fully conscious, established the fact that it was malignant. It was mesothelioma, a cancerous growth in the lining of the lung caused by exposure to asbestos. My days in the fire rooms and engine rooms of destroyer escorts had caught up with me. Major surgery was called for.

Thus the battle, probably my biggest, was joined. Remembering the words of MacArthur, "In war there is no substitute for victory," I hastened to assemble the best possible allies. In my mind, there was only one best place to find them: the Cox Building at the Massachusetts General Hospital.

Bill and Jessie Cox had lived just down the road from our house in Cohasset, in a beautiful mansion where they hosted some fabulous parties. Bill was quite talented, in a quiet way, as an amateur actor and singer, and could always regale the assembled company with a humorous song. Jessie and I sometimes recreated a duo from the chorus line of the Vincent Club Show of many years ago. Bill had often come to our house to get Carl, to play with his grandson, Bumpy, who was about the same age. Jack Bishop and I were very kindly invited to keep our 210s in the Cox barn each winter, before I moved my boat in with Ed Hills' 210 for extensive keel work, which required more equipment. In the spring I would be working furiously, sanding and applying the latest smoothing materials, and finally painting. In these efforts I was usually assisted by five young helpers, whose enthusiasm and good humor made up for lack of skill and experience. By noon we would all be covered from head to foot with dust and paint, when Bill would arrive, immaculately dressed, to check on progress, and invite us all over for appropriate drinks on the front lawn.

The Coxes were always most generous with their elegant house, putting up visiting 210 racers from Marblehead or New York, hosting tennis matches for charity or helping with any worthy cause. The Guttersons, who lived right on the water further down Atlantic Avenue, made an unfortunate choice of a wedding day for their daughter, Janet. They had set up a huge tent and had completed all arrangements the day before. A menacing dawn on the big day ushered in Hurricane Carol. While I was joining in the exciting adventure of trying to rescue boats down at the harbor, the fierce winds turned the Gutterson tent into a giant spinnaker, which promptly blew away in shreds, along with everything in it. Jessie Cox insisted that the reception be held in her spacious house and provided an ample supply of candles to replace the departed electricity. That is the way she was.

One very windy winter night we heard the fire alarm, and, counting the siren calls, came to the unmistakable conclusion that it was close by. Looking out the window, we were horrified to see the great Cox house enveloped in angry flames, goaded into added fury by the fierce wind, just as the blower had made white hot the coals in our old forge at the Shoals. We hastened to the scene, and I helped to pull the fire hoses as near the inferno as safety would permit. Several onlookers solemnly lamented that this was the end of an era: the Cox mansion could never be restored. I thought otherwise, and my thinking was soon confirmed, when Bill and Jessie returned from Europe and immediately set about restoring the damaged section just exactly as it had been. Jessie personally removed the black soot from hundreds of books which had escaped the flames. Later I rode my bicycle down the road a few hundred yards to attend a huge reception at the Cox house for Pat Nixon and David Eisenhower. I was most fascinated watching the Secret Service men, steely eyes darting suspiciously from guest to guest, guns ill concealed in pockets. Quite a scene for our peaceful little seacoast town.

When Bill died of cancer, Jessie donated the money to make the great cancer center in his name. The honest profits of Dow Jones and *The Wall Street Journal* were put to good use in a noble cause, far more efficiently than any government bureaucrats could employ confiscated taxes. Once more I was to be the recipient of the Cox generosity.

Surgery was to be the first form of attack, and I was confident that I was to get the best. I was serene in the knowledge that I was giving the enemy the best opening shot, confident that my excellent health, the skill of Dr. Mathisen and his able assistants, together with a little help from upstairs, would be able to pull me through the major surgery without undue complications. And so it turned out. In the intensive care unit, a few hours after the operation, they said that if I could lower my feet at the side of the bed it would help my circulation. I promptly stood up and started to do some knee bends, to the astonishment and horror of some of the attendants.

My first question to the good surgeon concerned when I could row again. He suggested eight weeks, which seemed insufferably long to me. I knew that I could row in calm water with minimal effort, and, taking no painkillers, my body would soon warn of any excessive strain. So I began rowing in two weeks, gradually increasing the pressure each time. My health returned with remarkable haste. I was able to ski all winter, as well as or better than ever before, without any further treatment. When the snow melted, Marjorie and I drove down to North Carolina, to commission the Energy 48, and enjoy some warm weather cruising, swimming, and rowing. We returned to Kittery in May for a dealer clinic, and then to attend the fiftieth reunion of my class at Webb, where I did the honors with a shovel to plant our class tree. I also showed off a total knee bend, on one leg, which I think impressed Admiral Stabile, the latter day and far superior successor to Admiral Rock.

But Dr. Mathisen had warned that traces of the cancer lingered throughout the lining of the lung, out of reach of his scalpel. Periodic X-rays were called for, the next one scheduled for June. I decided to get the jump on any possible growth of the malignancy and have the X-ray in May. Unlike the previous pictures, this one showed definite growth, and I cancelled my return to *Barnacle IV* in the sunny South.

I was re-admitted to Massachusetts General, to begin the first infusions of a new and promising chemical, called DHAC for short. It was still experimental, and I was warned of dire side effects, for which various drugs were available. I brought an Oarmaster with the X-oar-cizer attachment in with me, figuring that keeping in good condition would obviate the necessity for any drugs other than the experimental chemical. Whether from the exercise, Shaklee vitamins, optimistic attitude, or help from above, I escaped the severe side effects, and endured five days of infusions each month for five months. There were various objections to the rowing machine at first, but this to me was a vital part of the fight against cancer. The patient must never relinquish his prerogative to be in charge. Any loss of will is tantamount to a surrender to death. Doctors and nurses are an important part of the defending army, but, within reason, the patient must make as many decisions as possible. In addition to rowing I paced the hall vigorously, towing my constant companion, a stand on castors containing the chemical and the electric fusion machine which continuously pumped it into my vein. I sometimes raced the nurses down the long hall. When they needed me in another area for various tests of heart and lungs, someone would arrive with a wheelchair. My opposition to this form of locomotion, regardless of how badly I felt, was at first met with stiff resistance, but I never did have to ride in the chair. When a gurney (bed with wheels) was required, I wound up pushing it to the next building, much to the amusement of onlookers.

The new chemical proved to be ineffective, and the cancerous cells continued their murderous growth. It was disappointing to lose, but it was only one battle. Victors in war usually lose many battles, but not the last one. So the fight goes on, with another chemical and undiminished resolve.

If the big C finally claims another victim? I repeat the prayer from Alcoholics Anonymous, which can be applied to all of us mortals:

God grant me the serenity
To accept the things I cannot change,
Courage to change the things I can,
And wisdom to know the difference.

I look back on a long life of mostly happy memories. I am most grateful for the opportunities I have had to enjoy the love of family and friends, and the beauty of the natural world which God created. However long one lives, many of the world's greatest gifts must be passed by in the pursuit of others. My choices have emphasized blue water more than most, for which I make no apologies nor have any regrets. From my perspective, my life has been deeply rewarding. After all it is the quality of life that matters; not the length of time the heart can be kept beating. When cancer is discovered, many surrender, and spend what time they have left submerged in self-pity which spreads gloom among all with whom they come in contact, and surely reduces the body's capacity to fight the enemy. Since the confirmation of my mesothelioma, I have rowed for many a happy and meditative mile, sailed countless times in the Appledore 19, sometimes with Marjorie and sometimes alone. I have seen Dizy get married on a beautiful ketch in international waters. I have been blessed with three more grandchildren. I have spent a winter skiing at Sugarloaf Mountain.

But most lives include some impossible dream, destined to remain a fantasy until the spirit departs. The subject of my lifelong dream was the great challenger for the America's Cup, *Endeavour*. As a boy, I devoured voraciously every picture and word of the mighty J-class cutter. To me, and doubtless many others, she was the most beautiful yacht that ever was built, or ever would be built. I salvaged her lines from *Yachting*, and whittled out a little scale model with my jackknife, as Mr. Brewster had taught me. I painted it just like the original: red bottom, white boot top, and blue topsides. This particular shade of dark blue came to be known as Endeavour Blue. I painted *Barnacle II*, *Barnacle III*, and *Barnacle IV* this color, as well as my 210, all of our kayaks, and all of the first Alden Ocean Shells. We offer this color on all of our boats to this day, although other colors are available. I never saw *Endeavour*, nor any of the other mighty J class boats. When the huge yachts were replaced for America's Cup races by the smaller 12-meters years ago, *Endeavour* became a more remote vision than ever.

But then along came Elizabeth Meyer. A doting Concordia owner, she wrote articles, and finally a book, about these magnificent boats that meant so much to me. I had heard all about her, and even rowed an Alden past her Concordia, *Matinicus*, but had not had the pleasure of meeting her. I learned that she, although born after the J-boat era, had fallen under the spell of the neglected, rusting, and half submerged hulk of *Endeavour*. She spent five years and twelve million dollars restoring her to her former glory, sailing her across the ocean to the land of her defeat by an inferior *Rainbow*. Would it be possible for me to see at last this beautiful boat, between my "vacations" at Massachusetts General?"

My lifelong friend, Fran Loutrel, had met Elizabeth at a Concordia get-together. Knowing well my interest in the boat, to say nothing of his own, he asked Elizabeth if we, our wives, and his son Steve, who had designed some of *Endeavour's* new rigging, could possibly visit her gem. She very kindly invited us all to go sailing, just a few days before I was scheduled to return to the hospital. As the great day approached, I watched with apprehension as several beautiful days in a row went by. Surely a "breeder" for foul weather. Problems with the boat caused further delays. I feared that the chance of a lifetime would be lost forever.

But Saturday, the final chance, blessed us with clear blue skies, and a brisk northwest wind. As we neared the familiar Newport waterfront, we could see a great mast, towering above the buildings and surrounding spars, its three stainless steel spreaders, jumper struts, and rod rigging glistening in the sun. My heart jumped out of control, as I realized this was really happening. As we walked down Bannister wharf, I struggled to take it all in at once: the graceful bow, sharp as a spear, the steel topsides, not rough from welding, like so many steel ships, but smooth as a mirror, and painted the familiar dark blue, the mast, reaching 165 feet above the water into the clear sky, the spotless teak decks, dotted with ventilators, small varnished teak deckhouse, and endless winches, sheaves, blocks, color-coded lines, all colossal by my standards.

As we awaited the arrival of the owner, suspense increased by the minute. Finally, Elizabeth arrived, an animated, diminutive figure with eyes of a color halfway between the blue of the sea and the blue of the sky. As we followed her aboard, more and more impressions of the grace and perfection of the yacht crowded in. A muffled rumble far below announced the coming to life of the big Caterpillar diesel, and we cast off the dock lines. With the aid of the bow thruster, the captain eased the one hundred and thirty-foot giant out through the crowded harbor into Narragansett Bay. Elizabeth seemed to be everywhere, taking in fenders, coiling lines, and instructing guests on the proper procedure for handling the all-important running backstays, without which the huge mast would collapse in that wind. In open water, we came up into the wind, and the unbelievably heavy mainsail, already reefed, climbed up the mast, thanks to a hydraulic winch. Then the small jib (not the quadrilateral in this wind) and the forestaysail were set, and we were off, the wind dwarfing the power of the now silent engine. The feeling of so many tons of magnificence suddenly coming to life, and plunging wildly but gracefully through the water is impossible to describe.

Soon Elizabeth took the wheel, with unmistakable delight, controlling the huge mass of sail, hull, wind and water like the expert she

Endeavour. *A youthful dream was finally fulfilled when Elizabeth Meyer very kindly invited AEM to take the helm of the mighty America's Cup challenger. Photo: Marjorie Martin.*

certainly is. I walked carefully forward on the angled teak deck, now partially wet from spray, and occasionally under water at the lee rail in the gusts. I lay on my stomach, as near as possible to the sharp bow, watching the foaming bow wave, and the mist on the looard side, forming a miniature rainbow. Then back to the stern to watch the tremendous waves we were making and note the readings on the sophisticated instruments: true wind velocity in the gusts, 24 knots, maximum boat speed, 12 knots. Helping to set up one of the two huge running backstays on each side as we came about, listening to the thunder of the headsails, flogging wildly until they filled on the new tack.

Then, to my astonishment, and everlasting ecstasy, she invited me to take the immense wheel. Needless to say, I was far up on cloud nine, a million miles away from Massachusetts General. I will be forever grateful for the generosity of Elizabeth Meyer in adding so much to the quality of my life with cancer.

Whether God grants me many more years or only a few more months in this world, I would hope that the quality of that additional time be undiminished, though I cannot hope to duplicate the excitement of sailing on *Endeavour.* When I leave this world, I hope it will be none the worse for my brief presence here, and that some of you who remain may enjoy it as much as I have.

If you are a philosopher, and not in too much of a hurry to stop and dream a little, picture yourself as an oarsman, in the calm of early evening, when the glaring sun has receded in the West and with it the wind, gliding along through the clear water, arms, legs, and back moving in near-perfect rhythm, the silence complete but for the regular click of the oars in the oarlocks, and the water rippling and swirling away from the shell and the blades. Above your own aerobic breathing, you can hear a fish in the distance, slapping the water with his tail after a leap for a hapless prey. You will see your wake in the dim light, bubbling away in a straight line from under the stern, rising to a crescendo at the end of each stroke, and fading away at the start of the next one, and in the darkening sky above you will see a lone seagull returning to shore. You will not be in a hurry, for you already are where you want to be. You will not be bored, for the challenge of the sea is eternal. You will not be worried, for there is no room in the boat for the heavy burdens of life ashore. You will not disturb the marine ecology, for your silent passage discharges no poisons on the water nor harms a living thing.

You will feel humble in the grandeur of your surroundings, but you will be envious of no man. You will be completely alone, but not lonely. You will have an inner glow and peace that neither power nor alcohol nor drugs can duplicate. You will be living.